Markets and Civil Society

Studies on Civil Society
Edited by **Dieter Gosewinkel,** *Wissenschaftszentrum Berlin*
and **Holger Nehring,** *University of Stirling*

Civil Society stands for one of the most ambitious projects and influential concepts relating to the study of modern societies. Scholars working in this field aim to secure greater equality of opportunity, democratic participation, individual freedom, and societal self-organization in the face of social deficits caused by globalizing neo-liberalism. This series deals with the multiple languages, different layers, and diverse practices of existing and emerging civil societies in Europe and elsewhere and asks how far the renewed interest in the concept can contribute to the gradual evolution of civil society in the wider world.

Markets and Civil Society

The European Experience in Comparative Perspective

Edited by

Víctor Pérez-Díaz

berghahn

NEW YORK · OXFORD

www.berghahnbooks.com

Published in 2009 by
Berghahn Books

www.berghahnbooks.com

© 2009, 2014 Víctor Pérez-Díaz
First paperback edition published in 2014

Library of Congress Cataloging-in-Publication Data

Markets and civil society : the European experience in comparative perspective
/ edited by Víctor Pérez-Díaz.
    p. cm. — (European civil society ; v. 5)
Includes bibliographical references and index.
    ISBN 978-1-84545-607-8 (hardback) -- ISBN 978-1-84545-937-6 (institutional ebook) -- ISBN 978-1-78238-338-3 (paperback) --
ISBN 978-1-78238-339-0 (retail ebook)
    1. Civil society—Europe. 2. Capitalism—Europe.
3. Entrepreneurship—Social aspects—Europe. I. Pérez-Díaz, Víctor.
JC337.M26 2009
300.94—dc22

2009014622

British Library Cataloguing in Publication Data

A catalogue record for this book is available
from the British Library.

Printed on acid-free paper

ISBN: 978-1-78238-338-3 paperback
ISBN: 978-1-78238-339-0 retail ebook

CONTENTS

PART II: CIVIL SOCIETY IN TRANSITIONS TO
MARKET ECONOMIES AND LIBERAL POLITIES

TABLES

CONTRIBUTORS

Peter J. Boettke is the BB&T Professor for the Study of Capitalism at the Mercatus Center, Arlington, VA, and a Professor of Economics at George Mason University. Professor Boettke is the author of several books on the history, collapse and transition from socialism in the former Soviet Union as well as books and articles on the history of economic thought and methodology.

Laszlo Bruszt, a recipient of a PhD in Sociology from the Hungarian Academy of Sciences, teaches at the European University Institute (Florence). He has taught in the United States at Notre Dame University, at the New School for Social Research and at Cornell University. His recent publications include 'Multi-Level Governance – The Eastern Versions' in *Regional and Federal Studies* (2008); 'Organizing Technologies: Genre Forms of Online Civic Association in Eastern Europe' (with Balazs Vedres and David Stark) in *Annals of the American Academy of Political and Social Science* (2004); and 'Making Markets and Eastern Enlargement: Diverging Convergence?' in *West European Politics* (2002).

Christopher J. Coyne is an Assistant Professor of Economics at West Virginia University. He is also the North American editor of *The Review of Austrian Economics* and a Research Fellow at the Mercatus Center, Arlington, VA.

Javier Díez-Hochleitner, born in Washington, DC, holds a PhD in Law and is a Professor of Public International Law and European Union Law. Former Deputy General Director for European Union Legal Affairs and Deputy Chief of the Legal Department of the Spanish Ministry of Foreign Affairs, former Vice Chairman of the Independent Media Commission for Bosnia Herzegovina, he is now the Dean of the Faculty of Law at the Autonomous University of Madrid. He is also a member of the Madrid Bar Association. His recent books include *Derecho Internacional* (with A. Remiro, 2007) and *Derecho de la Unión Europea* (with C. Martínez, 2001)

Irina Olimpieva works at St. Petersburg Center for Independent Social Research as a research fellow and the head of the Social Studies of Economy research department. She is the author of numerous articles and an editor or co-editor of three books on informal economy in Russia: *Informal Economy in Post-Soviet Space: Problems of Study and Regulation* (2002); *Informal Economy of Logging in Irkutsk Region: Participants, Practices, Relationships* (2006); and *Fighting against Windmills: Socio-Anthropological Approach to the Study of Corruption* (2007). Her current research interests are focused on informal economy, civil society development, organizational studies and the problems of post-socialist transformation.

Víctor Pérez-Díaz received his PhD from Harvard University and is now Professor of Sociology at the University of Madrid and Director of the ASP Research Center. He is a member of the American Academy of Arts and Sciences and a founding member of the Academia Europaea. He has been Visiting Professor of Political Science at Harvard University, MIT, the University of California, San Diego, New York University and the Institut des Sciences Politiques; a Fellow Member of the Institute for Advanced Study, Princeton; a Visiting Research Professor at the Wissenschaftszentrum Berlin für Sozialforschung; and a member of the Committee on Western Europe, Social Science Research Council, New York. He is the author of more than thirty books, including *The Return of Civil Society* (1993), *Spain at the Crossroads* (1999), *La Lezione Spagnola* (Il Mulino, 2003) and *Europe and the Global Crisis* (2012).

Jesús Remón is a state lawyer and lectures on constitutional law. He is the head of area Law, Litigation and Arbitration in Uría Menéndez. He focuses particularly on commercial litigation, domestic and international arbitration, and legal advice on public law and constitutional issues. He is a member of the Corte Civil y Mercantil de Arbitraje, Corte Española de Arbitraje and the London Court of Arbitration. He is also a founder of the Spanish Arbitration Club and Vice-President of the Spanish section of the International Law Association.

Akos Rona-Tas received his PhD at the University of Michigan and is an Associate Professor of Sociology at the University of California, San Diego. He is the author of *The Great Surprise of the Small Transformation: The Demise of Communism and the Rise of the Private Sector in Hungary* (1997) and various articles on the post-communist transformation and economic sociology in journals such as the *American Sociological Review*, *American Journal of Sociology* and *Theory and Society*. His current research is on the formalization of credit assessment, the use of statistical prediction in society and the policy implications of scientific uncertainty.

Andrzej Rychard is Professor of Sociology at the Warsaw School of Psychology and head of the Graduate School of Social Research at the Institute of Philosophy and Sociology of the Polish Academy of Sciences. He specializes in political and economic sociology and in the sociology of institutions. His recent publications include 'Polska. Jedna czy wiele?' (Poland: One or Many?) (with H. Domanski and P. Spiewak, 2005), and 'Social Capital and Institutions: A Tentative Analysis of the Polish Case' (2006).

Balazs Vedres is an Associate Professor in the Department of Sociology and Social Anthropology, Central European University. He holds a PhD in sociology from Columbia University. His research develops new methods that bring network analysis into historical sociology and historical sensibilities into network analysis. Vedres's research interests include economic sociology, economic transformations, social networks, and historical and discourse analysis methods. His recent publications concern the interdependence of strategizing agents and evolving network structures in large-scale social change in the fields of business networks, political discourse and civil society organizations.

Stefan Voigt holds the Chair for Institutional and International Economics at Philipps University Marburg, where he is also the director of MACIE (Marburg Center for Institutional Economics). His research deals with the economic effects of constitutions. More specifically, current research focuses on the economic effects of the judiciary. In 2002, Voigt published a textbook (in German) on the new institutional economics, and in 2003, he published a two-volume set on critical writings in constitutional political economy. Voigt is a member of a number of editorial boards, including those of *Public Choice* and *Constitutional Political Economy*. He is a member of the CESifo Network.

EDITORS' PREFACE

Is there a 'European civil society' which cuts across national borders and spreads, though unevenly, through the continent? Does it help to form a European identity from below? Can it be seen as an answer to the obvious democratic deficit of the European Union?

For two and a half years, more than forty political scientists, sociologists, historians and other scholars from fifteen research institutions in ten different countries have worked together on the project 'Towards a European Civil Society'. They were supported within the 5th Framework Programme of the EU. The network was coordinated by the Social Science Research Center Berlin (WZB). The results of the project are published in the five to six volumes of this series, which include studies by other authors as well.

'Civil society' means many things – the concept varies and oscillates. To give a working definition, civil society refers to (a) the community of associations, initiatives, movements and networks in a social space related to but distinguished from government, business and the private sphere; (b) a type of social action that takes place in the public sphere and is characterized by non-violence, discourse, self-organization, recognition of plurality, orientation towards general goals and civility; (c) a project with socially and geographically limited origins and universalistic claims, which changes while it tends to expand, socially and geographically.

Civil society is a deeply historical concept. For a quarter of a century, it has experienced a remarkable career, in several languages. Having a long tradition of many centuries, it had nearly disappeared during most of the twentieth century before being rediscovered and reinforced in the 1970s and 1980s, when the concept became attractive again in the fight against dictatorship, particularly against communist rule in East Central Europe. But in non-dictatorial parts of the world, the term and its promise responded to widely spread needs as well. Western Europe can be taken as an example.

Civil society as a political concept of our time has come to formulate a critique of a broad variety of problems in contemporary society. To name three tendencies, first, the concept emphasizes social self-organization as well as individual responsibilities, reflecting the widespread skepticism towards being spoon-fed by the state. Second, civil society, as demonstrated by the phrase's use by present-day anti-globalization movements, promises an alternative to the unbridled capitalism that has been developing so victoriously across the world. The term thus reflects a new kind of capitalism critique, since the logic of civil society, as determined by public discourse, conflict and agreement, promises solutions different from those of the logic of the market, which is based on competition, exchange and the maximization of individual benefits. Third, civic involvement and efforts to achieve common goals are specific to civil society, no matter how differently the goals may be defined. In the highly individualized and partly fragmented societies of the present time, civil society promises an answer to the pressing question of what holds our societies together at all.

On the basis of broad empirical evidence, the project has analyzed a large number of core problems of civil society, among them the complicated relation between markets and civil society, the impact of a European civil society on a European polity and vice versa, and the importance of family and household for the ups and downs of civil society. The project has dealt with resources, dynamics and actors of civil society. It has dealt with questions of gender and other forms of inequality. It has compared developments in different European regions. It has begun to open up the perspective towards the non-European conditions, consequences and correlates of European civil society. It has reconstructed the language of civil society, including different semantic strategies in the context of tradition, ideology and power, which explain the multiple uses of the concept for different practical purposes. These are some of the topics dealt with in the volumes of this series. The authors combine a long historical perspective with broad and systematic comparison.

What does it mean to speak of a 'European' civil society? It implies a certain common European development, a parallel or even convergent trend towards the emergence of civil society in Europe. Such a development may be based on the activities of civil society groups. From the eighteenth to the twentieth century, civil society circles, associations, networks and institutions largely evolved in local, regional and national frameworks. However, transnational variants, which might contribute to the emergence of transnational coherence and similarities, remained secondary. It is in the second half of the twentieth century that the quality of the process changed. In this phase, the development of civil society in Europe increasingly assumed transnational, 'European' and sometimes global dimensions. This is a basic hypothesis of research in this series of studies. 'European Civil Society' will concentrate on transnational dimensions of civil society in Europe by comparing and reconstructing interrelations.

The evolution of a European civil society in the process of transnationalization is based on actors as well as on mobile concepts. The ideas and practices of civil society have evolved in a very uneven way, starting to emerge mainly in Western Europe, where it was initially restricted to a few proponents and to specific circles. In the course of its development, civil society spread to other parts of Europe (and into other parts of the world) and gained support within broader social spheres. As they expanded into widening social and spatial environments, the ideas and realities of civil society changed. Thus, the potential of an approach is explored which takes civil society as a geographically and socially mobile phenomenon with a good deal of travelling potential and with the propensity to become a European-wide concept.

'European Civil Society' focuses on Europe in a broad, not merely geographical sense. This includes comparing European developments with developments in other parts of the world, as well as analyzing processes of mutual transfer and entanglement. Europe in this sense transcends the institutional and spatial realm of the European Union. Yet, studying the emergence and dynamics, the perspectives and problems of civil society in Europe may produce insights into the historical process of European integration, which is underway, but far from complete, and presently in crisis.

'European Civil Society' is a common endeavor of European and non-European scholars. It centers on a topic that is the object of both scientific analysis and political efforts. The political success cannot be taken for granted. Scientific analysis, however, may help to work out the conditions under which the utopia of civil society in Europe has a chance of realization.

Dieter Gosewinkel and Jürgen Kocka

INTRODUCTION
Free Markets, Civil Societies and a Liberal Polity

Víctor Pérez-Díaz

This book is about connections between free markets, civil societies and liberal democratic polities. The point of this introduction is to highlight how these institutions should be seen as parts of an inter-connected whole. They refer to spheres of social life which tend to reinforce each other, and there are crucial institutional correspondences between them. From this view-point, these concepts point to, and complement, each other, and they belong in the same semantic field (Eco 1979).

This holistic view suggests a return of sorts to the past, to a variant of the old conception of classical liberalism; but such a view may also have increasing relevance for understanding our current times and the future. We live in times of worldwide transition to market economies; to a scenario of non-government, non-profit voluntary associations that amount to an emergent 'international civil society'; and to a complex web of governance in which liberal democratic politics (with limited and accountable govern-ments under the rule of law, elected representatives and respect for civil and human rights which are prior to, and independent from, the will of popular majorities) plays the central role. In other words, we are moving gradually away from a state-centered world towards ever more complex forms of worldwide social coordination which amount to some blend of free markets, civil societies and liberal democratic polities.

In the seventeenth and eighteenth centuries, some authors referred to an emergent system of analogous (if not identical) characteristics in the North Atlantic part of the world by the very name of 'civil society', broadly understood. They held to a very long tradition stretching back to medieval

---

Notes for this section are located on page 23.

and ancient times, and their conception was partly inherited from a tradition of natural jurisprudence and a civic tradition, which was rearranged to fit new circumstances in the parts of the Western world they inhabited. It was an ideal, a normative standard as well as a (descriptive, explanatory) theory for a system of decentralized decisions and voluntary exchanges under the law. The theory tried to explain the genesis of the system, as being the result of a complex and largely unintended evolution, as well as its functioning. It took as its basic units individual agents, which were understood by some as atomistic entities but by others as 'situated selves', as they were anchored in specific social and institutional context.[1] The anthropological assumption was that these individuals were neither omniscient nor overly benevolent, but of limited capacities and of mixed dispositions. They were fairly ignorant, but their knowledge could grow; and they were morally fallible, but they could improve themselves. Thus, they could go up in the ladder of social improvement leading 'from barbarism to civilization' (Pocock 1999) by increasing their limited understanding and limited trust in each other; or, to the contrary, they could go down. The institutions of liberty under the law – of limited and accountable government and elected representatives, free markets and plural associations – should help to shape their behavior, setting them on a sustainable upwards path. But the game remained open to other possibilities, including that of a vicious path leading them downwards. Thus, the language of civil society was descriptive, explanatory and exhortative all at once.

By the beginning of the nineteenth century, this concept of civil society broadly understood was still operating. Even in Hegel's complex and structured view, civil society remained a wide concept that encompassed markets (a system of needs) and corporations, but also included a state apparatus (the 'political state', composed of administration of justice and regulatory agencies).[2] As such, civil society broadly understood corresponded to a stage in the historical development of society, leading to the next stage of a higher form of ethical community (or 'state' proper; Pelczynski 1984). At the same time, Hegel unified the social, political and economic fields of that higher form of ethical community by placing the (political) state (with its rational bureaucracy) at its commanding heights, as he was quite sensitive to what in time would be known as market failures as well as the failures of corporations (to be counteracted by the state's remedial activities), but barely so to state failures.

From then on, there was a double tendency: to reduce the scope of the concept of civil society and to introduce a radical tension between its main components. On the one hand, Hegel, having been misread by his followers, was interpreted as if he had reduced civil society to markets and corporations (and taken public authority and administration of justice out of civil society). Then, Marx reduced Hegel's civil society ever more to market-based social classes. Finally, other theorists narrowed down civil society to a minimalist concept referring to corporations, or voluntary associations; in fact, as medieval corporations gave way to *corporations ouvrières*, many observers lost interest in Hegel's corporations and intermediary bodies, as they shifted their attention to unions and business associations, and lastly to voluntary associations in the conventional sense.

On the other hand, the second tendency was to introduce a radical tension between the main institutional components of civil society, and to assert that politics, the economy and society followed not only different but fundamentally conflicting logics. Thus, many settled for a disjointed view of society whose components tended to clash with each other. For some, conflicts and contradictions prepared the way for an overhaul of society's structures; for others, there was a tension[3] that might (or might not) give room for inconclusive, provisional compromises. For instance, markets and the state could combine against the life-world of society, by this meaning civil society in its minimalist sense; and, in this case, two things could happen: either a *modus vivendi* could be worked out between the different spheres, or a defensive war of sorts of civil society against the encroachments of state and markets would have to be envisioned.

By pointing to these tensions, these conflicting views of the whole of society had, and still have, a remarkable pedagogical and therapeutic value. They give us a useful, critical view of all the components of society as they have come about in real historical terms. They point, by turns, to the dark side of real markets as sources of predatory and exploitative practices; the dark side of real liberal democracies as they provide the grounds for oligarchical domination; and the dark side of real civil societies qua associations working, for instance, as transmission belts of authoritarian politics.[4]

A Holistic View of Civil Society

Civil Society in Its Broad and Narrow Sense

We must avoid 'verbal squabbles' (Popper 1992) and, for the sake of facilitating mutual understanding within a community of scholars, accommodate the dominant convention by using a narrow (even minimalist) concept of civil society qua voluntary associations, and social networks. There is no need, then, of trying to question and overthrow current usage.

However, we still need a name for denoting the entire semantic field, the whole; and a broad conception of civil society might do the job.[5] The concept of civil society broadly understood may have its advantages. It anchors the concept in a specific time and location. It helps Western inhabitants of the twenty-first century to engage in a conversation, foremost, with their recent ancestors, those of early modernity, and to understand their current situation as belonging in the long historical sequence then started; and it also helps them to continue that conversation further back, to the classical times of *societas civilis* and the *polis*, since, for all the differences between 'modern' and 'ancient' times, the analogies between them are striking and run very deep indeed. Besides, the fact of being anchored in a particular Western tradition does not preclude the concept being open to new transformations and varieties, as the experience it refers to migrates east and south and blends with other historical configurations.[6]

This said, we may arrange for a *modus vivendi* between the users of the word in its broad sense and in its narrow one. There is no reason, then, why the name of civil society in a narrow sense, meaning voluntary associations (and similar social groupings), should be avoided or rejected. A widely accepted term, it is used in the research agendas of many scholars and political and social activists and has become an accepted part of public discourse today.[7]

At the same time, the assumptions underlying the different uses of civil society in its narrow sense should be made explicit and put to open debate. The fact is that, underlying the different uses, there is a tension between different positions concerning whether or not the institutions of a market economy, the liberal polity and a plural society, as well as the cultural beliefs and dispositions that go with them, fit together, and, in the event that they do, to what extent and under which conditions they do so.

There is ample room for debate between authors who think in terms of an order of liberty which includes free markets and a liberal polity and a civil society (in its restricted sense), so that (this) civil society is expected to complement the workings both of a liberal state and of free, open markets; and those authors for whom civil society is merely *not* inimical to free markets and a liberal state (Keane 2005); and those authors who emphasize the tensions and conflicts between civil society, markets and the state, so that, for them, the *raison d'être* of civil society is to check and challenge the markets and, to a point, the state.[8]

This debate may prove most fruitful the moment we look into the relationships between markets, the state and associations and try to assess their fit – their degree of it or their lack of it – by examining the evidence with an open mind and asking the relevant questions.

A word on the character of the 'fitness' to be expected may be in order here. The spheres may be supposed to fit each other merely in the sense that they put limits to each other; that the markets, for instance, put limits to the power of the state, as Berger (1986: 79) suggests. Otherwise, they may be expected to fit each other to a substantially higher degree, in that they complement each other and reinforce each other, so that, when they put limits on each other, they do it *in a way* that favors the proper development of that other sphere on which a limit is imposed. Thus, by limiting state power, markets and civil societies favor the development of a liberal state – by, for instance, checking the eventual proclivities of its power holders to rule in an authoritarian manner or to collude with social, economic and cultural elites.

Civil Society, Public and Private

A common trait shared by markets, liberal states and civil society in its narrow sense (associations) is that they all have a foot in the public arena and another in the private one. The case is clear for civil society. Voluntary associations come under quite different forms and guises, but the attainment of their goals usually includes the consideration of general as well as particular interests. Formal organizations, social movements and informal networks may have different degrees of formality, closure, authority structure and permanence; but, one way or another, they all are supposed to solve, or contribute towards solving, social problems of various kinds. And, in the process of doing so, they are engaged in a mix of a particular and a general endeavor, and this, even if they focus on a particular segment of the population. Because, even if they push forward a particular interest, they have to frame it in a language of accommodation to a common good, or, at least, in a language in search of a *modus vivendi* with other segments, as they look for prospective allies or potential support outside their own ranks. If they assert a particular identity, they try to put the group concerned somewhere into the larger picture, and, at least by implication, they assert something general about the nature of this picture; for instance, that, in it, rules for mutual tolerance, or for a fair distribution of resources, or for the inclusion of those so far excluded, should apply. Particular and general pursuits come hand in hand, in an explicit or an implicit way. By means of the performance these associations engage in, as opposed to their mere words, they express a commitment to normative standards; as they try to make their voices heard in society, those values get a hearing, less by what the associations say than by what they do.

Both dimensions, public and private, are inextricably linked to each other in civil society. The same happens, also, in markets and liberal politics. Hence the difficulty, on the one hand, of defining civil society only by its public character, and by its orientation to a public common good and its acting in the public arena; and, on the other, of understanding markets with no reference to their public dimension. That markets talk loudly and clearly in the public sphere is obvious;[9] and, today, the point is brought home continuously by the consequences of capital movements over a wide range of polities all over the world, for better or worse. Politics, as well, is engaged in as a mixed endeavor of public and particular interests, public and particular identities, by politicians, civil servants, media participants, lobbies and social movements. All of them have their own agendas in which the two dimensions loom very large. They may occasionally parade as pure public-spirited agents, but if they do, the name of the game for the alert citizen is to see through the political theater and to discriminate the public and the particular interest in every political move and policy proposal. Nobody is exempted from having both, not even the citizens, who know it first hand, those trying to indicate otherwise being either naive or hypocritical.

The double dimension, public and private, applies equally to associations and to political parties, particularly when these parties are not in power. Firms, as well, are engaged in matters involving their social responsibility, corporate citizenship or civic concern; they are in between the worlds of politics and civil society, or markets and civil society. In addition, professions may play a complex game of being party to the schema of governance, looking after a segment of the markets and bearing a fiduciary responsibility for serving the needs of society; they stand abreast of all three worlds. Sometimes, the media plays, or tries to play, a similar role. Courts of arbitration for the adjudication of conflicts are located between the world of markets and that of a system of governance; and an analogous consideration applies to juries, which are a significant component of civil society within the system of administration of justice.

On Civil Virtues

The institutions of a civil society broadly understood (that is, the rules of markets, plural societies and of liberal democratic politics) do not 'act'; they shape, constrain and offer incentives for human agents to do the acting. By doing so, in a way fitting to those institutions, in a habitual manner, these agents, individuals or associations, are expected to develop a civil character, a set of civil dispositions or civil virtues. Prominent among them is what we may call 'civility': the virtue of living together, and communicating and interacting with other members of the community with a modicum of mutual recognition and benevolence.

As the several spheres of society differ from each other, so civility appears under different modalities in each of them. At the very least, this virtue of mutuality would mean that interaction takes place without recourse to violence and fraud in the sphere of the economy, without treating the political adversary as an enemy to be excluded from political society, and with due sensitivity to situations of dependence and vulnerability in the social sphere.

At the same time, since human agents tend to (or try to) develop a coherent moral character, and because of the correspondences that exist between all these spheres, it is to be expected that there will be some fit between those different modalities of civility.

In the political domain, civility implies a commitment to the kind of (modern) *civitas* which allows for, and rests on, individual freedom, respect for the citizens' private domain and emphasis on a limited government. Here lies the unity and, at the same time, the tension between civic-ness (a civic spirit) and civil-ness (a moral sentiment of interdependence and mutual respect and toleration among autonomous agents). In the economic domain, civility emphasizes the virtue of *iustitia*; in the social domain, that of *liberalitas*. Civility acquired in the domain of the economy may provide the foundations for other forms of civility in other domains. For instance, markets should be provided with some basics of political education. The practice of accountability (monitoring and enforcement) for economic decisions requires accepting the risks and rewards concomitant to them, and prepares people to hold political leaders responsible for their actions. By the same token, that practice makes people inclined to refusing a role of victims for themselves when the leaders they have chosen reveal themselves to be corrupt, or worse. In turn, political and social virtues, such as civil virtue and sensitivity to people's circumstances of dependence and vulnerability may prompt people to be alert to the political and social externalities of their economic activities.

Opposite to situations in which civility prevails, we find situations of various degrees of violence, exploitation or domination, and mutual indifference. There may be, and there have been in modern, contemporary societies, relatively frequent extreme cases of incivility, such as the ones associated with totalitarian regimes. This applies also, in particular, to situations of civil war – for instance, to that of Spain in the 1930s and of the Balkans in the 1990s. The example of Spain in the 1930s and its aftermath leading to the democratic transition of the 1970s, indicates a protracted yet virtuous path for taming the fratricidal passions of that war; the key lay, in good part, in the prosperity associated with the growth of a market economy (and, in connection to it, other demographic, social and cultural changes) both in Spain and in Western Europe, to which the Spanish economy was closely linked. Today, many envision the prospects for a complete pacification of the Balkan countries as being linked to an ever-greater integration of their economies with those of the European Union. The contrast between the degree of violence of a totalitarian system and the relative pacification of social life that comes with the spread of a (still, passably turbulent) market experience seems corroborated by the Chinese and the Russian cases; whatever turmoil is caused by the transition to a normal market economy, it looks rather mild as compared to the hundred or so million victims of their all-too-recent totalitarian past.[10]

Leaving the extreme cases aside, we may focus on the shades and grades of civility. For instance, there may be a low degree of civility where markets are subject to continuous interference by state officials and associated corporatist partners. This provides grounds for patterns of political deference and timidity on the part of businesspeople, and for their transformation from entrepreneurs into rent seekers. The practice of dwelling in the corridors of local, regional and national governments pushes businesspeople to look for friends in government in order to make a profit at the smallest possible risk by averting competition. In turn, this influences other middle classes such as professionals, teachers, academics, and public intellectuals to gravitate towards the state and miseducate themselves in the practice of being careful with the expression of their political ideas; otherwise their careers might be in jeopardy. This reinforces the engagement by the entire social milieu of business and its entourage in the practice and sentiment of a court society, and entails a low degree of both entrepreneurial spirit and civil virtue.

The theme of civility alerts us to the importance of building the agents' moral character, and of the weakening of it in the course of time. The agent's attempt to achieve a modicum of moral coherence, and be able to make a meaningful narrative of his or her own life, tends to reinforce the fit between the different spheres of the agent's life. Once these attempts are put in context, we may reach a better understanding of their aggregate results, and, therefore, of the dynamics of the reproduction and change of the interconnected whole to which these spheres belong. On the other hand, the process of losing that moral character, of loss of civility, may bring ruin on any sphere of life – a liberal democratic polity, for instance – and have repercussions on all the rest. This may happen in a short period of time; as attested by the many instances of breakdown of liberal democratic regimes in Europe and Latin-America during the twentieth century. By contrast, the building of that moral character, even in the face of largely unpropitious institutions, may be the way to build up a civil society, broadly speaking. A moral character may be built around an experience of truth as opposed to prevailing custom; this is the case of moral conversions, which, in turn, are embedded in supportive dissenting communities. Such was the experience of truth which Václav Havel appealed to in the face of the modern communist state. An analogy could easily be drawn here to the European religious tradition, and to Tertullian's dictum, 'Christus veritatem se, non consuetudinem nominavit' (Christ called himself truth, not custom),[11] which may be construed as referring to a contrast between an experience of truth and the customs of the old Roman state.

Major Themes, Leading Questions

Processes and Mechanisms

As a way of conceptualizing the problematic of markets, civil society and liberal politics as a unified field, we may focus on three general themes: (1) processes and mechanisms, (2) agency, and (3) the dynamics of reproduction, gradual evolution and drastic change. This exploratory overview will include occasional references to the contributions to this book, and will point to possible topics of interest for further inquiry.

Markets, civil societies and liberal democratic politics are processes of human interaction having both a strategic and a communicative dimension, and, as such, they contain a series of mechanisms, that is, of frequently recurring, patterned ways in which things happen (Elster 1989). They take place between basic units, individual agents who are engaged in an endless endeavor of mutual adjustment and mutual dissent, of imitation and experimentation. They unfold through a period of time, and may be subject to a dynamics of reproduction, gradual evolution or drastic change.

Markets, societies and liberal democratic polities follow to a large extent a similar logic, that of decentralized deliberations and decisions (even though, often, much less so in the case of politics). They should be expected to reinforce each other to a large extent. In fact, markets are helpful to democratic governance, for instance, in various ways (see Pérez-Díaz *infra*). They may lead to a growth of wealth, and to its dispersion among autonomous units, which, in turn, are prone to defend their own interests and assert their autonomy, and, therefore, may be inclined to do so by entering the political and social fields. The likelihood for them of doing so is enhanced by processes closely linked to the market operations which lead to the development of people's cognitive and moral resources. They know more and know better as markets spread knowledge and, at the same time, focus people's mind on the matter at hand and provide multiple, continuous feedback mechanisms to test their theories about the world. They become more sensitive to ever-larger networks of inter-dependence, and require unremitting attention to the needs, wishes and resources of others. In the end, people may use those economic and cultural resources (wealth, knowledge, morals) in the terrain of civil society and politics. They may finance and participate in voluntary associations. They may play a part in the political process, support a political party, engage in political actions, develop a political career. And, vice versa, participation in civil society and politics may increase people's resources and opportunities to enter other fields, the market included, when they are willing to do so.

Thus, economic, social and political (as well as cultural) resources accumulated in one field can be re-invested in another one. The ability of people to engage in this new investment depends, however, on one crucial cognitive and moral factor: on their familiarity with, their know-how regarding, the basic rules and general mechanisms of an order of freedom, whatever the field. If they know how to deal with other free agents, to respect their room for maneuvering, to assert themselves in a world of equals, to make decisions, to implement them while following the rules of the game, to pay the price of breaking those rules and being caught, to accept risks and responsibility for their actions, to monitor others' behavior, and, in the end, to hold on to this know-how, this culture, *not* as an inventory of tools[12] but as a way of life.

These mechanisms have to be explored, described and explained in their context; and some of the chapters in this book can be read as contributions to this exploration. To begin with, there are mechanisms of deliberate coordination and mutual adjustment. In their discussion of civic combinations, Laszlo Bruszt and Balazs Vedres allude to a mechanism of joint action, of mutual adjustment, between business, associations and government agencies. These segments presumably profit from their collaboration; at least, associations are said to do so. In his analysis of the Polish situation, Andrzej Rychard explores the subtle play between people as citizens and this same people as market participants (producers, consumers) and members of civil associations. Here, coordination refers to the action taking place within the agents, between their own different dimensions. In an initial period, these dimensions look like they supplement each other: strong participation in the market somehow substitutes for a lack of involvement in politics, for instance; while, at the next stage, there seems to be a parallelism in the development of the three dimensions: they all languish, or flourish, at the same time. This could be read as suggesting an increase in people's ability to coordinate their own behavior. Akos Rona-Tas looks at the mechanisms of mutual adjustment between a particular kind of entrepreneur and its clients, at the conversation taking place in the market for consumer credit. He shows how the banks increase the level of formalization and standardization in the communicative process in an attempt to increase their power resources. The communication follows impersonal, abstract procedures and becomes less dependent on a local network of people who know each other well. In the end, something is gained in terms of the bank's efficiency, but the effects are mixed in terms of people's access to consumer credit, and some segments of the population may suffer as a result of it. This may create an opportunity for civil associations to step in and open another, complementary line of communication.

A crucial part of the conversation, in all the spheres, evolves around the mechanisms of accountability, that is, of monitoring performance and enforcing the rules. As regards the accountability of the entrepreneurs, Peter Boettke and Christopher Coyne suggest that there are strong analogies between the monitoring and enforcing mechanisms of economic entrepreneurs and those of social entrepreneurs. Loss and profit mechanisms are quite effective in making the economic entrepreneur accountable for his decisions. Losses and gains in the level of trust or reputation in a local setting would be a proxy of that economic mechanism, which applies to social entrepreneurs; the implication being that no similar mechanism applies to a larger setting.[13] The authors tend to think that there is no equivalent mechanism in the case of politics. Electoral campaigns, opinion polls, voting and, in the end, a turnover of the political elites would not be enough. Still, this discussion may be pursued further, looking at different scenarios according to the scale of politics, the policy area and the character of the citizens. For instance, local and sectorial policy can be subject to closer and more informed scrutiny the more the political abilities of the citizenry improve by means of education and training.

Mechanisms for establishing normative standards and standards for producing and assessing relevant evidence in cases of conflict adjudication and administration of justice are supposed to belong in the political sphere, and be part of a state system of governance. But, in fact, we find variants of these mechanisms in settings located in between the state, markets and civil society. Stefan Voigt discusses the case of juries, which are a segment of civil society inserted within a state system of justice. Juries are aware of the legal procedural angle of the process, but they are supposed to act according to basic standards of common sense and decency, and follow their own moral intuitions and personal judgement while being open to persuasion by the rest. In the case of the arbitration system, discussed by Javier Díez-Hochleitner and Jesús Remón, experts such as merchants, retired judges and mercantile lawyers are watched over by a world of international professional associations acting on a fiduciary basis; they adjudicate conflicts of interests according to a *lex mercatoria*, or a derivation from it. The situation is close to that of self-regulation of markets *cum* a strong component of civil society.

Processes in Time: The Agents' Strategies and the Dynamics of Reproduction, Gradual Evolution and Drastic Change

Individual agents are the ones who do the mutual adjustment and the communication of the processes and mechanisms of markets, civil societies and liberal polities. What they do are both practical engagements (working, making a profit, solving social problems, holding power, etc.) and verbal or non-verbal statements. By making use of a verbal and a non-verbal language, they express identities, describe states of the world, explain them, and exhort people to behave properly. In so doing, these agents imitate others, or take others as role models, choosing between those who play by the rules and those who deviate from them; or, alternatively, they take a distance from any model and compare and experiment among several possible courses of action before making their choice. Imitation, or diffusion, of best practices may occur, for instance, between economic and social entrepreneurs, or between courts of justice and arbitration courts. Civic combinations may allow for mutual imitation between firms, associations and government agencies.

Imitations of best practices may lead to experimentation with general institutional patterns. For instance, the diffusion of mechanisms of accountability in different fields may lead to experiments with changes in the scale and the scope of governance pointing to a reduction of the range of power and responsibility of the national state. Policy areas can be unregulated, left to the self-regulation of markets or associations, or they can be watched over by some partnership between government, markets and civil society. Local government may seem easier to be held accountable by ordinary citizens. The end result of the reduction in scope and scale of state governance is a tendency towards the dispersion of power, ultimately reinforcing the system of decentralized decisions, which is characteristic of an order of freedom or civil society broadly understood.

The aggregate result of the agents' strategic and communicative interactions are processes of stability and change in society. Path dependency is the closest thing we find to a process of reproduction in an open system; it corresponds to processes with strong positive feedback mechanisms, and increasing returns for the participants provided they follow the rules. According to neo-institutional economists, once property rights, basic rules of justice and enforcement mechanisms are in place, this is what happens with free, open markets (North 1990). A similar argument can be made with respect to politics (Pierson 2003; Thelen 2003). A liberal polity rests on basic institutions which provide incentives to stay on course. Expectations of satisfactory results are attached to the workings of a liberal polity; under normal conditions, a consolidation of democracy should take place. This is most likely when the democracy delivers its promise, and fulfills people's expectations of peace and prosperity. Civil society (qua associations) is expected to have similar consequences: to increase both governability and economic prosperity, one way or another (Putnam 1993, 2000, 2002).

Gradual evolution suggests a mix of continuity and change that leads to important transformations in the long run. Evolution of consumer credit markets seems a long-term evolution, that goes beyond the initial set of rules (Rona-Tas, *infra*); but the transformation is gradual, *pari passu* with the slow-motion processes of geographical expansion and demographic changes as well as changes in the technology of communication, storage of information and the like. A similar slow-motion change seems to apply to the expansion of the arbitration system, *pari passu* with development of global, worldwide markets (Díez-Hochleitner, Remón, *infra*).

Drastic changes may occur in unsettled times. Cumulative process are punctuated by critical junctures, and what often follows is a mix of path dependency, slow-moving transformation, and crucial choices. Institutional transitions take place, then. They may go in every direction, including that of democratic transitions or of democratic breakdowns. Every part of the whole comes together at these transition times.

In the case of transitions from a situation of markets-cum-authoritarian regimes, the transition may imply a slow-motion evolution of social, economic and cultural institutions, to which the markets provide a crucial impulse. This was the case, for instance, of Spain (Pérez-Díaz 1993). Twenty years of transformations in the economy, society and culture created the conditions for a political transition in the mid-1970s. Then there was a critical juncture at which some crucial decisions were made; they transformed the political scene, but they were little more than an accommodation to the social, economic and cultural scenario that came from the past; and rightly so, we could add, from a normative standpoint, since this scenario contained already the basic ingredients of an order of freedom.

The situation may be different if the transition starts from a situation in which we have almost no markets (or the very distorted black, informal markets in the fringes of a command economy) and almost no civil society (through there may be families, neighborhoods, churches, informal networks, etc.), and on top of that stands a totalitarian political regime. Establishing the proper setting for markets and capitalist firms as well as for civil associations is a fairly complicated affair, and, here, we have to look not only to the formal rules but also, and mainly, to the informal ground rules. In this regard, Rona-Tas examines the peculiarities of establishing a consumer credit business in the East European countries; Boettke and Coyne discuss to the role of the media in helping the political transition; and Irina Olimpieva analyzes the strategic and communicative interactions between government officials, firms and associations of various kinds in their efforts to learn how to solve the problem of corruption or live with it.

Ground Rules and Habit Formation, Normative Debates and Ways of Living

Unifying the field of markets, civil associations and liberal polities implies a research agenda combining several disciplines; and one way to proceed farther along that road is by being alert to the problems associated with the (combined) processes of transition to a market economy, a plural society and a liberal polity. Transitions provide a propitious setting to see more clearly the connections, correspondences and complementarities between the different spheres; this is one reason why transitions loom large in this book. Solving the many problems of transition requires attending to the whole social world, the entire semantic field, and touches on a large range of transversal institutional and cultural issues – for instance, issues referring to the prevailing ground rules, habit formation and normative debates.

Formal institutions and ground rules should fit each other but may deviate from each other, and they often do. Sometimes, very illuminating historical comparisons between macro-institutional frameworks lack specificity because they leave aside the analysis of the rules on the ground, and miss how interactions and mutual adjustments and dissent are worked out at the micro level. The basic institutions of democracy can be established, but if there is rampant intimidation and corruption at the local level democracy cannot take root. Different modes of coordination may be set up at the top – for instance, a 'liberal' one or one based on state intervention and corporate pacts of unions and business associations to regulate, say, the labor market, the training system and a large sector of welfare services (Hall and Soskice 2001). In the end, however, we must look at the rules on the ground. Historical cases which look similar at a national level may work quite differently on the ground, and vice versa; countries with very dissimilar modes of coordination may function the same, or nearly the same, at the micro level. For instance, whether or not the documents pertaining to the working of the state bureaucracy (and the other partners) are available for the public and easy to get access to, may have enormous effects in the way the state bureaucracy behaves. It marks off an honest, competent, responsive bureaucracy from a corrupt, incompetent and arrogant one: a world of civil servants from one of 'uncivil masters'. The details, therefore, are of enormous importance. This shows in Olimpieva's discussion of the Russian case. Here, the final results hinge on the solutions given to problems of everyday, petty corruption and intimidation by local government agencies; and attention is focused on various ways to handle the problem, and the role of various kinds of associations in doing so.

Ground rules cannot be enforced on a daily basis by external enforcement agencies. The transaction costs will be too great. Usually, enforcement takes place through mutual monitoring at the local level, in the immediate surroundings, by means of continuous acts of approval and disapproval of local participants and observers, and, mostly, by the internalization of rules, by people acquiring habits of proper behavior on their own. This is the result of a process of education in which families and schools play a role, but one which is probably less important than the role of peer groups particularly at the critical, vulnerable time of the adolescence (Pinker 2002). In these settings, habituation to threatened tit-for-tat sanctions may be linked to the recognition of positive long-term benefits of remaining on good terms with the other party (Benson 1998: 213). The habits of cooperation, imitation and innovation (or experimentation) formed in the spheres of a civil society and a market economy would spill over to politics: they would tame people, and, eventually, would help them to put their memories of past violence in the proper perspective and time frame.

Particularly in times of transition, but not only then, the entire field of a civil society broadly understood, and every component of it, should be open to scrutiny and debate. It may be attacked as an ideological construct that confuses normative, analytical and empirical dimensions. Some people may think it should be demystified, so to speak, at least enough to uncover its underlying power struggles. These criticisms are quite legitimate, and, in fact, quite useful for the proper functioning of an order of freedom. The entire semantic field of a civil society broadly understood should be open to and include its intellectual critiques, which point to alternative institutions and ways of living. These (apparently external) criticisms can be incorporated into the process of immanent, rational critique of institutions and practices, which is required for the development of a tradition of liberty. They help people not to lose sight of the inconsistencies of, and the tensions between, the spheres of the economy, society and politics. In real life, they may help to reinforce each other, or, alternatively, hurt each other. People should be on the watch and look with a critical eye at every local, specific situation.

Let us remember one basic point in a communicative process, namely, that language, verbal or otherwise, has several functions, and all of them should be attended to. Signaling, expressing, describing, arguing: these are language's classical functions; but to this we must add others, such as the exhortative, normative function (Popper 1992). This dimension is of extreme importance. We live in an ideological, rationalistic, discursive era (Oakeshott 1991), and just 'doing things right', as a matter of custom or tradition, is not enough. A moral reasoning has to be incorporated into the picture, in order to ensure the legitimacy of an order of liberty in the eyes of the population.

Two remarks may be in order as regards this normative dimension. Firstly, for the reasons just stated, an explicit normative debate is needed. Let us notice, however, that a (paradoxical) difficulty to this debate may lie in the very success of a quasi-moral discourse incorporated to everyday public talk, political rhetoric, commercial imagery and so on. This common-place normative language may be so pervasive that it may be taken for granted, and, somehow, get unnoticed. In fact, nowadays, we witness a rapprochement in the current discourses about the proper, the better, the more successful way to conduct politics, the economy and civil associations. They imitate each other. Thus, politicians talk of trying to reach out to society, engage in partnerships and promise not to interfere, only give society a helping hand, solicit its help, sing the virtues of markets and civil society, and show themselves to be friends of both. Leaders of civil associations express themselves in a more guarded manner, but usually they behave in a way that suggests they are on the watch for funding from government and business (provided there are some limits to the government's and business's involvement in their own management), and that they are all for a *modus vivendi* with all of them, even if this requires them, sometimes, to tame their initial anti-capitalist, anti-system rhetoric. Others speak all the time of social capital, and civic community, taking economic capital as the standard reference. Businesspeople say they assume a modicum of social and corporate responsibility, and declare themselves ready to take care of both shareholders and stakeholders. They urge politicians to do their job and guarantee the functioning of the markets, but, at the same time, they say they are disposed to shoulder the burden of governance if and when needed. They declare themselves ready to be all inclusive, sensitive to gender, ethnicity, and whatnot.

The rapprochement in the discourses of all these political, social and economic leaders is reinforced by their sharing a common attitude. The perceived increasing complexity of the challenges they meet and the high risks of their (joint) goals of, say, peace and prosperity being compromised by events out of their control, make them rather humble or, at least, put them in the path of some humility. Perhaps this is because even though they talk about the future non-stop, they rather know, or suspect, that what the future really looks like must remain unknowable.

However, secondly, an explicit normative debate is not enough. Classical moralists have taught us that ethics is not so much about normative discourses as it is about ways of living. This shows most forcibly in the ground rules that apply to the immediate situation, in the agents' actual behavior, in habits acquired as a result of frequent activity and in the character which is the result of a combination of such habits.

The different chapters of the present book can be read as being engaged in a conversation of sorts with each other, and in relation to the general themes mentioned above. But, certainly, they go beyond these limits, engage in a variety of related topics, and converse with a variety of other scholars and disciplines, including the fields of sociology, law, political philosophy, economics and political science. The book is divided into two parts. In the first part, two chapters take a broad, theoretical and comparative view of the entire field, as they focus on markets as conversations (Pérez-Díaz) and various forms of entrepreneurship (Boettke and Coyne). The next two chapters deal with institutions and organizations of civil society as they are parts in systems of governance: juries (Voigt) and arbitration courts (Díez-Hochleitner and

Remón). In the second part, four chapters discuss markets and associations in particular sectorial, local and political settings, in the context of processes of economic, social and political change, and with particular attention to Central and Eastern Europe. In one of them, changes in one market in particular (consumer credit) are put in a large historical and comparative context (Rona-Tas). Other chapters analyze complex patterns of relationships between associations, business and government agencies in Hungary (Bruszt and Vedres) and Russia (Olimpieva), and ways in which people handle their different roles in the market, civil society and the political scene in Poland (Rychard).

Summing Up the Book's Contributions

A line of argument provides unity and coherence to the various contributions to this book. The underlying assumption is that exploring the relations between markets, civil societies (qua associations) and politics, or the public sphere, provides a key to better understanding, and eventually solving, problems of social coordination at a time of increasing complexity in an ever less state-centered world.

Thus, I argue (in chapter 1) for a broad, holistic understanding of civil society as a way to point to the underlying unity of markets, a liberal polity and a world of civil associations. I refer to markets, a liberal polity and civil society as parts of an entire action field, and broaden my view to encompass a large historical context. I engage in a debate in a conceptual history which is open to diverse interpretations; and suggest a way for understanding the interconnection between conceptual history and context in our contemporary societies. Then I move to the key question, namely, an understanding of markets as communicative processes, or, as I put it, as conversations. By this approach, I try to convey the message, first, that there is a need for putting together both linguistic and extra-linguistic means of communication, markets being crucially important in this last regard; second, the crucial feature in the communicative process is not so much direction but discovery; third, the process is open to progress as well as to regression.

The idea of markets as conversations applies to diverse stages of the economic process. This view of markets helps us to understand the formation of different conversational spaces, large and small; and it facilitates the understanding of their moral effects, in the extended orders as well as in the small worlds. Then, I suggest that similar communicative process are at work in various social and political settings. This leads to a reassessment of the role of markets with respect to politics, which intimates that, on the conditions of proper markets operating under the rule of law, in the absence of fraud and violence, they should be expected to have a rather civilizing effect on politics, and help to improve a liberal democratic polity. There are indications about the ways in which markets shape and foster civil dispositions, check the tendency to understand politics in terms of friends and enemies, and tame the violent passions associated with that kind of politics. An account is given of some of the resources markets provide citizens in terms of holding their magistrates responsible, and for participating in the city. They provide lessons in fast learning, decentralization of decisions and favor a politics of mutual adjustment and accommodation.

Peter Boettke and Christopher Coyne contend that the entrepreneur is an agent of social and cultural change. They consider the entrepreneur in the economic, social and political settings; and they back their argument by referring to several pieces of evidence located in different parts of the world. They are interested in the role of the entrepreneur insofar as he or she is able to play a crucial role in the communication process that drives the economy, society and politics. This the entrepreneur does by being able to shift the focus of people's attention and by shaping common, public knowledge. The authors' purpose is to understand how entrepreneurs create anew or shift existing focal points and how they make these changes salient.

As Boettke and Coyne examine the ways the entrepreneurs accomplish their role in the three settings, they conclude that the desirable aspects of entrepreneurship in economic settings are transferable to non-market and political ones to the extent that there are proxies for prices and profit/loss mechanisms. They argue that while reputation serves as a soft constraint in non-market settings, there is a complete absence of a disciplinary device in political settings. Next, they examine the overlapping of settings that come with the entrepreneurs, social or economic in particular, being able to operate in several settings, with the help of several examples.

Stefan Voigt argues that lay participation in judicial decision making can be interpreted as an element of civil society in adjudication. He deals, then, with a segment of civil society as it is involved in matters of adjudication of conflicts and the administration of justice, namely, juries. The latter are prominent in both criminal and civil cases in a number of countries, and Voigt addresses the issue of the jury's contribution to governance in a liberal polity under the rule of law – first, by taking into account some of the classical literature on the matter, and, then, by providing an operational schema for stating a number of hypothesis and suggesting ways to test them empirically. The chapter contains, then, a theoretical part in which hypotheses on the likely effects of juries are developed, while at the same time it offers an overview of the uses that European societies make of trial by jury.

Following hints from Montesquieu, Hegel and Tocqueville, Voigt suggests that juries can be useful on two accounts. First, in a direct way, they can improve the administration of justice. Second, in an indirect way, and above all, they can improve the quality of political life. This can be achieved by different means. By checking the executive's temptation and proclivity to overstep its authority; by reinforcing the independence of the judiciary; and by educating the public in the knowledge and respect of the law, which may result, in turn, in less crime and less litigation. Civil society follows its own rules of deliberation based on the rules of a conversation when it is geared to a well-ordered and focused debate, and trusting on the arts of mutual persuasion among equals to testing alternative hypothesis against the facts of the case, and applying logical reasoning. Here, we may be witness to a niche of the system of governance, that of the adjudication of conflicts in civil cases, and of the application of the law in criminal ones, being imbued with, or 'colonized' by, the basic rules of the game of civil society.

Javier Díez-Hochleitner and Jesús Remón refer to arbitration courts, which have become more and more salient in global business; they talk about a 'tidal wave' of arbitration. They see the phenomenon as part of the emergence of an international civil society within the context of globalization. Many observers contend that this international civil society has penetrated the structures of international power interacting with states and international organizations; this has pushed forward, also, private regulatory schemas, so that a new private authority emerges side by side with those states and international organizations. Díez-Hochleitner and Remón argue that a situation of this kind is occurring in the area of dispute resolution, where arbitration has grown dramatically within a context of increasing international commercial transactions.

Díez-Hochleitner and Remón trace the origins and development of international arbitration, and analyze the various positions adopted by the states with regard to arbitration. They suggest that the prevailing pattern is one of continuous mutual accommodation between state jurisdictions and arbitration courts, since arbitration depends, in fact, at least to some extent, on recognition by state courts. At the same time, national states, their legislative bodies and courts included, depend on world markets, foreign capital and investment, for providing the goods that their own legitimacy depends on; and this requires of them to take an accommodating attitude towards the arbitration courts, which may be seen as a fairly flexible, accessible and competent, and, in the end, reliable system of adjudication of conflicts.

As the following authors look into the relationships between markets, civil societies and local governments in a variety of sectorial and local settings, they observe a similar pattern of reciprocal influence and mutual checks, and the emergence of a common conversational space.

Thus, Akos Rona-Tas deals with a particular set of economic entrepreneurs, the banks, as they handle the world of consumer credit. Here, he follows, first, the process by which banks have replaced a system of communication between lenders and borrowers based largely on tacit knowledge of local social networks of information and trust, by more formalized, impersonal, explicit forms of knowledge, gathered and disseminated on a vast, mass scale. Rona-Tas goes into the details of the operations of classification, codification and numerical precision that come with this process of instrumental, formal rationalization. He provides us with a careful description of the various steps of the process of formal rationalization, and its operations of classification, identity, recording, quantifying, productivity and information.

Rona-Tas's analysis is sometimes reminiscent of a quasi-Foucauldian approach to the process of codification as struggles for control and power; but the other side of a struggle for control is, as any reader of Hegel may remember, a process of mutual recognition. In a sense, the controlling process can be re-construed as a way to enlarge the circle of trust. Boettke and Coyne had argued for the scope of social entrepreneurship being reduced, based on the need for relying on local reputation and the difficulty for finding a proxy to the mechanism of profit and loss in a social setting beyond local communities (even though they point to the Ashoka experience, and in general to that of micro-credits as a promising development in this regard). Therefore, the reader may be allowed to draw the conclusion that Rona-Tas suggests a way in which the business practices themselves provide an instrument which is, by its very nature, a mix of profit and loss and of personal reliability – a hybrid of market logic and the logic of personal recognition. In a final stroke, Rona-Tas points to the fact that even though there may be a number of failures in that process of formal rationalization that amount to a loss of relevant but intricate information and the introduction of bias, part of these failures could be made up by the intervention of new forms of social networks, possibly of civil associations, which could provide a dose of additional, compensatory information and fairness.

Laszlo Bruszt and Balazs Vedres discuss the experience of non-governmental organizations which pursue a variety of goals such as solving social problems related to issues of economic growth and social cohesion, and which may be involved in partnerships with state agencies and/or business, the whole of such arrangements being referred to as 'civic combinations'. The question the authors try to answer is whether these organizations lose their autonomy and narrow their goals once they enter such combinations, as part of the literature suggests.

After a careful reading of the results of a survey on a representative sample of Hungarian non-governmental organizations, Bruszt and Vedres conclude that most of these organizations feel at ease with these experiences; they do not narrow their goals nor do they lose autonomy. Of course, questions could be raised regarding the efficacy and efficiency of these arrangements for solving social and economic problems, and doing it efficiently; these are in fact questions which have been traditionally raised *à propos* of all sorts of corporatist arrangements in the past. But it is important to realize that, from the viewpoint of the organizations involved, those civic combinations seem a satisfactory move that provides them with access to resources with no loss of autonomy on their part.

Irina Olimpieva opens a vista on the complex, ambiguous dealings between non-governmental organizations, business and state officials under current conditions in Russia. Some authors, such as Shleifer and Treisman (2005), for instance, have remarked that, in a sense, the degree of corruption and arbitrariness documented in the functioning of markets in Russia may not be that different, all things considered, from what we might observe on the ground in Brazil, Mexico, China or India; they suggest that we should see these conditions as 'normal', so to speak, for countries at this stage of development. The point, however, is how to correct or improve this 'normalcy'. Here, Olimpieva offers us a view at close range of some of these mechanisms and strategies that may remedy the situation, based on recent survey data from the business scene in Saint Petersburg. Her main findings suggest that much depends on the informal rules on the ground, and the way, and the extent to which, these informal rules can be challenged, and changed. The state bureaucracy in place, inherited from the previous regime, manages the everyday monitoring of, and intervention in business affairs in such a way that business is hostage to a discretionary application of dysfunctional regulations, and arbitrary sanctions, to be avoided only by being party to corruption schemes of all kinds. As a way to handle, if not to solve, this problem, a number of strategies are being tried, other than the most obvious and most difficult ones – namely, bureaucratic reform and a better administration of justice.

Olimpieva points out that businessmen seem to rank the strategies available to them in terms of efficacy in the following way. They rank as low the strategy of civic associations, or civic non-governmental organizations, which make an argument on the public sphere to this effect. Many of them seem resigned to live with the situation more or less as it is; but those willing to do something about it opt for trying to balance the rapport of forces with bureaucracy by means of business associations that bargain with it, and/or by tapping a growing market sector of services firms that specialize in dealing with the public authorities, handling all sorts of issues (complying with zoning laws, obtaining importing licenses, getting access to public utilities, doing a creative reading of the maze of local regulations and taxes, licensing for all sorts of activities, etc.). In the end, the range of options for coping with the state, regional and local bureaucracies makes for some mix of resorting to markets and associations of various kinds, in the expectation of solving immediate problems, and, possibly, establishing some sort of long-term, predictable relationship with the state at various levels. Business and civil society, thus, converge, to a point, in either checking the excesses of politics and/or taming or educating the state officials, so far with limited results; or, alternatively, in getting used to markets and associations operating in a milieu with a modicum of fraud and violence.

Andrzej Rychard suggests, in his chapter, that the Polish experience is one of quite limited involvement of Poles as citizens in the workings of the political system, as demonstrated by a low turnover in a series of elections plus a lack of interest in politics and of trust in politicians (which are, in fact, fairly widespread phenomena among many populations in the West, and one which, to a point, may be compatible with stable democratic institutions). At the same time, he is inclined to think that Poles have become considerably more involved in the operations of the market, even if this does not translate into an overly optimistic explicit assessment of the virtues of the market system as such. The fact is that well into the 1990s, entrepreneurship spread and multiplied all over, giving birth to a popular capitalism, of sorts, consumers taking eagerly to buying all variety of consumer items typical of advanced Western societies; and even unions, for all their ritualistic contests with private or public enterprises, were tuned to the mood of their affiliates and the moderate stand of the workers themselves. That way, involvement in the market (as employers, consumers and producers) made for a prudent, moderate political position of the population concerning the basics of the new social and economic policies, thus averting the risks of populism.

By looking into the experiences and attitudes of the community base of civil society associations, Rychard submits that there is a connection between people's performances in the economic, social and political settings, so that participation in one of these worlds would compensate for the lack of participation in the others and would, moreover, shape the contents of that participation. In this case, it would do so by reducing the probability of support of populist policies and even possibly, we suggest, by easing the transition from the social movements of the 1980s to the third-sector type of associations of the late 1990s. This may not be enough in the long run, and here Rychard enters in his final discussion, in a complex debate among Polish scholars, public intellectuals and other observers, about the difficulties they perceive for a complete development of a full-fledged liberal democracy, an advanced market economy and a robust civil society fifteen years down the road since the Round Table negotiations of the 1990s.

Notes

1. See Taylor (1995) on the distinction between ontological issues and advocacy issues regarding the relevant units of society.
2. See, in particular, Hegel ([1821] 1963: paragraphs 209 to 249).
3. Such as the one by which the bureaucratic state and the capitalist markets combine as against the life-world of society.
4. For instance, see Keane's (2005) comments on the dark side of markets, and Field's (2003: 71ff.) comments on the dark side of social capital (and by implication, we may assume, of civil societies).
5. This much is asserted in one of the chapters of this book (see Pérez-Díaz *infra*).The suggestion to stick to what sounds like an eighteenth-century use of the terms may have a provocative flavor to it, as it seems to imply the conceptual development of the theory during two centuries has been more a detour than an improvement. Even so, it could be argued that a detour may also be construed as part of God's wisdom, a ruse of reason (as Hegel would say), a way of learning. Having gone astray from the right path and lost the way to freedom quite a few times, Europeans could have learned to appreciate it most once they recovered their senses. To name it 'civil society' may be a provocative move on another account, too, since today's academicians are prone to creating neologisms to mark off the new-new from the simply new, not to speak of the old. (Neo-corporatism and neo-liberalism were ways to avoid, or mitigate, the connection with corporatism and classical liberalism. Should we speak, then, of a 'neo-civil society'? But maybe we are running short of 'neo-names'.) Certainly, other names could be used: an order of liberty, an abstract society, an open society, a free society, civic capitalism and so many others.
6. I will not attempt to pursue the matter any further here (I do, to a point, in Pérez-Díaz, *infra*); but whatever the name adopted, the point is not to miss the contents to which the name refers: the inter-connected whole to which free markets, a liberal polity and a world of voluntary associations belong.
7. Provided that confusion is avoided between the two versions of civil society, in a broad and in a narrow sense.
8. Possibly by means of helping to create the ground for a deliberative political society (Wagner 2006). Let us notice, however, that a commitment to the development of a deliberative political society may also be congruent with a holistic view of civil society.
9. Granted that the way of talk and the degree of explicitness and elaboration of the argument of markets and associations are different. More on this later.
10. See the estimates in the book by Courtois et al. (1997).
11. Quoted in Ratzinger (2005: 120).
12. 'A tool knit', as Swidler (1986) puts it.
13. Even though the experience of international, transnational civil associations suggests that there may be ways to go beyond the local scene and still have an accountability mechanism in place.

References

Benson, Bruce L. 1998. 'Economic Freedom and the Evolution of Law', *Cato Journal* 18, no. 2: 209–232.

Berger, Peter. 1986. *The Capitalist Revolution*. New York: Basic Books.

Courtois, Stéphane, et al. 1997. *Le livre noir du communisme*. Paris: Robert Laffont.

Eco, Umberto. 1979. *A Theory of Semiotics*. Bloomington: Indiana University Press.

Elster, Jon. 1989. *The Cement of Society: A Study of Social Order.* New York: Cambridge University Press.

Field, John. 2003. *Social Capital.* London: Routledge.

Hall, Peter, and David Soskice. 2001. *Varieties of Capitalism: The Institutional Foundations of Comparative Advantage.* New York: Oxford University Press.

Hegel, Georg Wilhelm Friedrich. [1821] 1963. *Hegel's Philosophy of Right.* Trans. T. Knox. London: Oxford University Press.

Keane, John. 2005. 'Eleven Theses on Markets and Civil Society', *Journal of Civil Society* 1, no. 1: 25–34.

North, Douglass C. 1990. *Institutions, Institutional Change, and Economic Performance.* Cambridge: Cambridge University Press.

Oakeshott, Michael. 1991. *Rationalism in Politics and Other Essays.* Indianapolis, IN: Liberty Press.

Pelczynski, Z. A. 1984. 'Introduction: The Significance of Hegel's Separation of the State and Civil Society', in *The State and Civil Society: Studies in Hegel's 'Philosophy of Right'*, ed. Z. A. Pelczynski. Cambridge: Cambridge University Press, pp. 1–13.

Pérez-Díaz, Víctor. 1993. *The Return to Civil Society: The Emergence of Democratic Spain.* Cambridge, MA: Harvard University Press. First Spanish edition 1987.

Pierson, Paul. 2003. 'Big, Slow-Moving and … Invisible: Macrosocial Processes in the Study of Comparative Politics', in *Comparative Historical Analysis in the Social Sciences*, ed. James Mahoney and Dietrich Rueschemeyer. New York: Cambridge University Press, pp. 177–207.

Pinker, Steven. 2002. *The Blank Slate: The Modern Denial of Human Nature.* London: Penguin Books.

Pocock, J. G. A. 1999. *Barbarism and Religion, II: Narratives of Civil Government.* Cambridge: Cambridge University Press.

Popper, Karl R. 1992. *The Open Universe: From the Postscript to the Logic of Scientific Discovery.* London: Routledge.

Putnam, Robert. 1993. *Making Democracy Work: Civic Traditions in Modern Italy.* Princeton, NJ: Princeton University Press.

_____. 2000. *Bowling Alone: The Collapse and Revival of American Community.* New York: Touchstone.

_____. 2002. *Democracies in Flux: The Evolution of Social Capital in Contemporary Society.* Oxford: Oxford University Press.

Ratzinger, Joseph. 2005. *Introducción al cristianismo.* Trans. José L. Domínguez Villar. Salamanca: Sígueme.

Shleifer, Andrei, and Daniel Treisman. 2005. 'A Normal Country: Russia after Communism', *Journal of Economic Perspectives* 19, no. 1: 151–174.

Swidler, Ann. 1986. 'Culture in Action: Symbols and Strategies', *American Sociological Review* 51: 273–286.

Taylor, Charles. 1995. *Philosophical Arguments.* Cambridge, MA: Harvard University Press.

Thelen, Kathleen. 2003. 'How Institutions Evolve: Insights from Comparative Historical Analysis', in *Comparative Historical Analysis in the Social Sciences*, ed. James Mahoney and Dietrich Rueschemeyer. New York: Cambridge University Press, pp. 208–240.

Wagner, Peter. 2006. *Languages of Civil Society.* New York: Berghahn Books.

Part I

MARKETS, CIVIL SOCIETY AND POLITICS

Chapter 1

MARKETS AS CONVERSATIONS
Markets' Contributions to Civility, the Public Sphere and Civil Society at Large

Víctor Pérez-Díaz

The economy is embedded in politics and society, as today's neo-institutional and Austrian economists as well as economic sociologists point out (Boettke and Storr 2002; Granovetter 1992; North 2005; Swedberg 2005a, 2005b), and historians have known for long (Braudel 1973: 444), but the reverse is equally true.[1] We should understand the different ways of functioning of these spheres and how the boundaries between them are maintained, but also how these spheres complement and reinforce each other and how their boundaries are continually crossed. Markets are influenced by politics and society while market experiences shape each one of them in return. The connection going from the markets to the other spheres is the focus of this chapter. I am also interested in understanding how markets and these other spheres may cohere in an orderly whole.

Coherence, or orderliness, is a matter of gradation. But while the development of society brings with it a growing complexity and institutional differentiation, yet a modicum of internal compatibility between the different institutional spheres of society is necessary for society to hold together and continue to grow; otherwise, it may retrogress and, in time, disintegrate. Of course, one way or another, societies continually change. They change because real, individual agents pursue manifold strategies and make use of the existing repertoire of meanings, rules and resources for achieving certain aims or for upholding certain values, that may be at variance with each other.[2] In so doing, institutional and cultural tensions develop which, in turn, combine with the effects of pressures originating in the environment to push change even further. Nevertheless, the proposition that, for sustained periods of time, a minimum institutional fit is necessary holds true, as individuals need it for making their own life plans, engaging in their particular strategies and standing up for their values.

In trying to understand this process of change, we should be aware that the neatness of ideal-typical modelling is not to be confused with the untidy facts of real life. Still, some conceptual ordering is required both for theoretical and practical purposes; even though ideal types are not supposed to correspond to actual developments, they may help us to understand and evaluate them. However, not all models have equal value when it comes to making sense of historical experience, and, eventually, many reveal themselves to be inadequate to the task, and are disregarded. Thus, the realities of socialist life may weaken our current interest in Marxism as an analytical and normative model, while this may not be the case as regards some so-called bourgeois ways of thinking; even the 'messy experiences of bourgeois life' (Habermas 1989: 329) still allow us to keep an interest in that seemingly most archaic specimen of 'bourgeois ideology', namely, the theory of civil society in its old-fashioned, Scottish variety.

A Brief Summary of the Argument

The points I intend to make are, basically, three: (1) that markets should be understood, in an ideal-typical manner, as part of a general social order which I refer to by the ancient expression 'civil society'; (2) that markets may reinforce that order by shaping and influencing politics and society so that they proceed, or function, in a civil manner; and (3) that we may get a better grasp of the way markets act and achieve this effect by developing an understanding of markets as conversations.

Markets are part of, and shape, civil society understood (in ideal-typical terms) in a broad sense. This broad view of civil society (henceforth, CS)[3] has an institutional and a cultural dimension. As a set of practices and institutions, CS brings together, in a systemic whole, the spheres of free markets; of a liberal (and democratic) polity defined by the rule of law, limited and accountable government, and a public sphere-cum-free elections and a representative body; and of a plural society in which voluntary associations and other communities (civil society in a restricted sense: Pérez-Díaz 1995, 1998) play a crucial role. Markets, free polities and plural societies are processes of strategic and communicative interactions which operate within given institutional frameworks, but these institutions cannot be sustained in the long run unless people develop civil (and civic) virtues which provide them with the proper abilities and inclinations to participate in them.

The broad and composite view of CS belongs to a living tradition anchored in the peculiar historical experience of certain seventeenth- and eighteenth-century Euro-Atlantic political communities. That time and place provided the relevant historical context for the Scottish thinkers who put the various pieces of the theory of CS together.

Of course, we must distinguish between an analytical and normative model and the actual workings of any given society. An economy of free and open markets that is subject to the rule of law and proscribes fraud and violence is a model, a regulative idea, that helps us to understand a historical situation and may eventually inspire policy. But it is not a substitute for reality; in fact, there are abundant records showing how the real economies of so-called capitalist democracies of our time incorporate the survival, and even revival, of collectivistic and authoritarian practices.

The historical record shows that markets as well as liberal democratic governments can fail, and do fail. It is not only a matter of under-performance. Economic entrepreneurs may collude with public magistrates to defraud and exploit a gullible and passive public. They can make a mockery of the rule of law by controlling the administration of justice. Oligarchic parties may enter into an unholy alliance with media conglomerates of the left or right, and they may distort a liberal democratic polity and lead the way to corruption, tyranny, Caesarism or authoritarian politics. The public space may be polluted by lies and threats, propaganda and violence. All such developments are deviant and pathological from the viewpoint of a normative theory of CS, but they should be expected to happen under certain conditions.

These practices show ways in which business, government officials, big unions, media conglomerates and the like conspire to reduce the scope of, and distort, a market economy; and, of course, explaining these practices, in their historical context, implies a change in the level of analysis and the use of an array of complementary theories to that of CS as such.

In this chapter, I keep my discussion at a rather general level while I attempt (in the second section) to restate the traditionally broad conception of CS and suggest its relevance for a better understanding of our times, while also reinforcing our links to our historical roots.[4] Then (in the third section), I develop a view of markets as conversations, that is, as a system of communication (mostly, but not entirely, by non-linguistic means) which works as an educational mechanism shaping people's habits. In turn, these habits may help them to develop a complex of capacities and dispositions, of civil (and civic) virtues, which we can bracket together under an ample rubric of 'civility'. Again, a caveat is included here regarding the obvious possibility that real markets depart from this ideal-typical discussion, and due acknowledgment is made to the 'dark side' of real markets (which, by the way, is analogous to the dark side of real liberal democratic polities and of real voluntary associations). Finally (in the fourth section), I explore the scope and the limits of the civilizing effects that free markets, thus understood, have in the realm of politics and the public sphere: on the development of civic capacities, on the formation and preservation of fairly well integrated political communities, and on the relations between citizens and public magistrates as well as the political class at large.

A last word of caution. As presented here, the theory of CS is neither a substitute for reality (as indicated) nor a substitute for a theory of a good society as such. It denotes a reasonable set of institutional arrangements that allows for people with different comprehensive views of the good to live together, peacefully, while trying to enact their ultimate moral views in the various spheres of social life.[5] In a sense, civil society is not so much a good society as it is a superficial order which is 'good enough' for the purpose at hand.

Back to Civil Society in Its Broad Sense

The Scottish Philosophers' View of CS in Context

A broad, composite understanding of the term 'civil society', encompassing social and political institutions, has been part of Western tradition for many centuries, dating back as far as classical political philosophy, civil jurisprudence, medieval political theory, the new scholastic and the Renaissance humanists. The Dutch and Anglo-Saxon thinkers of the seventeenth century, and, in particular, the Scottish philosophers of the eighteenth century, were the starting point for a new avatar of the concept of CS in modern times; but in order to understand this modern version better, we must put it into historical and intellectual context.

During Europe's early modernity, an expansion of overseas markets and profound demographic and agrarian transformations came along with far-reaching cultural and technological changes. As a result, a mosaic of small, circumscribed local or regional worlds (of micro-cosmos in Fernand Braudel's terms; 1990: 114) became parts of a network of larger political units and of extended, spontaneous orders of economic and social exchanges of all kinds, so that, by the eighteenth century, Europe had become a system of states (Pocock 1999: 2, 20, 310), in which governments engaged in a certain amount of dialogue with significant segments of their subjects-citizens, religious and political dissent was gradually permitted, markets and commercial transactions multiplied, and a cultivation of manners spread among increasing numbers of the educated, wealthy sectors of society. Thus, a society based on markets, limited government, a public sphere and voluntary associations was *not* a mere theoretical construct, no more than an analytical or normative model with a distinguished intellectual tradition behind it: it had become the historical horizon, the plausible, attainable reality of significant parts of Europe at the time.

Even then, this world had to be thought out and understood by the people concerned. The Scottish philosophers of the eighteenth century had that world-historical experience within their grasp, and they attempted to theorize it. From their own singular half-local, half-cosmopolitan perspective (midway between Glasgow or Edinburgh and London so to speak), they put together the different narratives and conceptual schemas which they had inherited from a civic tradition, the tradition of natural jurisprudence and the discourse on civility and manners of a polite society. In this way, they constructed a new discourse of the genesis and structure of modern 'civilized' societies.

At the same time, their choice of arguments was not merely theoretical; it had a normative and evaluative, and lastly an existential dimension to it. In a fairly deliberate way, while trying to understand the historical situation they faced, they engaged in it and, in a sense, they embraced it as well. They made the choice between clinging to the independent nation that Scotland had been in the past, and being part of the United Kingdom. They chose the Act of Union (1707) as a vehicle for a different Scotland in the future, which meant opting to engage in a system of expanding markets, representative government and public debate, and in a new social world in which the so-called mingling classes would play an ever-increasing role. They chose to do all of this along with most of the middle and upper strata of the Lowlands to which they belonged.

Furthermore, the Scottish theorists were brought various theoretical languages through a variety of institutions and recent experiences (exiles returning home after a sojourn in Dutch universities, and a milieu of professors, civil servants and Whig aristocrats, among others), which provided them with the tools to articulate a new current of thought; while, at the same time, the historical situation itself provided the challenge, the motivations, a repertoire of institutional mechanisms already to hand, and the climate of intellectual debate for doing so.

At the heart of the Scottish intellectual project lay the tradition of natural jurisprudence as it was transmitted from Dutch scholars of the seventeenth century. This was primarily built around the principle of justice ruling the social exchanges between autonomous actors, based on respect for their private property and the fulfillment of their contracts and promises, but it was complemented by other principles. *Iustitia*, for one, might be a key virtue of that civilized, civil society (CS), particularly in the economic sphere, but it was not the only one, since it must combine with some form of benevolence in the social sphere as well as civic virtue in the political one. Together, justice, benevolence and civic virtue constitute a broad moral character of 'civility' understood as a combination of those civil virtues which fit into and facilitate the proper workings of a CS in its broad sense.[6] In fact, the Dutch experience of the seventeenth century bore witness to this combination of *iustitia*, benevolence and civic virtue. These were assumed to be characteristics of the *burghers*, who were engaged, on the one hand, in their economic pursuits, family life, neighborhood activities and associational experiences of all kinds (in their churches, philanthropic societies, etc.), and, on the other, in city and political affairs (Schama 1988: 7). The view of society in the tradition of natural jurisprudence, dating as far back as Cicero, is that of a self-governing system of social, spontaneous coordination among rational, autonomous agents, but only up to a point. In fact, the whole cannot work unless there is a balance between the free, private arrangements of the individual actors, the institutional framework, and the attending role of legislators and those same individuals insofar as they are *cives*, that is, citizens. In turn, in order to be worthy citizens, individuals should be endowed with a certain amount of civic virtue as well as of *liberalitas* or generosity, which may be implied by bonds of fellowship, and may extend to the moral sentiments of sympathy and empathy which played such a central role in the thought of Adam Smith and Adam Ferguson (Philipson 1983; Robertson 1983).

Social and economic exchanges between individuals need a legal, political framework of rules, and a domain of public goods, to provide for protection for private property, the enforcement of contracts and the defense of the city, plus a substantial modicum of social cohesion; in fact, in the case of the United Kingdom, one of the main rationales put forward for an economic policy favoring free markets was, originally, that of procuring the betterment of the poor classes (Hont and Ignatieff 1985). In any case, the political domain and government could expand to the extent that they did not erode, much less destroy, the very order of freedom – free markets included – they were supposed to uphold.

The civil tradition of the Scots (inspired by civil jurisprudence) allowed itself to be influenced by a civic (or republican) tradition (Robertson 1983: 141ff.), but with a caveat. The Scots were keen on the effects of an institutional machinery which they felt would allow the principles of justice to prevail in the long run; and some of them (Ferguson, for instance) thought civic virtue could reinforce these effects. But they also wanted to tap into people's moral sentiments. As the Scots were inclined to make as realistic an assessment of human nature as possible, they were sensitive both to people's cognitive limits and to their moral weaknesses: their opportunism, predatory tendencies and proclivity to envy, idleness, hubris and resentment. 'Limits', however, are only one half of the human condition; the other half lies in people's 'human potential' for good or benevolent moral sentiments. These might be favored by the institutions which the Scots tried to describe and explain as a result less of conscious design than of complex evolution.

The practical question facing the Scots may be summarized as follows. How could reasonable people, subject to conflicting feelings and desires, organize their conduct in such a way that the (partially intended but mostly unintended) results of their activities and interactions would contribute to a social order which, while adapted to their environment, would exclude a central, directing power and therefore allow the maximum degree of freedom for the individual? The Scots' answer was a repertoire of prudent recommendations. These included an appeal to heed traditions, tempered by the use of immanent, rational criticism and an attempt to design and revise such institutions, an appeal to political moderation and civil virtues, and a judicious assessment of the capabilities and inclinations of different social strata, including a strata of *burghers* or mingling classes.

The same urge to attain a dispassionate, realistic understanding of human beings in general applies to social aggregates as well. Thus, the Scots (and Smith, in particular) tended to consider the different orders of society with mixed expectations. We might say, not one of these groups (gentry, financiers, bureaucrats, the mingling classes, nor the deserving poor) qualified for the leading role, but most had some significant redeeming features, which could grow into full-fledged virtues under the right conditions. The Scots accepted them as they found them, as people with mixed proclivities, and proceeded to make the best institutional arrangements, while recognizing the fact that a CS is and would always be (to put it in Humean terms) a rather precarious undertaking (Robertson 1983: 157, 167).

Thus, the Scots tried to be as realistic as they could in their appraisal of the different strata. They had no illusions regarding bureaucrats, proletarians, political leaders or the intelligentsia: none of these deserved the title of either 'universal class' (*more* Hegel, or Marx), or charismatic leaders (à la Weber), endowed with a prophetic, historical world vision. At the same time, the Scots were appreciative of competent and honest civil servants, prudent legislators, resilient and industrious workers, and helpful experts and *philosophes* (in fact, they themselves tried to fit this particular description). As for the mingling classes, they saw them with a mix of sympathy and detachment but did not consider them to be a universal class, the bearers of a historical world project aimed at realizing an order of freedom on earth. They looked at their historical performance, and examined their constitution, with a clinical eye. They found their state of moral health, in modern times, tended to oscillate between moderately good and unwell. The record showed that they might conspire with others, and act as accomplice to the government, to defraud and coerce the public or, alternatively, to play fair within the rule of law. By the same token, they could act like egotistical, greedy, predatory animals, or, alternatively, be driven by good (and complex) moral sentiments, possibly rooted in a humanist education, classical examples or Biblical teachings.

A word may be added concerning the relations between legislators, civil servants and *philosophes* as leading characters of the public sphere. In it, selected groups and, ultimately, the public at large held government to account, tested the limits of government action and participated in the deliberation and decision-making processes of policy, including negotiations concerning the mode of governance of society as well as the economy.

From the very beginning, there was significant variation in the way in which the public sphere was related to the world of politics and policy in Western societies. Reinhart Koselleck (1988, 2002) has insisted on the point that, at least for the Enlightenment period, the public sphere appeared in quite different modalities in the United Kingdom compared to the European continent (and there were also significant variations on the continent, between France and Germany for example). The crucial distinction lay in the way in which governments, or states, and societies interacted, and this boiled down to differences in the public's access to politics and policy, and to differences in the public's familiarity with, and understanding of, them. This showed in differences regarding the institutional settings of public opinion, the public's self-understanding as a political actor, the criticisms it made of politics and society and its general attitude to politics.

In the United Kingdom, the bridges between public opinion and the political classes were frequently and regularly crossed, as there was no neat separation of the two worlds. Pocock (1999: 164) has referred to this situation as one of a symbiosis of state and society, in contrast to a prevailing pattern of distance, or even of separation, between the two in continental Europe. In the United Kingdom, there was ongoing, fluid communication between court, country and city which led, in due course, to the rise of a massive press readership, the development of political parties with a relatively large following (Pocock 1999: 165), and, gradually, to a culture of mass consumption attuned to continuous changes in taste (Campbell 1987). Under these conditions, criticism by the intelligentsia could be turned into responsible political action since its political opinions found their way into actual politics and policy. The intellectuals-turned-politicians were judged by the practical effects of their proposals on all avenues of life by a public of attentive peers, listeners and debaters.

By contrast, in continental Europe, intellectuals (jurists and the clergy partially exempted) tended either to be cut off from the mainstream of state power or were marginal to it. Most of their debates were conducted in a parallel world of salons, coffee houses and academic settings. No doubt, there was some overlap, (more or less) extended contact and (at times crucial) mutual influence between the two worlds of political deeds and political words, but, on the whole, the logic of debates tended to be quite different in each one. In the world of politics, action brought about real consequences; but in the ideal world of the intelligentsia, criticism was unburdened by the constraints of real politics (Koselleck 1988: 11) and often proceeded in accordance with an ethics of convictions. In the continental tradition, quite a number of writers assumed the role of public intellectual not far removed from that of preacher or moral prophet, particularly if they were addressing a large audience. To the extent that they confined their influence to more restricted circles, many of them found a niche as advisors to the prince and courtiers in aristocratic circles, and, were we tempted to extend the analysis to them, we could add that, in later times, they found their niche as experts in the bureaucratic state machinery, officers in corporate bodies, cadres in party apparatuses or professional revolutionaries in radical parties. The point is that, in one way or another, they tended to shun the role of responsible politicians who could be held to account for their decisions in a public forum.

Various Intellectual Roadmaps for a Way Back to CS

The Scottish philosophers of the eighteenth century understood CS as a type of society which was the result of a largely unintended historical development and was composed of several institutional components which fitted together (in a more or less problematical way). They saw it as a conceptual and normative model for some contemporary societies (Great Britain, the American colonies, the Netherlands, and even France) which were partly, or in the process of becoming, such a type of society. This view has since become entrenched within the liberal tradition right up to our own times, and is in practice, and in a diluted, vaguely ideological way, almost taken for granted in English-speaking countries. However, even in the Anglo-Saxon world, the challenges of nationalism and socialism on the domestic front, and imperialism and world politics in the international arena, as well as gradual questioning of the moral foundations of the liberal order, have obscured this view of the whole. Thinkers in the prevailing empiricist tradition have tended to neglect the systemic character of the links between the different parts of the system. Several generations of pragmatic politicians, civil servants and businesspeople have dealt with institutions as if they could be managed and understood as a *de facto* miscellaneous arrangement of loosely connected parts, useful and resilient in practice but left largely un-theorized as the parts of a whole. In time, the term 'civil society' for denoting this whole has been all but forgotten, and the concept of CS has undergone a protracted process of wear and tear to the extent that, to many, the Scots' original views seems *passé* and archaic. Thus, the scene has been gradually set for a semantic shift in the application of the term from the whole to some of its components, first, to the non-state parts of the whole (markets and associations), and, later, to just the voluntary associations.

The fact is, however, that a closer look at the intellectual history of the discussion suggests a baroque trajectory, with an intriguing ending to it. Eighteenth-century theorists (Montesquieu being an outstanding example of it) used to have a systemic view of human affairs and theoretical disciplines. The Scots' focus on the whole was facilitated by their ability to be conversant with, and try out their ideas in, different fields: jurisprudence, moral philosophy, economics, government and sociology; and Hegel was able to do the same, and his views were focused, too, on the unity of the social system. Hegel substituted the modern state for the Scottish, more traditional view of CS to denote the systemic whole. He made a distinction between a 'strictly political' state and a (more reduced) version of CS, and, in a sense, 'separated' state and CS; but then, he engaged in an attempt to keep the unity of the social-political system. Thus, Hegel's CS encompassed not only markets (the so-called system of needs) and corporations but also courts of justice (and juries) as well as regulatory and welfare public agencies, and, furthermore, he made CS subject to a strictly political state in which civil servants (and, to a point, the representatives of the 'estates') played a key role.[7] In the end, Hegel depicted CS less as 'separated' from the political state than as a 'moment' or a stage in the development of the state proper (Pelczynski 1984: 1). Tocqueville (another example of Montesquieu's influence) also tried to keep a vision of the whole as he looked at the transition from the Ancien Regime to modernity, and at the American experience. He, too, was interested in the role played by intermediate bodies and voluntary associations in the whole system, even though he saw their relationship with the state in a more complicated and sophisticated way than Hegel did.

However, thereafter, every discipline in social sciences has tended to move in different directions. In the case of sociology, for instance, the prevailing tradition focused on the problem of how to maintain or achieve social order under modern conditions. References to the whole remained clear in Émile Durkheim and among structural functionalists and system theorists; and they were present, too, in Max Weber's views on the cohesive effects on modern society of a combination of value orientations, markets and politics, even though Weber was more interested in exploring the tensions between, and the disjunctive logics of, the different spheres of social life (as it has been the case with other sociologists, e.g. Daniel Bell 1976). At the same time, sociology also developed a particular interest in groupings such as intermediary bodies and voluntary associations, which were seen as part of the solution to problems of social order. They had already loomed large in Hegel's and Tocqueville's views, and also in Durkheim's understanding of the limits of organic solidarity and the role of corporations in overcoming these limits in the late nineteenth and early twentieth centuries. The themes of community and societal institutions (and, in particular, of fiduciary professional organizations), and of their contribution to a cohesive and dynamic social system, played a crucial role in the development of American sociology throughout most of the twentieth century and inspired the work of structural functionalists like Talcott Parsons (Brick 1996; Gouldner 1980: 363ff.). Those themes were prominent, too, in the work of small-group, exchange theorists like George Homans, and in most of the latest research work on social movements and networks, and on social capital and non-governmental organizations which has been built on that sociological tradition. The current trend is now to look into the way in which associations, markets and states relate to each other, and to explore their connections in increasing dialogue with the disciplines of law, economics and history. This suggests a return of sorts to the same problematic as that of the eighteenth-century thinkers, although with a different vocabulary. For them, CS stood for the social whole, and that was followed by a semantic shift towards markets and associations, then to associations; now, associations are seen more and more in connection with markets and politics, and the question is whether (and how) they fit together in a systemic whole or depart from it.

The Marxist tradition followed a different path. Marx opposed the unitary views of Hegel and the Scottish philosophers and developed his own dualistic interpretation of modern (and, for that matter, ancient and feudal) society. Marx decomposed Hegel's highly complex, structured concept of CS, and reduced it even further to the economic sphere (Pelczynski 1984: 3). For him, CS in the Scottish, even Hegelian, sense became an ideological label that stood for a bourgeois society which should be understood not as a systemic whole but as a location for radical contradictions and clashes between social and political enemies. Because the bourgeois class exploited a proletarian class, and this exploitation was the *raison d'être* and defining trait of the bourgeoisie, both classes were locked in a fierce struggle with each other which would only end by the proletariat's final victory and a new, now fully cohesive, socialist and communist society. The unraveling of Marx's dualistic, agonic view of bourgeois (civil) society has taken a considerable length of time. In time, the grand strategy of Marx-inspired socialist and communist parties leading a revolutionary proletariat towards a new, more cohesive society became less and less plausible, resulting in a series of strategic retreats.

Marx saw the inner contradictions of the market economy as the driving force for change and, therefore, minimized agency, trusting the proletariat would fulfill its role in due time, with a helping hand from a revolutionary party. But capitalism did not follow Marx's script, and it survived and prospered enough to make room for a moderate industrial working class by the 1920s (as the German case showed: Moore 1978). The historical actors that Marxists assumed to be the bearers of a future, orderly society, such as revolutionary parties and the working classes, lost direction and became contaminated, in the eyes of some followers of the Marxist tradition, by their accommodation to the logic of the market and state bureaucracy. Workers engaged in a process of *embourgeoisement* and were more and more dependent on the welfare state, while unions and parties either followed suit or went down a path leading to authoritarian and even totalitarian regimes.

From a Marxist viewpoint, those developments amounted to 'recalcitrant experiences' (to use W. O. Quine's terms) which refuted long cherished expectations derived from Marxist theory, and asked for changes in the theory. One response was to shift emphasis from the economy to politics, society and culture, and from structure to agency. The shift provided the grounds for a revival of interest in, and a redefinition of, civil society within a marginal segment of the Marxist tradition. Antonio Gramsci saw civil society as the arena for a struggle for cultural hegemony, preparing the way for those thinkers of the Frankfurt school who interpreted civil society as a public sphere in which a selected section of voluntary associations or social movements would play a main role as the bearers of a neo-Marxist, critical moral project. In the wake of this, by the 1960s, Jürgen Habermas advanced a new version of the Marxist scenario. He had already come to the conclusion that the property-less masses could no longer gain control of their own lives and secure a measure of autonomy through participation in markets (Habermas 1992: 434). He seemed oblivious to the fact that these masses had secured a significant amount of economic, political, social and educational resources (in short, they were no longer 'propertyless'); and that there was significant inter-generational, even intra-generational, social mobility in those very Western societies where the markets played a crucial role. He was also suspicious of the state and ultimately came to believe that market and state formed a system of integrated fields that followed its own reified logic. Its two driving forces, money and power, tended to replace language as a mechanism for coordinating social action and instead used sanctions (rewards or punishments) to induce behavior. In contrast with this 'system' there was what Habermas called the 'life-world' comprising the realm of public debate and voluntary associations. Here, life followed the liberating logic of linguistic communication and mutual understanding and recognition.[8]

On the basis of that contrast, Habermas advocated opposition to, and the uncoupling of the life-world from, the integrated system of the economy and the state, and use of the life-world to create a democratic barrier against that system. However, three points qualify that opposition. First, Habermas was reluctant to advocate reform of the system, since he thought the market economy and the state could not be reformed without damaging their own internal logic. The implication here is the double recognition that damaging market logic could have negative consequences for the propertyless masses, and that allowing the market to play its role largely unimpeded can only mean this role is useful or valuable. Second, the erection of a democratic barrier against the economy and the state (or resistance to the colonization of the life-world by the economy and the state) requires collective action and, in particular, access to the welfare state and participation in democratic politics. This leaves the way open for mutual influence between the life-world and the system. Third, Habermas has since come close to subscribing to the position taken by John Rawls with his program of political liberalism for a plural society, in the knowledge that Rawls's program is but a variation of one of the core traditions in the U.S. experience, which gives equal weight to *la liberté des modernes* and *la liberté des anciens* (Habermas and Rawls 1998; Rawls 1996).

The main line of Habermas's argument suggests that the pathologies of the system, or of bourgeois life, can be hard to live with but that they are not that threatening, and certainly not lethal. In this, he takes a position far removed from that of French sociologists such as Pierre Bourdieu, who comes across as much more critical. In Bourdieu's view, there are no opposing logics since one prevailing logic pervades all spheres of life. The structural homology between politics and the economy permeates society and culture down to the heart of the personality system and there is no escape from it. The agent's *habitus* is the internalization of the structural conditions the actor lives under; for this agent to be part of a dominated/dominating segment of a dominated/dominating class (in whatever combination) provides him with a fairly limited repertoire of strategies. The argument applies indifferently to liberal, democratic societies and to illiberal, undemocratic ones: for Bourdieu, these are merely variations of the same structural schema of power games and social domination.[9]

Apart from people with extreme positions, most Marxists came, however, to realize that a view of markets and the state as a unified system subject to a reified logic was at odds with their life experience, with their own specific life-world, so to speak, and with the moral engagement that flowed from that life-world into a long-term strategy of finding a niche in, and accommodating themselves to, bourgeois society. For 'the fortunate few', this meant living in the protected environment of academic establishments. For people who employed themselves in a variety of occupations in the real world, this led them to what came to be known as the 'long march' of the 1968 generation through the institutions. In this process, the cognitive dissonance of living within the system and applying the logic of strategic action, while also living in another world according to the logic of mutual understanding, could hardly be maintained. The *coup de grace* came a little later, with the collapse of the socialist system towards the end of the twentieth century. All in all, there has been some learning along the way which people involved in this retreat from the Marxist tradition could still cling to. They recovered the concept of civil society in a restricted sense, as being a part of the social and institutional infrastructure of the public sphere (in Gouldner's terms; 1980: 371), and, in turn, they could regard the public sphere as the location where society could debate on the game rules for a well-ordered society, perhaps endlessly or until many people eventually rediscovered the old truths of an order of liberty (in other words, of CS, in a broad sense).

In these conditions, and through a baroque sequence of events, we witness a return of sorts to the eighteenth century's broad, composite conception of CS, while, at the same time, a new emphasis is put on the non-political components of CS, namely, associations (civil society in a restricted sense) and markets. This arrangement may fit in with a significant part of the sociological tradition and its current research programs, for instance, that on social capital (Field 2003; Putnam 2000), and may accommodate some of the insights of the critical tradition. Thus understood, the broad conception of CS may provide a conceptual schema that illuminates the links between the different components of the social system, while being sensitive to the gaps between a normative institutional system and the actual workings of those institutions in given historical settings. It may also respond to an increasingly perceived need for an analytical and normative theory which corresponds to the systemic whole that brings together free markets, limited and responsible government under the rule of law, and a plural world of voluntary associations.

On the Current Historical Context

Historians of political thought urge us to see theoretical shifts, discoveries and rediscoveries, and innovations and deviations from semantic conventions within context (Pocock 1999), and social scientists suggest that we look at the contexts of plausibility of different cultural constructs and social interpretations of reality (Berger and Luckmann 1991). The fact is, the need for a semantic shift-in-reverse in order to return to some version of the broad eighteenth-century concept of CS is taking place with simultaneous changes in the intellectual climate and, even more, with changes in historical conditions. We can point to four robust, partly interconnected, current developments.

First, for most countries, diffusion of liberal democracies and globalization are pointing the way towards the future, while authoritarian and socialist experiments seem to be a thing of the past. The wave of transitions to liberal democracy and the reinforcement of market economies in different parts of the world in the 1970s and 1980s made clear the institutional complementarity of a free polity and a free economy and, at the same time, bore witness to an explosion of free associations. In turn, the crisis that led to the final collapse of socialist experiments (authoritarian or totalitarian politics *cum* socialist economies *cum* weak civil societies in the narrow sense of the term) in the Soviet Union and throughout Central and Eastern Europe in the late 1980s and 1990s, made equally clear the failure of the socialist alternative in the face of a combination of free polity and free economy. All over the world, more and more societies are experimenting with different ways of putting together a liberal democracy, a market economy, and the other essentials of CS (the rule of law, an array of voluntary associations, and a civil disposition); they are rediscovering, in word and in deed, the broad concept of CS.

Second, more and more people have realized that most 'third-way' experiments are versions of, or variations on, CS. The failure of third-way regimes to stand on their own had already been anticipated in the collectivistic (socialist, nationalist) experiments in developing countries, but it has since been brought home to Europeans, both West and East. In the West, this learning followed on from a better understanding of the limits of its own neo-corporatist and welfare state arrangements. In the East, from the difficulties experienced by alternative social movements to define and implement a new type of post-communist society other than a version of the 'bourgeois' one. In fact, every formerly socialist country in question has gone down the road of a democratic transition coupled with a transition to a market economy. For the people involved in the social movements of those countries (think of Solidarność in Poland, for instance), their best hope has been in their ability to adapt to this process, to imitate the Western world and become part of it, and, therefore, for them to enter political parties, voluntary associations, the judiciary and the business community. They either had to learn to compete with post-communists in leading the country or to become part of a complex system of checks and balances (inherent in a CS, in its broad sense). In so doing, their ability to counteract the uncivil proclivities of arbitrary government, corrupt firms and overly domineering cultural institutions allowed them to continue, in a new context, their old fight against uncivil practices and institutions which were a legacy of the communist past. This experience has resulted in a new, more realistic understanding of their own role, and may be similar to the one that David Hume attributed to religious enthusiasts in the seventeenth and eighteenth centuries. In effect, they were successful in challenging the rule of a new priestly caste, the communist *nomenklatura*, they subsequently harbored over-inflated views of their own role and only later came to their senses.

The two above-mentioned developments come down to a reassertion of civil ('bourgeois') society in the face of the failure of its socialist, historical alternative, and the pseudo-hybrid of third-way societies. To this we may add a third factor, namely, the need of the West to respond to the challenge to CS coming from a quite different and unexpected quarter in the form of Muslim society. In this respect, it is worth noting the contribution of Ernest Gellner (1994). Gellner was attracted to the use of the term 'civil society' in a broad sense precisely because he was attempting to contrast CS with a variety of closed societies, not only Marxist *but also* Muslim societies. Gellner's aim was to make a sharp conceptual distinction between two systemic wholes: between CS defined by the institutional *pluralism* of its economic, political and social-cultural spheres, and those societies defined by a *fusion* of the economic, political and ideological hierarchies ruling over the rest of society. By the early 1990s, few matched Gellner in his anticipation of a new challenge to CS coming from the Muslim world.[10]

Finally, globalization in the form of worldwide markets integration and the diffusion of new techniques of information and communication is giving a new impulse to a historical mutation 'from polis to cosmopolis' at a world scale. This world may no longer be understood in terms of a collection of (national) states and societies, and their interrelations. The United States, Japan, China, Russia and so many others are, or try to be, players of that character; but Europe seems to be in an ongoing transition to a different kind of historical entity for more than half a century, and large parts of the rest of the world cannot be understood in those terms either. Their predicament suggests fluid political and social architectures, in which networks of fragile compromises play a crucial role. More and more, the most vital problems of governance, economic growth, migrations, social cohesion and geo-strategy are tackled in this fuzzy context, from many institutional angles and at many territorial levels. This is a situation that requires rethinking the connections between world markets, an international civil society (in a restricted sense; see Kaldor 2003a, 2003b; Keane 2003), governments of various kinds, and international law. A thoughtful return to the old schema of CS may provide some cues for a better understanding of the institutional fluidity of these new times.

Markets as Conversations and Educational Institutions

The Civilizing Effects of Free Markets, with a Caveat

Markets are processes of coordination among individual agents who are engaged in a variety of activities including investing in, producing, distributing, exchanging and consuming a large array of goods and services that they provide for each other (Swedberg 2005a). These agents are embedded in social networks of various kinds; they are 'situated selves', to employ the terms used by some communitarian thinkers (Sandel 1982; Taylor 1995) as well as by liberals in the Hayekian tradition (McCann 2002; Pennington 2003). In principle, markets should foster the development of CS and therefore have civilizing effects, but, of course, in practice they may not. It depends on what the agents choose to exchange with each other, and which rules they actually follow in doing so; this, in turn, depends largely on the kind of social and political arrangements that they are embedded in, and on the repertoire of cultural meanings and motives they use. At the same time, for markets to work properly, fraud and violence must be checked by legal controls which are guaranteed by public authority, by social sanctions and by a shared cultural background; in the end, they must all provide with a minimum of mutual understanding and mutual trust.

According to the Scottish philosophers, historical experience suggests that, under the right institutional and cultural conditions, allowing markets to function relatively freely (by avoiding a high degree of state intervention and/or collusion between political and economic elites) tends to increase society's chances of freedom, survival and prosperity. It should reinforce an order of freedom, or CS in its broad sense, and thus have a civilizing effect, at least in the long run. In Smith's words, for a civilizing process to go forwards it would be just enough to enjoy peace and justice, and 'easy taxes', presumably referring to a protective yet limited state. In the words rendered by Dugal Stewart: 'Little else is required to carry a state to the highest degree of affluence from the lowest barbarism but peace, easy taxes, and a tolerable administration of justice; all the rest being brought about by the natural course of things' (quoted in Rae [1895] 2005: 2). The right institutional conditions mean that the game rules exclude violence and fraud, and the right cultural conditions mean ordinary people are expected to behave as if they were passably decent and no-nonsense, most of the time and under normal conditions. This degree of cognitive realism and moral decency (including self-control and sensitivity to others' needs) creates the required minimum of mutual understanding and trust, in the absence of which the best institutions, left to themselves, cannot do their job and a CS cannot be sustained.

Institutions may fail, and in real life they often do so, because, in the final analysis, they don't act but are acted out by human agents who have limited cognitive and moral capacities. First, these agents may misperceive and misunderstand the situations they are in, and prove unable to correct their misinterpretations.[11] Besides, they perceive and articulate their desires, interests and goals in life in all sorts of ways. In a sense, humans are always, by definition, under-socialized,[12] and they may come to believe in quite different parts of the range of institutions and beliefs at their disposal, either agreeing with or deviating from prevailing rules and values, or plainly upholding the wrong ones. So, on top of the due acknowledgment of the eventual failures of the markets, we have to attend to the possibility of a 'dark side' to actual market operations at any time or place.

This dark side of the market may come in different ways. Firstly, market practices can be gravely distorted by violence or fraud, perhaps as a result of collusion practices between predatory and opportunistic economic entrepreneurs, demagogues or fanatics of various kinds, corrupt state officials or mafia-like gangs, revolutionary guerrillas or drug traffickers, and so on. In fact, markets incorporate violent and corrupt practices to varying degrees, and, for instance, the markets for hired assassins, slave labor and child prostitution as well as for drugs and weapons have thrived at one time or another.

But, secondly, we may think there is no need to focus on such extreme cases since distorted markets are often the rule rather than the exception in many places. As Andrei Shleifer and Daniel Treisman (2005) have argued, many of today's middle-income developed and developing countries (and they point to Brazil, Mexico, China and Russia) have weak judiciary and law-enforcement institutions, poorly performing liberal democracies with authoritarian leaders (or authoritarian regimes *tout court*), frail social and media controls, and a precarious public sphere. Under these conditions, it is hardly surprising that they also have market economies in which corruption and coercion play, at least for the time being, a significant role; in fact, this is what can be considered their 'normal' (frequent, sustained, predictable) state of affairs.

Finally, we may even consider that well-established markets in advanced capitalist democracies are far from being free from still significant doses of violence and fraud that may creep into the workings of the economy in either ostensible or insidious ways, hence the need for watchful civil and civic vigilance and continuous remedial action. Indeed, next thing in the agenda of a research program that starts from an ideal typical view of markets as conversations is bound to be an examination of those problematic situations.

However, there is nothing odd in these disparities between an ideal type and real life. The same applies to liberal democracy, the rule of law or voluntary associations (the so-called third sector, or civil society in a narrow sense), or to a community of discourse, not to speak of universal religions as well as of science: they have all been distorted and put to uncivilized uses on many occasions.

The ideal community of discourse, for instance, may be geared towards testing the claims to validity, sincerity and truth of the participants in a process of deliberation, or in a reasonable conversation; but this is far from what we may find passing for a conversation in most cases. In his 'Hints towards an Essay on Conversation', Jonathan Swift ([1758] 1977) sets out to portray *not* the ideal type of conversation in its perfected form, but rather the way it was (in his words) much neglected and abused in his own time. He describes people given to the folly of talking too much, talking to themselves, running over the history of their lives, lying in wait to hear themselves praised, deciding matters in an abrupt, dogmatic way, never at ease but when they can dictate and preside, overcome by pedantry, prone to singling out a weak adversary and raising a laugh at his expense, impatient to interrupt others, troubled with the disease of wandering thoughts: the list goes on and on. And Swift was writing at almost the same time and place, eighteenth-century Great Britain, as the modern philosophers were adumbrating their theory of CS, which included the sphere of public debate and polite conversation as one of its key components.

Words and Deeds, or Statements and Practices, as Communicative Acts

From an ideal-typical viewpoint, markets may be seen as processes of exchanges between situated individuals who are rational enough to understand each other's signals and moral enough to trust each other so as to keep the exchanges going. Markets are processes of interactions with strategic and communicative dimensions which are inextricably linked to each other. As communicative processes, they are like verbal as well as practical conversations, and as such, they are conducted by linguistic as well as extra-linguistic means. These verbal and practical conversations are expansive, unending and open-ended. In fact, market practices are not fixed practices, role or *habitus* performances: simple responses to inducements by a price system considered as a steering mechanism. They are one variety of human engagements, of manners of being-in-the-world, which involve practices and social interactions that can only be partially and imperfectly understood. This limited understanding consists of knowing how to handle the (social, material, cultural) world at hand, around us, and is implicit in a repertoire of coping skills that can only be grasped in the process of doing things, exchanging things, interacting with people, and trusting them, to a point. Both limited understanding and limited trust are tested in the market process and may, consequently, either increase or decrease. Meanwhile, they are also influenced, as all human engagements are, by the sort of moods people are in (light-hearted, detached, anxious, resolute, etc.); and they incorporate, also, many levels and forms of interpretation, as regards the background of relevant (formal and informal) rules, the angle or perspective from which the situation is approached, and the process of time involved in the form of expectations, possibilities and projects (Dreyfus 1991).

The market process may be seen, then, as a range of social practices by means of which people's understanding and trust of others evolve (by growing or shrinking); these partially understood practices are partly revealed to others by various means of both conversation and communication. In this respect, Georg Simmel's ([1917] 1964: 409ff.) discussion of conversation and Paul Grice's (1989) exposition of the rules of an ideal conversation are both useful. Simmel makes a distinction between content-oriented conversation and the art of conversation. Both modalities are relevant but there is still something missing from Simmel's account. Content-oriented conversation focuses on a matter to be debated (Simmel ([1917] 1964: 409ff.) whereas the art of conversation points to a larger situation. It is more open-ended. Changes of subject do not restrict themselves to following the direction of the conversation (as Grice would say). They may, and are expected to, deviate from it. The message, the implication, is that there is more than content as a rationale for engaging in conversation. It is a performance for being together, marking social distinctions, intimating a plurality of possibilities and life projects, the sharing of an entire world or an encounter between a multiplicity of worlds. Furthermore, beyond the linguistic exchanges of speech acts in the contents debate and the art of conversation, there are also gestures, body language, silences, ironies, exits and re-entries. Strict conversation (the debate and the art) is followed and preceded by, and is part of, a process of communication which is much broader, and takes place in a longer temporal frame. Seen from this viewpoint, linguistic exchanges combine with signals that are exchanged by means of actual conduct of, say, market, social and political activities and even cultural activities, which are carried on with little or equivocal linguistic support, or none at all.

In this context, Paul Grice's rules of truth, sincerity and validity should be thoroughly revised, as far as their applicability to those situations is concerned. It is not a matter of arriving at the truth by means of an explicit argument, but rather of engaging in an open-ended process of discovery of the truth, in which thousands of hypotheses or statements of plausibility are tested again and again, and which still only give us, at best, nothing more than an approximation to the truth. The rule of sincerity becomes a rule for engaging in a process of self-discovery, by means of increasing one's awareness when confronted with the gradual unfolding of several levels of intentionality as the process of communication goes on; and of taking stock of the criticism and dimensions of self-reference implied in our own criticism of others. The rule of validity changes too. It is, rather, a matter of testing the intensity of our commitments, and their consistency with each other, in a world of pluralism concerning our own values and those of others. Thus, it is also a process of discovery that goes beyond simple imitation to a better understanding of our own choice between the different models to be imitated. Besides, these statements concerning truth, sincerity and validity cannot be abstracted from performances. Discovery means experiments and tests, decisions and risks; and the same applies to self-discovery and the discovery of values. Thus, a relaxation of Grice's values follows: the more we are embedded in a flow of social interaction, the more latitude we apply to the rules related to the direction of the flow of conversation, in line with the art of conversation, and move on to a process of communication combining linguistic and extra-linguistic means. Conversation becomes part and parcel of a package of linguistic and extra-linguistic communication, in a process of discovery and self-discovery with no end in sight, that could go awry any moment. This allows us to move towards an ideal-typical account of conversation which is closer to reality, more relevant for understanding things as they are, and may also help us to make a more persuasive argument in normative terms.

Some Illustrations of Linguistic and Extra-linguistic Communication in the Art World, the Urban Scene and Politics

In Rilke's ([1907] 1984) portrait of Cézanne (in his letter to Clara from *la rue Casette*, 7 October 1907), he describes Cézanne in an angry mood, battling with every one of his own works. But Cézanne's works are like words to him or like sentences in a conversation of which he is a part. He starts painting with the more somber tones of his palette, then he superposes a lighter tone, going just slightly beyond the surface of the previous one, repeating the operation again and again, covering the surface while changing the tonality and the atmosphere, so that his visual perception of the motif and the appropriation of what is perceived go hand in hand. However, they do not go as amiable partners; they fight each other all the way, talking at the same time, interrupting each other, while Cézanne himself has to bear their discord. In the end, he finds refuge in 'work and only work', facing something so enormous that he is left speechless and immensely distrustful of the power of words to grasp his experience. Rilke adds that he is also distrustful of the flood of explicit, articulated words his friend Zola used to render Cézanne's experience and, in fact, to falsify it (though, no doubt, with sincerity and in pursuit of truth). In Rilke's account, Cézanne could not respond with words to Zola's misinterpretation, but only by pointing his finger at his breast, speechless and overcome by emotion; and the next day, by waking up early and returning to work, lonely, silent and resolute, to make his work speak for him. In the same vein, we may add that Proust's aesthetic feeling was of a different (and, to this reader, higher) quality than Zola's, but Umberto Eco (1979: 173ff.) has suggested that even Proust could render, almost, the range of feelings and values embodied in impressionistic painting only because he analyzed an *imaginary* painting, by 'Elstir', since a *real* painting would have carried on portions of content his words could not cover. This allows Eco to conclude that non-linguistic devices convey portions of a general semantic space than verbal language does not.

In a different terrain, there is the eloquence of utterances which are not words, and of words which are treated as 'material' for other words. For instance, an episodic *fou rire*, like the one Proust and his friend Lucien Daudet indulged in when they were together and heard a commonplace (Raczymov 2005: 157). The message is not that different from what Proust suggests himself when, in his analysis of '*le gratin*' of the Faubourg Saint Germain, he remarks,

> when [Madame de Guermantes] talked [interestingly about] Faubourg Saint Germain, she provided my spirit with literature [that is, with matter for Proust's imagination to translate into a different communicative block, with its own emotional and ideational implications, a different piece of conversation between himself and his readers], while I could only hear her [rather stupid] 'Faubourg Saint Germain' when she talked literature [that is, Proust decodes her words as a game of social distancing that she shared with her own world in dealing with each other and everyone else]. (Proust [1921] 1954: 496)

What this means is that the initial conversation is taken to pieces and its various components duly transformed into utterances with other implications and reoriented to other destinations and other audiences, and given different meanings by their connection with a variety of practices.

Proust's handling of his cultural material is a way of conversing with, and engaging in a social performance with, a number of social networks. He is responding to people of his milieu as well as to the unknown reader with whom he also tries to establish a social and a moral bond. By means of words, he tries to express his emotions in a way that touches on, and engages, the reader's emotions, thus creating an atmosphere of mutual understanding and trust. What Proust does is analogous to what Jane Jacobs ([1961] 1992: 56) observes in a completely different setting, in the formation of casual public trust on the city sidewalks. There, trust is formed over time as the result of many little formal and informal contacts, which create an ambiance of moral and physical safety for everybody to pursue their own errands and to connect with each other. In the end, a social situation is created, in various domains, in the way in which the familiar social networks of giving and receiving operate everyday, mixing linguistic and extra-linguistic means to accomplish their task. These social networks allow for the development of a 'practical knowledge of thoughts and feelings of others which arise from complex social interactions ... as a matter of responsive sympathy and empathy elicited through action and interaction … and involve pre-linguistic recognitions' (MacIntyre 1999: 14ff.).

Moving onto politics, politicians speak partly with their words but mostly with their deeds, and it is not possible to understand what they are saying unless it is within the context of what they do. In the extreme case of war, the best speeches are the shortest and form part of the ongoing action: just a brief reminder of where one is and what being there means. Pericles' oration was eloquent if somewhat argumentative, in a very Greek way. Nelson's words at Trafalgar are like an elliptical summary of the same argument. 'England expects that every man will do his duty' sounds as if to fight and be ready to die for one's country is a matter of course. But what else can you do as a British sailor facing the French and Spanish when the fighting starts? In general terms, the usual, implicit reference to the means of coercion is only a small part of the leader's performance; it must be fine-tuned to the audience and the situation and it risks being counterproductive. What Theodore Roosevelt once suggested may be sufficient: 'talk softly and carry a big stick', but even then both the soft words and the big stick are needed. At the other extreme, twenty-five centuries earlier on the other side of the world, Lao Tzu said 'one who assists the ruler of men by means of the way does not intimidate by a show of arms', and he added wistfully, 'that which goes against the way will come to an early end' (Lao Tzu [sixth/fifth centuries BCE] 1962: 35).

Political performances can be peaceful or war-like, even though, in general, the better governed a society is, the smaller the role of political violence. Resort to violence is the very last, exceptional thing to do, and in Roosevelt's times in the United States it was of no use even to win an election. Politics is not defined by violence but by the very fact that violence is left on the margins of the game. Political language is not a veil masking the truth; power is not a medium that coerces or induces people's behavior. Political authority, or any political agency in general, communicates by means other than rewarding obedience and punishing deviance; it makes statements of value, assertions of identity, descriptions of alternative courses of action and assessments of rapport as a means to shared goals. Obedience or the lack of it in politics are just a part in a communicative process, and go back and forth between political rulers and their constituencies. Of course, in an Orwellian world, if the dominated segment of the dominated class (to employ Bourdieu's strict, slightly mesmerizing terms) has been thoroughly indoctrinated and trained to obey, their *habitus* reduced to playing by the rules of the dominating segment of the dominated class plus those of the dominated and dominating sectors of the dominating class, there is no alternative but to submit to a combination of physical and symbolic violence. However, the best illustration of this extreme situation is not any variation of a CS, but rather a concentration camp in the Gulag, for instance, and the best description would not be provided by sociological literature but by a personal witness, as in Shalamov's (1994) *Kolyma Tales*.

Performances in the sense of communicative action that I am referring to are *not* in the manner of ritual, play or text as Clifford Geertz (1983: 23ff.) presents them. Neither are they in the manner of a ritual drama, with a largely foreseeable outcome, nor of a drama in which various agents play games with masks they put on or take off, largely in control of their performance if not of the final outcome. Lastly, they are not in the manner of conduct as text understood the way Ricoeur (1981) suggests: that they are a text insofar as they are subject to inscription and being fixed. They are more in the manner of an open-ended, shifting discovery process, in which small, gradual changes are introduced at any moment by those who, while being participants in the ritual drama, the dramatic performance or the inscripted text, are ready to depart from the script.

Markets as Conversations: The Way They Work at Various Stages of the Economic Process and in Different Conversational Spaces

A view of trade as an exercise in debate and oratory was a commonplace in the discourse of the classical economists. In Turgot's words, as Emma Rothschild (2001: 8ff.) reminds us, free commerce is 'a debate between every buyer and every seller', in which individuals make contracts, listen to rumors, discuss the values of one another's promises, and reflect on 'the opinion and the reality of risk'. Adam Smith described exchange as a sort of oratory in which 'the offering of a shilling, which to us appears to have so plain and simple a meaning, is in reality offering an argument to persuade one to do so and so as it is for his interest.... And in this manner every one is practicing oratory on others through the whole of his life'. The point to be emphasized is that markets are ongoing (verbal and practical) conversations, which proceed in time, change direction, and display an open-ended, unpredictable character.

They are not debates in which a state or a point of equilibrium is reached on some common agreement on any given matter, as if supply (the solution to the problem) and demand (the problem to be solved) were to meet once and for all. In fact, they constantly coincide, and diverge. Knowledge flows from relative prices, signaling relative scarcities, temporary and changing desires and available means. There is a process of discovery and mutual adjustment that goes on indefinitely; disequilibria are endemic, checked by attempts at an always elusive equilibrium. Agents are endowed with varying, and limited, degrees of brilliance (knowledge, information, wisdom) and benevolence (Boettke and Leeson 2003). Their search for truth, their sincerity and the validity of their findings are tested over and over again; as they may be tempted by opportunism or hatred, and enter in collusion with politicians and fanatics to use violence and fraud. At best, peace, justice and limited government provide a level playing field for nonviolent, non-fraudulent economic exchanges, allowing a conversation to go on.

Thus, markets may work as procedural mechanisms whereby the relative scarcity of goods and services is discovered and communicated, allowing for multiple examples of action: doing rather than talking, observing and emulating behavior, imitating what is successful and avoiding what is not. Market practices go some way to protecting the playing field for the game of economic, social conversation, because, on the cognitive side, markets may provide a reality check on the wishful thinking of politicians, civil servants or academics, and refute or expose the shortcomings of their ill-conceived policies by means of capital movements, employment decisions or shifts in consumption patterns. On the normative side, markets give a voice to the public's full range of value statements and limit the effect of the moral imperatives of the few.

Markets make use of both linguistic and extra-linguistic communication, but the core of market communication is non-linguistic (Horwitz 1992; Pennington 2003). The way market processes, *qua* social conversations, work is by means of exchanges of not so much explicit verbal statements as actual performances. These include imitating and innovating, giving and receiving, buying and selling, producing and consuming; even though these activities may be accompanied by performative utterances, partial explanations and occasional exhortations.

Extra-linguistic and linguistic communication can complement each other. Formal, explicit, deliberate discourses of analysis and justification play a role in the whole conversation; and can be put to use for modeling, pattern prediction, *post facto* explanations, piecemeal experimentation with various institutional designs and statements of general principles, all of which can make them helpful for educational purposes. There is even an interpretive dimension which may add coherence and depth to market experiences, and provides additional tools for a Humean-like, immanent, rational critique of these practices (Horwitz 1992). If market exchanges are seen as exchanges of tacit statements (performing, giving, receiving, etc.), then they must be placed in context, and the decisions they embody (whether spontaneous or deliberated) should be seen as responses to understood situations, even if that understanding comes only in a tentative, limited, tacit way. The point is that most decisions made by entrepreneurs, investors, managers, employees, distributors or consumers have little or no explicit justification, but this does not mean they do not convey some of the reasons, diagnoses, normative orientations, priorities, expectations, hopes and predictions of the participants, based on their local, practical, tacit knowledge and moral wisdom.

Markets can be seen as part of an endless, society-wide, global conversation which encompasses an infinite number of bilateral transactions within an ever-wider network, but the extent of their scope is matched by the intensity of their penetration into every stage of the economic process: of production, distribution and exchange, consumption, and investment (Swedberg 2005a). At the stage of distribution and exchange, prices guide our choices by providing us with knowledge of relative scarcities, by indicating the success of our choices and thereby discovering opportunities for profit. By so doing, markets go beyond the limits of rational discourse and enrich the range, quality and complexity of our communication process (Pennington 2003).

At the production stage, for instance, the engineer employs a discourse of applied science, applied economics and so forth, to his task of fitting things together and making them work (Hapgood 1993: 28). In doing so, he is just one among many technicians, skilled and not-so-skilled workers involved in the design and production process, who talk to each other through what they actually do. This conversation is surrounded by talk of a similar kind with the salesmen, and through them with the consumers of the product, as well as with the financiers, and through them, with the stock markets and other sources of capital.

Mass production may be seen as requiring simple, repetitive tasks that incorporate little knowledge; but this is far from the usual, let alone the only, way of working in complex market economies. In many situations, there is a moral professional side to work, in that many producers of goods and services aim at the attainment and preservation of the highest possible skill. In the words of Joseph Conrad, such skill is made up of accumulated tradition, is rendered exact by professional opinion and, like the highest arts, it is spurred on and sustained by discriminating praise. Such skill goes beyond efficacy and efficiency, and presses into art of ceaseless striving to raise the dead level of current practice (Conrad [1906] 1988: 20).

An analogous situation can be observed at the stage of consumption. By buying a product, the consumer sends a signal, which is very complex and wide-reaching, to many agents and institutions. But additionally, by deciding to buy, he has reached a conclusion as the result of a conversation which is part and parcel of the workings of the micro-society of which he is a member, together with other family members (Perez-Díaz 2000: 27ff.), colleagues, friends, neighbors, and so forth. The peasant farmer who buys a piece of agricultural machinery does so within the context of a family conversation. Maybe he responds to his boy prompting him to do so because otherwise he may as well pack up and go elsewhere. The same farmer, performing in the same complex role of *pater familias*, may buy a household appliance within a similar conversational context with his wife and daughters, eager to lighten their workload, and embrace the standards of modern life.

'Markets speak' means 'people speak', that is: they express values and preferences, analyze situations and make forecasts by exchanging goods and services and information, thus creating conversational spaces. These spaces can be as extensive as a large national community, even a transnational community, and as circumscribed as a business firm or a family unit.

It can be argued markets have been extremely important in undoing the decades of authoritarian, collectivistic practices that led some fairly civilized European nations into barbarism. For instance, it is true that in the very hard times of unemployment and social crisis of the late 1920s and early 1930s, the Germans tried to overcome a sense of loss of direction by putting their trust in a charismatic leader who was intent on uniting the country behind him and engaging in a search for vital space and world domination. But, as Ludwig von Mises ([1944] 2002) has argued, the Nazis' success in winning the hearts and minds of a majority of Germans till near the end of the war was the final stage of an unfolding drama and was built on experiences that could be traced back to the second half of the nineteenth century. While fighting each other, national conservatives and socialists had deep elective affinities with each other and, for decades, they pushed for state intervention in the economy and for a *modus vivendi* between state officials, business associations and unions around ideas of protectionism, regulated markets and a welfare state. Many of them interpreted the historical situation as one of a worldwide contest for natural resources and foreign markets, and for the final victory of one or another set of ultimate values, a particular *Weltanschauung*. It all ended in a terrible episode of violence and war, destruction and self-destruction that led to the hugely demoralized society of post-war Germany.

We have a poignant artistic evidence of this loss of direction in Germany, during the first years immediately after the war, in the film *Germania, anno zero*, by Roberto Rossellini. The lovers of old movies may remember the film was made in the spirit of the Italian *neoralismo* of the 1940s, a sort of *cinema verité avant la lettre* with a touch of a Pascalian or Augustinian Catholic view of human nature. It tries to be, however, an eye-witness account of a hugely demoralized society. Germany has just suffered an absolute and crushing defeat. In a devastated Berlin, the name of the game is now survival, and survival pitches a childish-looking boy of twelve against all the odds. The boy wanders from one place to another in search of shelter. People sharing an apartment reject and manipulate each other, they resent being close to an ill person and, in due course, gather around his dead body, anxious to get rid of it while saving the garments for further use. Fittingly, people gather in the street around the corpse of a dead horse eager to get a piece of meat from it. Adolescents come around in a display of exploitative behavior by stealing from each other. Small children playing in the streets reject the boy wanderer. The inner circle of his family is made up of a lamenting father, an aimless girl and a fearful older brother, with the boy as the only plausible chance for the survival of them all. When he happens to cross paths with his former teacher, he's exposed once again to a lesson in the ways of the jungle, and to the 'survival of the fit' rhetoric of Nazi days. Putting together his teacher's lessons, which may resonate from his own school days, and his sick father's endless lamentations about being a burden on his dysfunctional family, leads the boy to kill his father and then commit suicide.

This gruesome tale stands up by virtue of the documentary likeness of the movie. The sequences are brief and stark. The camera moves fast and follows the boy moving intently and aimlessly among the ruins, looking for some kind of emotional shelter. But society has collapsed. German society has not just been defeated. It has vanished. Through Rossellini's pitiless eyes, the time is not for preaching but just for looking. He looks for a society. Instead, he finds a series of social black holes, and the boy is just swept away by and whirled down to the bottom of one of them.

The point is that the way the country emerged from that kind of nightmare involved a combination of economic and social 'miracles'. Within a very few years, the Germans were able to make a comeback. They worked hard, and pulled themselves back up, abiding by rules of mutual toleration and looking destiny in the face. All of this was crucially dependent on the new rules of the economic game put in place by the Germans themselves. Ludwig Erhard bet on an open, free market economy and let the spontaneous forces of supply and demand work their way through the frail and demoralized society of post-war Germany. He achieved this with the support of a German Chancellor who had very limited political authority at that time, and by taking advantage of the fact that the highest political authority, the American military commander, was caught in a lapse of absence. With politics sidelined, the way was open for individuals to play their game of endless, ever-renewed, mutually advantageous economic exchanges. By doing so, they rebuilt a social fabric, woven of mutual trust, from the bottom up. It was done partly before and partly *pari passu* being formally stated in laws, political programs and corporatist arrangements between the political, economic and social elites.

In general terms, the whole of continental Europe had lost direction in the years preceding World War I and the inter-war period, and the result was a drift towards authoritarian politics, heavy state intervention in the market economy and feverish nationalism leading to fascism, corporatism and socialism, followed by Nazism, communism and outright war. Rising up out of this descent into madness took a huge amount of political and economic liberalism on the part of the Western European nations over the next half century, with a determining role being played by the markets. Furthermore, markets have created, or strongly contributed to the creation of, a European common space. They have checked the protectionist, inward-looking tendencies of the economic structures of every country, and they have made people all over Europe more aware of each other and to the opportunities originating among their neighbors. They have largely replaced competition through war, that is, by way of death, rape, torture, invasion, humiliation and other displays of aggressive behavior, by the more peaceful endeavor of competition through trade and investment. And they have done so generation after generation for the last sixty years.

At the opposite end of the spectrum of social forms we find small groups, or small worlds; there, the markets can also be seen to enhance communications and the sense of community, in social settings such as business organizations and families. The firm, for instance, is quite often seen as a sort of community only when management is able to strike a deal with employees who are considered as prominent stakeholders in the organization; but there are other possibilities for the firm to be understood as a community. It can also be seen as a matrix of contracts, a community of weak ties (Granovetter 1973), but still a community. For instance, recent experiences point to the possibility of business employees spending part of their working day trading in futures of their own company: on the future of sales, product access, supplier behavior, procedures (Kiviat 2004). This proves that useful information embedded within a group can be extracted and organized via a marketplace. This may well be the way that management, or leadership, is downgraded within firms, and partly replaced or complemented by people speaking in a direct, and possibly eloquent, way, instead of through their union representatives.

By the same token, the logic of social exchanges under the rule of *iustitia*, of norms of reciprocity and equal or nearly equal exchanges, can also apply to intimate relationships such as those within families, and between lovers and friends, as Viviana Zelizer (2005) has shown. In these settings, and in the context of what Zelizer calls 'connected lives', the logic of markets may be tempered, but it is not fully rejected, by the virtue of benevolence and by the pursuit of a common goal.

Civility and Two Morals, of the 'Small Worlds' and of the 'Extended Orders'

Communications go beyond giving information on facts, values and ideas to setting examples, issuing exhortations, and shaping the habits of heart and mind, to intimate moral behavior. The argument developed by Hayek

(1988: 18) suggests that we live in two different worlds to which different morals apply. One moral would be guided by the pursuit of a common goal and would typically apply to 'small worlds';[13] the other, by the rule of equal exchange between agents who wish to achieve their own individual goals and would apply to extended orders and large systems of social networks. But, in fact, the moral of mutual benevolence coupled with concern for a common good applies to *all* sorts of social groupings, big and small, and has a bearing on the extended orders too; while the moral of extended orders also applies to both very large and very small settings. According to circumstances, we apply morals that are different yet compatible with each other, so as to not endanger the narrative unity of our connected lives; and we may combine different moral viewpoints to apply to mixed situations. We may do this in dialogue with our 'autobiographical selves' (Damasio 2000) and with friends, curious onlookers and, hopefully, some impartial spectators who may come along. Under those conditions, making the right choices is what prudence or practical judgement is all about.

It is true that the morals of the small world tend to apply more easily to networks of families, friends and close acquaintances, tribes and villages, and possibly to traditional, segmented societies or modern, closed ones (Gellner 1994). The small world has been the main setting for ordinary moral behavior in most of Europe throughout the second millennium, and has continued to be so well into the second half of the twentieth century in rural areas (half of the population of France or Italy, for instance) (Braudel 1990). The views of MacIntyre (1999) on networks of giving and receiving, in which he finds a prominent role for voluntary associations and local communities as a source of morality apply here, and so do remarks by Boettke and Rathbone (2002) on local reputation as a disciplinary mechanism for associations and face-to-face communities. However, it is also possible to design a system of trustworthiness that goes beyond local boundaries and applies to national or transnational social networks, global non government organizations, credit systems and international institutions.

Large social ensembles have been often understood as small worlds writ large. So has a nation-state with its appeals to brotherhood, a strong public authority playing the role of *pater familias*, a common goal and shared substantive values as well as a circle of trust circumscribed to the national community, along with the corresponding feelings of fear and hatred of strangers. In times of war, this has been seen as quite a normal moral development. It may also underpin the task of building a welfare state as if this were a normal trait of a nation-state understood as a big family house, a people's house, a *Folkhem*. This can take different forms. In a very robust form, it may reflect the Myrdals' view of a maximalist welfare state in which 'the most important task of social policy is to organize and guide national consumption along different lines from those which the so-called free choice follows', aiming at 'a socio-political organization and control not only of the distribution of incomes but also of the focus of consumption within families' (quoted in Rojas 2001: 16). It could also adopt the extreme form of a 'therapeutic society' in which state interference is complemented by an army of what Edgley and Brissett (1999: 215ff.) have called 'meddlers and virtuecrats', eager to tell others how to behave and what values they should adopt, as these authors think is the case in certain social milieus in the United States.

Contrary to those who think of the market is full of *anomie*, a jungle where the 'law of the jungle' (i.e. no law) applies, it can be shown that the law of the jungle and market law are complete opposites. Gains made in the jungle at another's expense, by seizing their property, for example, contrasts with gains achieved in the market by serving another in peaceful cooperation (Rothbard 1970: 1325ff.). In fact, a modicum of trust in each other is the normal disposition of those who participate in well functioning markets. Without trust in the quality of products, in the contracts binding employers and employees, in the rules of lending and borrowing, and in the game rules of corporate governance, markets would come to a stop.

Again, a literary reference may serve to illustrate the point. In Joseph Conrad's *Typhoon* ([1902] 1962), MacWhirr, the captain of the ship, sees a typhoon approaching. Though a man of deeds and not words, MacWhirr explains himself and what he is about to do. Freely summarized, his explanation might be as follows:

> I see the typhoon coming but until it hits us I cannot weigh up the danger it involves. At the same time, I'm under an obligation to make the trip profitable, keep an eye on the costs and save coal. I must stay on course. How could I explain taking a costly detour to avoid a danger I cannot measure? I must trust my contractors have provided me with a solid steamer, built with the strength to sail the high seas; and the builders, carpenters and other craftsmen who made the different parts of the ship to last: they will not let me down. And the seamen will do their duty.

MacWhirr's motto could be 'In men I trust', in other words, in their commitment to do their work properly, and in the social arrangements, contracts and mutual promises which are behind their personal endeavors. This includes trust in people we know personally, but also trust in a worldwide division of labor, in an abstract world of professional obligation, commercial honesty and social arrangements of many kinds. Of course, we, as readers, need all the words that Conrad offers us to understand the players and the situation they respond to, but for MacWhirr himself, we gather, most of these words were not needed. He would prefer to let his deeds speak for themselves, or let the words be torn from his lips as 'broken shouts' (Conrad [1906] 1988: 281).

Markets' Morality Not as Ethica Docens but as Ethical Life, and Markets as a Character-Forming Institution

It follows from previous remarks that the morality of the market is not an *ethica docens* that comes to us in the form of a moral discourse which can be articulated in a series of verbal, written statements, and taught and debated by similar means. It is more like a pattern of actual behavior, an ethical life. Morality is embedded in mores, habits, capacities and a cluster of dispositions, a moral character that results from continuous moral practice. The dispositions encouraged by proper and continuous involvement in the markets tend to be those of self-possession and self-reliance, readiness to assert our rights and respect for the rights of others, attentiveness to others' needs, trust and service, fulfillment of promises and contractual duties. There is also an inclination to follow the game rules while simultaneously taking the risk of making considered acts of dissent or deviance from established practice, and either paying the price for making mistakes or reaping the profits from the new opportunities opened up by that initial act of defiance (Barry 2001; Williams 2004). These dispositions indicate a life of peaceful co-existence, of live-and-let-live, with a minimal core of basic values that must be shared, since otherwise all these exchanges would be impossible to replicate or to sustain, but must be also unencumbered by excesses of moralism of either a superstitious or over-enthusiastic nature.

Let us take, for instance, the experience of Spaniards as they have been engaging in the European markets over the last few decades, in a similar way to many other European peoples before and since. Spanish workers were industrial and agricultural manual workers in France, Germany, the Netherlands and Switzerland. At the same time, they became familiar with the British, Germans and Scandinavians moving in to their own towns by buying a second home on the Mediterranean coasts and in the Canary Islands, and with the French and other European tourists holidaying everywhere. As consumers and producers, they have been increasingly engaged in commercial and financial exchanges with other Europeans. Their overall experiences have developed a corpus of implicit background assumptions which underlie attitudes of mutual toleration, an absence of xenophobic sentiments, and mutual, rational expectations of proper behavior as producers, consumers, home-owners, and bank customers and borrowers, etc. This has helped to produce elective affinities between Spaniards and other Europeans, and it is a basis for their mutual understanding and empathy for each other's predicaments in an ever-larger variety of situations, in the absence of which there would be fear and mistrust among them.

These basic, everyday, shared experiences may also provide the basis for a European demos as (and if and when) they become more widespread throughout Europe; in fact, shared experiences are a necessary condition for any community, and this also applies to a political community. Already, these shared experiences come together through basic, possibly barely articulated or even tacit understandings. But, at the same time, it may help if some articulated thoughts, political *topoi*, narratives, are added; for instance, if there is available a repertoire of discourses of justification transmitted through the media and other cultural constructs, for instance, including familiarity on the part of educated people with a shared high culture (which has played and still plays a crucial role in European self-understanding). Still, these cultural constructs should be internalized, thought out and understood by the moral agents; and this cannot be done without putting them to practice. Only so, there can develop the kind of self-understanding and immanent critique of practices and institutions which is the proper mark of moral reasoning.

Now, to the extent that markets help to spread the morality of an extended order among situated selves with cognitive, moral and emotional resources to engage in long-term, mutually beneficial exchanges, they make people realistic and morally aware of both their own interests and values and those of others: self-reliant, on the one hand, and alert to others' wishes, propensities and abilities, on the other.

Markets educate people in the sense of making them used to the idea that they are expected to pay a price for their mistakes. To the extent this is so, markets may reinforce the ethos of accountability at all levels and in all avenues of life, from the *pater familias* to social leaders and politicians. In that case, there is no easy way out from the consequences of mistaken decisions; others will be quick to expose and exploit them. It is the name of the game and has to be accepted. Lessons of realism happen and the principle of reality applies, any time. For better or worse, involvement in the markets allows little dream-time; less than the one people may get while waiting for the next election, the next book, or the next gathering of the chattering classes. The usual way of escaping from reality is cut off; and this may cause a hardening of the heart, an injection of courage. In fact, fear is often the first way people try to escape from a situation, which may be then followed by an attempt to reduce the appreciation of danger and ultimately by a denial of the danger itself, to the point of not naming it. Perhaps markets do not encourage people to search for danger, but they certainly make them clearly aware of the specific dangers from which they are trying to escape. They may be compatible with specific fears of specific dangers but do not plunge people into a diffuse sense of angst. The usual manner in which people's clouded thinking makes them unfocused and unable to ask questions or set priorities, and therefore become incapable of facing up to reality, is thus radically curtailed. Markets focus people's minds.

They focus them not in order to have a theory about reality but to do something with it. In order to do something, the actor must make a choice between several possible courses of action, and, to be able to do that, he must make his mind up about his values and priorities. Therefore, the market has a normative dimension which is inextricably linked to its cognitive dimension.

Discovery of new opportunities comes hand in hand with choices of morals, or prudence, which is, in fact, a mitigated form of morality. For this very reason, markets require and encourage the development of some form of moral discourse to justify, and build on, the decisions that are made. Otherwise there would be no action, and the market process would come to a stop. Moral nihilism, by contrast, can only end in a cultural morass and the pervasiveness of a lack of ability to make decisions. Moral nihilism encourages distrust of other people's intentions and deeds, and therefore stands in the way of a generalization of economic exchanges. In fact, a free flow of exchanges (economic or otherwise) can happen only in a climate of mutual understanding and trust; thus markets are mighty mechanisms for a spreading of trust.

To borrow from Hume's views (Gellner 1994: 46ff.), morality of the kind that markets favor encourages people to move from superstition to enthusiasm and finally to moderation. Superstitious people follow the lead of magical manipulators, be they charismatic leaders or priests; but markets make people use their intelligence to make their own decisions and accustom them to independent decision-making, obviating the need to defer to a higher authority in order to find their way. At the same time, markets are great equalizers in the long run, and their influence converges and combines with that of political or religious enthusiasts (Puritans, for instance) who are supposed to help liberate society from its superstitious domination by priests. Then comes a time for the markets to ease the way to moderation as they lead society away from the excesses of these enthusiasts. Markets cool people's thinking, make them more rational and more prone to use a kind of instrumental rationality that erodes much of the halo around priestly kings.

This said, a reminder of the caveat stated at the beginning of this section may be in order. Markets may help focus people's minds and strengthen some moral dispositions in them, and assist them into becoming more rational and more moral, up to a point. In the long run, markets may help in making use of dispersed knowledge and transmit information. But people trade on noise and not only on information, may follow bad advice, and may understand their situation and form their expectations on the wrong premises; in short, they may behave in a rather irrational way (Shleifer 2000). Markets may help them to learn from their mistakes *to a point*; provided markets last, and are not overrun by all sort of events (political or otherwise), as they often are. As for the morality of the play, markets are just a system of incentives and social coordination, leaving people in full responsibility for what they want to do, and to trade; and therefore, they may become instrumental in people's attempts to achieve all sorts of goals, moral or immoral.

Markets' Civilizing Effects on Politics, Policy and the Public Sphere

Markets, Civil Virtue and the Political Community as a World of Shared Experiences or of Friends and Enemies

In real life, markets combine with other institutional and cultural processes, and their effects are mixed up with those of local politics, demographic movements, ethnic communities, religion and many others; the end result may well be an example of social disorder, such as the one conveyed by the image of messy, disorderly modern, metropolitan city, which has caused deep ambivalence among intellectuals of all persuasions from the outset.[14] But here we are engaged in an ideal typical discussion, trying to sort out the effects to be expected from markets as such, and, from this viewpoint, participation in markets can be seen to foster the development of several civil and civic virtues. On the cognitive side, I have already mentioned the customs of deciphering signals conveyed by the structure of relative prices, and acquiring a limited but clear understanding of changing and complex situations. There is also alertness to disparities between prices and the opportunities for profit that follow. Intellectual habits come together with the development of moral capacities. Hard, critical decisions have to be made on an almost continuous basis; lapses in *akrasia* or acedia, in weakness of will, can be punished. As people keep trying to succeed despite occasional setbacks and failures, their resolve may be strengthened, too. They should develop a sense of responsibility in the aftermath of their decisions, since they have to bear the consequences of them, whether success or failure. People have to get used to coping with limited knowledge, discounting risks, and relying on their own judgement. But the development of sound judgement can also be expected in a world in which reality checks are continually happening.

Engagement in markets should also be expected to bring home awareness of the fact that every individual is placed within an ever-expanding network of social relations. Interdependence of the market kind may involve belonging to communities with weak ties, but they are still real communities made up of real ties. Rules apply that people have to know and follow, concerning respect for private property and the fulfillment of contractual obligations and promises. Sensitivity to others' needs, desires, expectations and abilities is expected to increase along with a sense of moral reputation and a modicum of politeness, needed in order to smooth the deals and prepare the way for future exchanges.

On top of that, continuous involvement in the market, under proper conditions, is expected to favor civility, by strengthening a sense of justice and respect for the game rules as well as some (mitigated) form of benevolence, mutual understanding and mutual trust, and, in this way, to reduce the likelihood of violence. Montesquieu's ([1748] 1961: 8ff.) classical reference to *le doux commerce* points to habituation to peaceful practices in all spheres of life, leading to a general disposition to exercise them in politics, in particular.[15] *Le doux commerce* presumably reduced the pervasiveness and intensity of violence which had been usual in the heroic and military societies of the past, including that of the Ancien Regime. It did so by changing the general orientation of politics and policy, and by shaping people's manners and making them used to peaceful competition as a substitute for violent conflict. In turn, the effects of market-induced civility may be reinforced by the forms of civility linked to civic virtue.

Civility as required in politics qualifies the level and the form of the (legitimate) violence that is involved with crucial political performances. This shows both *ad intra* and *ad extra*: in domestic politics, and in the politics and policies aimed at foreigners. To begin with, the development of commerce inside the city offers a choice between two quite different interpretations of the political community. On the one hand, it rests on a world of shared experiences, and politics is supposed to reaffirm these foundations. On the other, politics is supposed to evolve around the dichotomy of friends and enemies, and the political community is alerted to watch over its internal enemies, which may mean the patrician class watching over the plebeians, the 'right' watching over the 'left', or vice versa. Now, commerce is biased in favor of the first definition of politics resting on a community of shared experiences. By contrast, the diffusion of a definition of politics in terms of friends versus enemies, à la Carl Schmitt ([1927–1932] 1996), in Germany and other continental European countries in the inter-war period, may be seen as already a symptom of how far removed these societies were from the ideal type of a CS. By the same token, it may also be argued that the survival of a vision of politics based on the dichotomy of friends/enemies is a symptom of weakness of the cultural and institutional foundations of today's liberal democracies, particularly during a period of transition to democracy, and possibly afterwards.

The fact is that, initially, these liberal democracies have to draw on political leaders whose habits were already shaped in their youth by totalitarian politics (fascist, Maoist, Stalinist, Trotskyist, and the like). They then carry these habits of sectarian politics and political hatred with them when entering the arena of democratic politics. All the same, violence when it comes in the form of defending the city against foreign enemies is neither marginal nor accidental to a CS but belongs at the heart of it and may epitomize civic virtue. An actual readiness to fight and die for the city, understood as an order of freedom, instead of just talking about it, was the mark of a true member of a CS in Pericles' Athens. 'Fight for the city, don't just talk about it' was the topic of Demosthenes' repeated warnings to his fellow citizens to strengthen their resolve. The warnings revolved around that distinction between deeds and words, because the failure to understand it and start fighting weakened the Athenians when they faced the Macedonian king and made them unable to take crucial decisions (Jaeger 1945: 156). The critical distinction here is between an uncivic and uncivil, endlessly deliberative society, an aggregate of chattering classes unwilling and unable to fight decisively at the right time, on the one hand, and a CS composed of individuals ready to stand up against a threat to their liberty, on the other. In this regard, Ferguson's remarks on the role of a militia should be seen as indicative not of a contradiction between a CS and the need for defense, but as a discussion of the forms of defense most fitting to a CS, the choice being between a standing army (Smith's preference), a popular militia or some combination of each of them (Pocock 1999: 348ff.). At the same time, civility affects the conduct of war and the forms of fighting. For instance, Frederick II's tactics of using troops in close formation was a statement of sorts about the ruler's deep distrust of his own army of soldiers who were supposedly inclined to escape if given half a chance. Making them stand in closed ranks reduced their opportunity to exit the battlefield. By contrast, trust in ordinary soldiers was to be a mark of the citizen armies of revolutionary France, and this allowed for a mobility and tactical flexibility that empowered them to win. In time, a mobile army of conscripts may come to be replaced by an army of professionals provided they remain subject to civilian authority.

Thus, civility is not only a check on violence, it is also part of the violence involved in the workings of CS. Civility in market operations does not nullify people's aggressive drives but it does shape them, reduce their intensity, provide an outlet for them and make them compatible with positive feelings towards rivals, partners, suppliers, consumers and so forth. In the realm of politics, an analogous reasoning can be applied to the task of enforcing law and order in a CS. Just because public business is conducted in a civil manner in no way makes the police or their work accidental, marginal or external to the functioning of a CS. In fact, CS could not exist without basic defenses against internal bullies and external invaders. There is an inescapable Hobbesian component in any understanding of what a CS is about, insofar as peace and security are basic preconditions for liberty. Hence, from the perspective of the members of a CS, the basic rules of justice should be followed, or otherwise enforced. For them, police work is not the work of 'aliens': policemen do 'their' work. This is the reason why, in a well-ordered CS, the police force is supposed to be trusted and respected, and is assumed to deserve people's willing collaboration in the performance of its duties. Of course, in real life, police forces may or may not act in a proper manner. They may act with civility or with brutality, in a way befitting their role in the maintenance of a CS or in a way that erodes or destroys it.

These considerations could be extended to the whole range of state activities. They could be applied to the performance of civil servants in the fulfillment of their duties and in their rapport with the public, as well as to political parties' handling of their mutual relations, and their relations with their constituencies. In each case, civility is a crucial and essential standard to be applied to them. On the one hand, civility establishes the difference between a society of deferent subjects and one of free and self-reliant citizens who look their public authorities in the eye. On the other, in regard to the character of the relations among the different parts of the body politic, things may oscillate between a fairly integrated political community and one on the verge of political strife. Depending on the degree of civility in its politics, every society find itself at some point along a continuum that goes from a CS proper, in which the political game is played between loyal adversaries, to an insidious and irate clash between seemingly irreconcilable parties bordering on outright hostility, right the way through to civil war (Pérez-Díaz 2002).

Markets' Placing Limits on the Excesses of Politics and Pointing to a Self-Governed Society

Markets provide some of the resources and cultural tools for people to enter the public sphere, and, by so doing, to engage in two crucial sets of activities: to put limits on government (democratic or otherwise), and to participate in the (thus limited) political process, by way of political deliberation as well as by sharing in policy decision making and policy implementation. By insisting on the limits of politics and by providing people with experiences of self-reliance and spontaneous coordination, markets provide them with intellectual and moral resources, and they offer them a repertoire of examples and meanings conducive to building a free society and shaping the cultural landscape accordingly. By providing individuals and voluntary associations with economic resources, markets reduce their dependency on public funds and political patronage to participate in the public sphere. In other words, markets make a decisive, indispensable contribution to the independence of the public vis-à-vis political power.

The long-term trend of increasing productivity has freed time for schooling. Affluence and schooling have freed people from habits of deference to leaders and parties, and empowered them by increasing their self-confidence. In fact, citizens can stand up to their rulers and hold them to account only if they develop a sense of political equality between rulers and citizens. Markets have provided people with the basic life experiences for understanding politics in terms of political exchanges between governments and political parties on the one hand, and a community of citizens on the other. They also allow them to envision the relationship as one between an agent (the politicians) and the principal (the demos), adding a sort of common sense, logical plausibility to the corresponding academic theories.

This is not an easy task, however, as the political spectacle tends to go in the opposite direction. Usually, public debate is vitiated by an asymmetry of information, understanding and interest, which benefits the insiders (politicians, civil servants and interest groups) at the expense of the outsiders (most citizens). The politicians face their poorly informed and mildly interested constituencies and tend to sell them a package of identity labels, charismatic leaders, ideology and a few scattered substantive policy positions. Thus, the only way a genuine political exchange can take place is often on the basis of politicians' arguing on specific issues that citizens are familiar with, interested in or sufficiently knowledgeable of.

The media have a mixed record in this respect. They can limit the power of the state only if they are independent of government largesse and good will, and only if they do not develop a political agenda of their own in combination with politicians. In fact, in today's Western societies, the media's civic effects are mixed. Their tendency to dramatize events inflates the importance of politics, gives an aura of plausibility to politicians and civil servants' pretenses to control fate, and entertains the delusion that the future hinges on the results of the next election. The media's partisanship leads them to attribute charismatic traits to the politicians of their liking and deny them to those they disfavor. Partisanship and the media's hostile attitude towards politicians reluctant to yield to the media's influence may lead to the spread of feelings of suspicion vis-à-vis the entire political class. Sometimes, this may help in cutting politicians down to size (Cowen 2000: 169), but it may also erode public trust and confuse people and their expectations. In the long run, the result might be educational, as it would promote people's detachment from hard forms of political partisanship; but, contrariwise, there could be an increase in people's cynicism and erratic moods leading to support of populist policies. In a benign scenario, the media's contribution to a CS may be extremely positive; in a worst-case, Paretian, scenario, media plutocrats would combine with demagogues to have their own way (Pareto [1921] 2000: 55). Loading the scales in favor of a benign scenario, markets may place limits on the concentration of power in the media and check their propensities to collude with the state and political parties in two ways: by introducing pressures for competition in the market, and by the development of a discriminating public which keeps its distance with regard to the media.

In the last decades, two interconnected developments have taken place in many Western polities: the rise of monitorial citizens (Schudson 1999a, 1999b) and of voluntary associations, thanks to a variety of factors. The markets generally encourage this but so, from the supply side so to speak, do the state's growing complexity, which has offered many access points to the public, and the decline of political parties, which have gradually taken a back seat at many public debates. Monitorial citizens would be a variant of the informed, interested citizens of a somewhat idealized past. They decline to know everything and make no pretense at showing an intense interest in all sorts of things public. They know that to master, or even to become familiar with, the details of any public issue takes an inordinate amount of time and energy; Schudson highlights this by drawing on his own experience: just studying the reports that made up the dossier for the completion of a single local road in a county of Southern California, affecting a reduced number of communities, took several months.

Monitorial citizens are the hard core of leaders and active, non-deferential members of voluntary associations (CS in a restricted sense). Many new voluntary associations have come to exist in the guise of non-governmental non-profit organizations, quite different from the hierarchical organizations of the past, typically supported by public authorities with public money and public privileges. They try to make their voice heard in public debates, express their identities and put forward the interests of local or sectorial constituencies, articulating their different views on the common good.

Thus, markets may benefit a healthy public sphere by supporting monitoring citizens and voluntary associations. They can check the concentration of power that comes from government, or rather from some combination of an ambitious government, rent seekers in the business world, and self-appointed opinion leaders in the media. The fact is, media and politics often come together in support of a political theater that encourages people in their delusion of obtaining a political consensus and absolute knowledge about the matter in hand. Markets, on the contrary, suggest that there are always limits: an inherent frailty to what can be achieved by means of public deliberation ending in a collective decision. In the final analysis, there are cognitive and moral limits for public deliberation to end in any lasting consensus. At most, there may be agreement on a core of values and practices in the absence of which there can be no proper working of the basic institutions of free markets and a liberal polity, as there can be contingent, prudential compromises on the issues at hand. Other than that, room must be left for as much experimentation as possible.

Involvement in markets may place welcome limits on the excesses of politics in several ways. First, by proposing a model for testing experiments in which there is multiple, continuous feedback on any attempt at solving individual or social problems, contributing to fast learning. This is in contrast to the very slow learning in politics, with limited and infrequent feedback on policies (Pennington 2003), limited choice between a few political parties, a confused clash of programs and ideological platforms, and ambiguous verdicts in the polls. In their market experience, people get used to comparing the speed of feedback to consumer or investor choices when business is concerned and it risks losses and cannot hide behind the government, as compared with the usual slack in cases where it can: in the utilities, the media or infrastructure, for instance, and possibly, education, health or the welfare services.

Second, by showing that a good measure of social cohesion may be the result of market processes, by challenging social inequalities and ensuring a significant degree of social mobility. Markets per se would be supposed to provide incentives for the lower and middle classes to develop alertness and move up and, vice versa, for the economic establishment to remain stuck in their old ways and lose relative power, wealth and status, possibly over one or two generations time, unless they combine with politicians and are able to shape politics and policy to suite their interests. Anyway, the validity of arguments about trends towards equality and inequality under capitalist conditions is, of course, contingent on the spatial and temporal frame of reference, and on disentangling the effects of political and economic factors; only with this caveat in mind, it may be pointed out that markets as such have a tendency to facilitate social mobility in the long term.[16]

Third, by emphasizing a view of the proper functioning of a system in a decentralized way, markets suggest a view of politics in which the state and society work together as a web of multiple instances for decision making and policy implementation. This is not just a 'new spirit of capitalism' in operation, as Boltanski and Thevenot (1987) suggest, but a return to an old tradition. This return has been enriched by the experience of nations such as the European ones, having lost their way many times in collectivistic and semi-collectivistic experiments during the last two centuries and having learned the hard way what a 'politics of faith' – unchecked by a strong dose of skepticism (Oakeshott 1996) – in the virtues of a central authority may mean. It is further reinforced by the erosion of communist regimes, such as the Chinese one, thanks to the penetration of markets (Nee and Lian 1994).

A modicum of abstract thinking, and institutional or constitutional design, may be helpful, but any pretense at knowing the totality, the whole of a situation, is doomed to failure. This is not just because of the inanity of the pretentious worldviews of totalitarian states and parties, but simply because there is no way of solving even a local problem in full knowledge of its causes and ramifications, and the full consequences of different courses of action. This is a well-known, familiar feature of the human condition, the fundamental limits of human reason, even if some enlightened people did lose sight of this for a couple of centuries. Karl Jaspers's (1946: 178) humble appreciation of what can be said and done when we accept and recognize that we are less than the 'involving whole' that we can never apprehend, and that not even being part of a successful mass party (or a 'society of knowledge' for that matter) can change the limits to our knowledge, makes for a different kind of good citizen. One who must focus on the task at hand, and accept that there is only limited, partial knowledge to bring to the here and now, to which he must be faithful.

In a CS, the government is supposed to rule subject to society's advice and consent, and to be sensitive and responsive to public opinion. This is not merely a matter of elections, referenda or parliamentary votes. It is a process of continuous accommodation to a largely self-governed society. In it, government should be kept on a short leash and submit to the basic principle of a free society, namely, that society is not to be led in any particular direction by anybody; and 'anybody' conspicuously includes any combination of government, business and the intelligentsia (with or without help from any particular voluntary association). Everybody is free to choose his/her own goals in life, and the institutional system, of which government is part, should allow individuals to pursue altruistic or self-interested business of their own choosing, unimpeded. Even if the public arena were populated by collectivistic or semi-collectivistic characters eager to meddle and make busy-bodies of themselves concerning others' choices, a proper civil government should keep the playing field level and open to all-comers, and respect the avenues that individuals decide, independently, to go down.

Civility is as much about persuading people, expressing sympathy and understanding, and coming to sensible agreements, as it is about allowing people room for maneuver in order *not* to be persuaded if they do not wish to be, or to dissent and cling to their own ideas. The spirit of civility excludes the *animus* of disputatiousness, which may prevail in meetings of scholars or religious sectarians, or in lawyers' courts; nor it is that of an endless time consuming effort to reach an agreement, near the time of the final judgement. There is no need for staying put and locked in a debate aimed at a consensus around the right collective choice that settles once and for all the matter; instead, the space is left to a multiplicity of choices, and experiments according to an immense, and changing, variety of specific circumstances. Civility implies an open and often erratic conversation, which may be interrupted by fits of distraction and absentmindedness, and in the course of which people stop talking to engage in manifold activities in the real world and then come back. Nor is it a fight to be settled by a majority vote, so that the right definition gets enshrined in the group's proceedings, the winners impose their definition and issue implicit or explicit threats of silencing and ostracism, followed by the group split and so on.

The attitude I have in mind is more in the manner of what some Victorian writers, Anthony Trollope, for instance, understood as civility, namely, in the manner of a mild disposition to settle for a truce, which allows for conversation to go on in a spirit of accommodation, self-restraint, curiosity and understanding, punctuated by decisions to exit from the debate which are, themselves, fairly eloquent. Thus, in Trollope's novel *The Warden* ([1855] 1994), the debate concerning the rights and duties of the wardenship is settled after being conducted in the press, in the open so to speak, according to the politically correct *topoi* of the time, in a formally deliberative, but in fact highly disputatious, manner. The settlement of the matter implies, however, the destruction of a small network of giving and receiving, built on long experience and mutual trust. But learning eventually comes in for everybody involved, thanks not so much to the warden's words, which are few and barely understood at the moment, as it does by the warden's simple decision to exit gracefully of the situation, and thus making people, himself included, to face the consequences of their moves. And then, life goes on in the community, with a minimum of governance and a maximum of mutual adjustments, by means of silences, a few wise words possibly unheard, long and vehement speeches, displays of authority good for little, examples to decipher, disappointments and provisional satisfactions.

In that literary micro-cosmos, the intimation is made that while politics may induce the mirage of a collective goal, reached through explicit debates and backed by a mix of ritual and coercion under the lead of proper authorities, and while, eventually, a deferent, submissive, insecure public opinion may encourage that authority to take the lead, by the end of the day, politics may be tempered and governments may be tamed and made to understand their limited role in a CS. For this to happen, people, in all stations of life, myriads of them, have to stand on their own, stick to whatever resources they have, of decency and common sense, of education and property, and use them, provided there are proper institutions around that allow them to do so.

Conclusion

Market processes are part and parcel of a larger institutional and cultural formation that we may call by different names, including that of a civil society in its broad sense, in case we stick to a particular conception that was fairly well articulated in the eighteenth century. I have made an argument for today's relevance of the main lines of thinking of the Scottish philosophers on civil society, and on markets. After a long detour away from the original conception, there has been a return of sorts to the old, broad conception, as a normative and analytical type. In fact, current historical developments allows us to think of market processes, the rule of law, democratic transitions, civil society (in the restricted sense of voluntary associations) and the public sphere all fitting together as parts of a whole; and the inner logic of the developments in social science disciplines encourage inter-disciplinary dialogue to a similar effect.

I have shown that markets have civilizing effects per se, provided the basic rules of the game (such as those of no fraud and no violence) are respected. Multiple experiments in discovery and self-discovery, and in the communication process by which these discoveries spread, allow for a gradual increase of knowledge and trust within society. Markets as conversations point to the complex nature of these communicative processes, by both linguistic and extra-linguistic means. The communicative experience goes beyond a content-centered debate and the domain of the art of conversation; it incorporates experiences of doing and performing, exchanging and interacting while dealing with a world of material artifacts enmeshed in a world of meanings. In so doing, it suggests some revision of the rules of the ideal conversation, such as those of truth, sincerity and validity, is required. In these conditions, understanding and trust can only be limited, largely tacit. In fact, some of the characteristics of market processes, in this regard, are analogous to those we find in other human engagements, in culture (painting, for instance), society, and politics as well, where there is a similar mix of linguistic and extra-linguistic forms of communication.

I suggested that the idea of markets as conversations applies to diverse stages of the economic process; and I indicated, with examples, how this view of markets helps us to understand the formation of different conversational spaces, large (nations, supranational communities) and small (firms, families). This view of markets may also facilitate our understanding of their moral effects, how they apply to both the morality of the extended orders and that of the small worlds, and how they work as a vehicle for the formation of moral habits.

As for the relationship between markets and politics, policy and the public sphere, I have suggested ways in which markets shape and foster civic dispositions among the population, and check the tendency to understand politics in terms of friends and enemies, and in so doing tame the violent passions associated with that kind of politics. They help to channel and shape the violence that may be necessary to defend an order of freedom in a resolute manner when the time comes to it. Then I gave an account of some of the resources that markets provide citizens with for the task of holding their public magistrates accountable and for participating in politics and policy in order to check excesses of partisanship and help develop the figure of the monitorial citizen.

Markets may provide lessons in fast learning, social cohesion, the decentralization of systems and, last but not least, a sense of humility in regard to the control of our fate. In the end, markets work in favor of politics as a process of continuous accommodation in a civil manner. Hegel thought his *Philosophy of Right* amounted to a reconstruction of modern ethical life, a totality of ideas and sentiments, practices and relations, which were regarded as valid, in a normative sense, by citizens of Hegel's time, and prevailed in fact (Pelzcynski 1984: 8); but historical experience has taught *our* contemporary citizens to be much more modest. In the end, the theory of civil society may be treated as a system of significations that stands in a larger semantic context where we find opposite types of society (socialist, totalitarian ones) and gradations, variations, even degenerations of civil society; there are many 'possible worlds', and civil society in its best form is just one of them. Indeed, in view of our past experience, it may be safe to think that the realization of civil society in its best form, should be considered the least likely.

Thus, the concept of civil society in its broad sense is more of a regulatory idea (useful on both normative and analytical grounds) than a description of things as they are, or ever have been, or possibly will be, at any particular point in time. It has come closer to the fact at times, and departed from it quite often. In this regard, so far, there has been progress, and there has been regression. As for the future, there is room for hope and faith, as there is room for skepticism. But anyway, even at its best, a civil society can only leave open the question of what a good society may be, as people with different comprehensive views of the good maintain the discussion alive. Within these parameters and limits, markets are crucial for the process of creating such a civil society, mainly because they are communicative processes that go to the heart of the kind of decent and reasonable community a civil society is supposed to be, or to eventually become, in time.

Notes

1. Prior versions of this research were presented at the CiSoNet (Civil Society Network) Workshop 'Markets and Civil Society in Europe', Madrid (23–24 September 2004) and, later, at the Minda de Gunzsburg Center for European Studies, Harvard University (30 May 2006). I am indebted to the participants at these seminars for their comments, and particularly to Emma Rothschild and Juan Carlos Rodríguez, as well as to Michele Salvati and John Keane.

2. Neither 'society' as such, nor 'atomistic' (or 'unencumbered') individuals, but rather 'situated selves'; see Taylor (1995: 181ff.).

3. I use the acronym CS for the sake of brevity, but only in reference to civil society understood in its broad sense (not for civil society in a restricted sense, that is, associations).

4. While not questioning the relevance of using, at the same time, the concept of civil society in a restricted sense applied to voluntary associations; see my Introduction to this volume.

5. By analogy to Rawls's (1996) argument on political liberalism, which is restricted to the political sphere.

6. A more restricted view of the virtue of (political) civility appears in Smith (2002).

7. In particular, see Hegel ([1821] 1963: paragraphs 209, 210, 219–249).

8. In drawing this distinction, Habermas thought he was expanding on Weber's diagnoses of contemporary societies, even though Weber's meaningful social actions – that is, actions which take account of and are oriented towards others – apply to all spheres of social life including the economy and politics, and this should put crucial limits to the effects of any supposedly reified logic of markets and bureaucracies.

9. Bourdieu insisted on this, most notably in a conference in East Berlin in October 1989, just a few days before a crucial march for regime change in Leipzig and a few weeks before the fall of the Berlin Wall; it seemed as if, for him, there was no (or little) qualitative difference between the two sides of the wall (Bourdieu 1994: 31ff.; see also Alexander 1995: 189).

10. Other developments would point to different kinds of encounters between the Western CS tradition and other non-Western traditions. See Randeria (2006) and Bruhns and Gosewinkel (2005).

11. See, for instance, Shleifer's (2000) discussion of the case of the financial markets.

12. But not 'un-socialized' (Granovetter 1992).

13. In fact, Hayek's (1988: 18) terms for the same concept are various: microcosmos, small groups, small bands, small worlds.

14. Even among those intellectuals whom one might expect to be sympathetic towards a commercial, entrepreneurial society such as the United States, as Morton Whyte and Lucia Whyte (1962) pointed out when they analyzed the ambivalent, rather hostile attitudes of a good part of the American intelligentsia towards urban culture.

15. By means of economic interests taming political passions, as has been emphasized by Hirschman (1997), but also by means of the views of the world which are implicit in market practices. A different view of 'commerce as a duel' is presented in Girard (2007: 114); and on the combination of commerce and war in Europe's early modernity, see Hont (2005).

16. Or in the short term; for instance, even in regard to a period of time which is usually seen as one of growing inequality in the United States, Young Back Choi (1999) has shown how, between 1979 and 1988, 85.5 percent of the poorest 20 percent moved upwards in just nine years, and the poorest 20 percent in 1979 had an equal chance of staying in the poorest strata or moving to the richest 20 percent in 1988. At the same time, it has been pointed out that, by the beginning of the twenty-first century, real hourly wages since 1979 have barely risen for most workers even though workers' productivity has increased by 60 percent; in fact, workers' productivity has increased 80 percent since 1960 but the average worker works about 200 hours a year more that he/she did at that time (Pastor 2007: 290).

References

Alexander, Jeffrey. 1995. *Fin de Siècle Social Theory: Relativism, Reduction, and the Problem of Reason.* London: Verso.

Barry, Norman. 2001. 'Ethics, Conventions and Capitalism', in *Capitalism, Morality and Markets,* ed. Brian Griffiths, Robert Sirico, Norman Barry and Frank Field. London: Institute of Economic Affairs, pp. 57–77.

Bell, Daniel. 1976. *The Coming of Post-Industrial Society.* New York: Basic Books.

Berger, Peter, and Thomas Luckmann. 1991. *The Social Construction of Reality: A Treatise in the Sociology of Knowledge.* London: Penguin.

Boettke, Peter, and Peter Leeson. 2003. 'Is the Transition to the Market Too Important to be Left to the Market?' *Economic Affairs* 23, no. 1: 33–39.

Boettke, Peter, and Anne Rathbone. 2002. 'Civil Society, Social Entrepreneurship and Economic Calculation: Toward a Political Economy of the Philanthropic Enterprise', *Working Papers in Economics,* George Mason University, WPE 02.02.

Boettke, Peter, and Virgil Henry Storr. 2002. 'Post-Classical Political Economy: Polity, Society and Economy in Weber, Mises and Hayek', *American Journal of Economics and Sociology* 61, no. 1: 161–191.

Boltanski, Luc, and Laurent Thevenot. 1987. *De la justification: Les économies de la grandeur.* Paris: Gallimard.

Bourdieu, Pierre. 1994. *Raisons pratiques: Sur la théorie de l'action.* Paris: Seuil.

Braudel, Fernand. 1973. *Capitalism and Material Life, 1400–1800.* Trans. George Weidenfeld and Nicolson Ltd. New York: Harper & Row.

_____. 1990. *L'identité de la France: Espace et histoire.* Paris: Flammarion.

Brick, Howard. 1996. 'The Reformist Dimension of Talcott Parsons's Early Social Theory', in *The Culture of the Market: Historical Essays,* ed. Thomas Haskell and Richard Teichgraeber III. Cambridge: Cambridge University Press, pp. 357–396.

Bruhns, Hinnerk, and Dieter Gosewinkel. 2005. 'Europe and the Other: Non-European Concepts of Civil Society', *WZB Discussion Paper,* Nr. SP IV 2005–406.

Campbell, Colin. 1987. *The Romantic Ethic and the Spirit of Modern Consumerism.* Oxford: Blackwell.

Choi, Young Back. 1999. 'On the Rich Getting Richer and the Poor Getting Poorer', *Kyklos* 52, no. 2: 239–258.

Conrad, Joseph. [1902] 1962. *Typhoon, and Other Tales.* New York: New American Library.

_____. [1906] 1988. *The Mirror of the Sea.* Marlboro, VT: Marlboro Press.

Cowen, Tyler. 2000. *What Price Fame?* Cambridge, MA: Harvard University Press.

Damasio, Antonio. 2000. *The Feeling of What Happens: Body, Emotion and the Making of Consciousness.* London: Vintage.

Dreyfus, Hubert. 1991. *Being-in-the-World: A Commentary on Heidegger's Being and Time, Division I.* Cambridge, MA: MIT Press.

Eco, Umberto. 1979. *A Theory of Semiotics.* Bloomington: Indiana University Press.

Edgley, Charles and Dennis Brissett. 1999. *A Nation of Meddlers.* Boulder, CO: Westview Press.

Field, John. 2003. *Social Capital.* London: Routledge.

Geertz, Clifford. 1983. *Local Knowledge: Further Essays in Interpretive Anthropology.* New York: Basic Books.

Gellner, Ernest. 1994. *Conditions of Liberty: Civil Society and Its Rivals.* New York: Allen Lane.

Girard, René. 2007. *Achever Clausewitz.* Paris: Carnetsnord.

Gouldner, Alvin. 1980. *The Two Marxisms: Contradictions and Anomalies in the Development of Theory.* London: McMillan.

Granovetter, Marc. 1973. 'The Strength of Weak Ties', *American Journal of Sociology* 78: 1360–1380.

_____. 1992. 'Economic Action and Social Structure: The Problem of Embeddedness', in *The Sociology of Economic Life*, ed. Marc Granovetter and Richard Swedberg. Boulder, CO: Westview Press, pp. 53–84.

Grice, Paul. 1989. *Studies in the Way of Words*. Cambridge, MA: Harvard University Press.

Habermas, Jürgen. 1989. *The Theory of Communicative Action*, vol. 2: *Lifeworld and System: A Critique of Functionalist Reason*. Trans. Thomas McCarthy. Boston: Beacon Press.

_____. 1992. 'Further Reflections on the Public Sphere', in *Habermas and the Public Sphere*, ed. Craig Calhoun; trans. Thomas Burger. Cambridge, MA: MIT Press, pp. 421–461.

Habermas, Jürgen, and John Rawls. 1998. *Debate sobre el liberalismo político*. Trans. Gerard Vilar Roca. Barcelona: Paidós.

Hapgood, Fred. 1993. *Up the Infinite Corridor: MIT and the Technical Imagination*. Reading, MA: Addison–Wesley.

Hayek, Friedrich. 1988. *The Fatal Conceit*. Chicago, IL: University of Chicago Press.

Hegel, Georg Wilhelm Friedrich. [1821] 1963. *Hegel's Philosophy of Right*. Trans. T. Knox. London: Oxford University Press.

Hirschman, Albert O. 1997. *The Passions and the Interests: Political Arguments for Capitalism before Its Triumph*. Princeton, NJ: Princeton University Press.

Hont, Istvan. 2005. *Jealousy of Trade: International Competition and the Nation-State in Historical Perspective*. Cambridge, MA: Harvard University Press.

Hont, Istvan, and Michael Ignatieff. 1985. 'Needs and Justice in the *Wealth of Nations*: An Introductory Essay', in *Wealth and Virtue: The Shaping of Political Economy in the Scottish Enlightenment*, ed. Istvan Hont and Michael Ignatieff. Cambridge: Cambridge University Press, pp. 1–44.

Horwitz, Steven. 1992. 'Monetary Exchange as an Extra-linguistic Social Communication Process', *Review of Social Economy* 50, no. 2: 193–214.

Jacobs, Jane. [1961] 1992. *The Death and Life of Great American Cities*. New York: Vintage Books.

Jaeger, Werner. 1945. *Demóstenes: La agonía de Grecia*. Trans. Eduardo Nicol. Mexico City: Fondo de Cultura Económica.

Jaspers, Karl. 1946. 'Sobre el espíritu europeo', in *Balance y Perspectiva*. Trans. Fernando Vela. Madrid: Revista de Occidente.

Kaldor, Mary. 2003a. 'The Idea of Global Civil Society', *International Affairs* 79, no. 3: 583–593.

_____. 2003b. *Global Civil Society: An Answer to War*. Cambridge: Polity Press.

Keane, John. 2003. *Global Civil Society?* Cambridge: Cambridge University Press.

Kiviat, Barbara. 2004. 'The End of Management?', *Time*, 6 July.

Koselleck, Reinhart. 1988. *Critique and Crisis: Enlightenment and the Pathogenesis of Modern Society*. Cambridge, MA: MIT Press.

_____. 2002. *The Practice of Conceptual History: Timing History, Spacing Concepts*. Trans. Todd Samuel Presner, Kerstin Behnke and Jobst Welge. Stanford, CA: Stanford University Press.

Lao Tzu. [sixth/fifth century BCE] 1962. *Tao Te Ching*. Trans. D. C. Lau. London: Penguin.

MacIntyre, Alasdair. 1999. *Dependent Rational Animals: Why Human Beings Need the Virtues*. Chicago, IL: Open Court.

McCann, Charles. R. 2002. 'F. A. Hayek: The Liberal as Communitarian', *The Review of Austrian Economics* 15, no. 1: 5–34.

Mises, Ludwig von. [1944] 2002. *Gobierno omnipotente: En nombre del estado*. Madrid: Unión Editorial.

Montesquieu, Charles-Louis de Secondat, Marquis de. [1748] 1961. *L'Ésprit des Lois*, II. Paris: Garnier.

Moore, Barrington, Jr. 1978. *Injustice: The Social Basis of Obedience and Revolt*. New York: Random House.

Nee, Victor, and Peng Lian. 1994. 'Sleeping with the Enemy: A Dynamic Model of Declining Political Commitment in State Socialism', *Theory and Society* 23, no. 2: 253–296.

North, Douglass C. 2005. *Understanding the Process of Economic Change*. Princeton, NJ: Princeton University Press.

Oakeshott, Michael. 1996. *The Politics of Faith and the Politics of Scepticism*. Ed. Timothy Fuller. New Haven, CT: Yale University Press.

Pareto, Vilfredo. [1921] 2000. *The Transformation of Democracy*. Ed. Charles Powers; trans. Renata Girola. New Brunswick: Transaction Publishers.

Pastor, Alfredo. 2007. *La ciencia humilde*. Barcelona: Crítica.

Pelczynski, Z. A. 1984. 'Introduction: The Significance of Hegel's Separation of the State and Civil Society', in Z. A. Pelczynski, ed., *The State and Civil Society: Studies in Hegel's 'Philosophy of Right'*. Cambridge: Cambridge University Press, pp. 1–13.

Pennington, Marc. 2003. 'Hayekian Political Economy and the Limits of Deliberative Democracy', *Political Studies* 51: 722–739.

Pérez-Díaz, Víctor. 1995. 'The Possibility of Civil Society: Traditions, Character and Challenges', in *Civil Society: Theory, History, Comparison*, ed. John Hall. Cambridge: Polity Press, pp. 80–109.

_____. 1998. 'The Public Sphere and a European Civil Society', in *Real Civil Societies: Dilemmas of Institutionalization*, ed. Jeffrey Alexander. London: Sage, pp. 211–238.

_____. 2000. 'El consumo, la conversación y la familia', in *El consumo en España*, ed. José Antonio Gimeno. Madrid: Fundación Argentaria-Visor, pp. 27–33.

_____. 2002. 'From "Civil War" to "Civil Society": Social Capital in Spain from the 1930s to the 1990s', in *Democracies in Flux*, ed. Robert Putnam. New York: Oxford University Press, pp. 245–287.

Philipson, Nicholas. 1983. 'Adam Smith as Civic Moralist', in *Wealth and Virtue: The Shaping of Political Economy in the Scottish Enlightenment*, ed. Istvan Hont and Michael Ignatieff. Cambridge: Cambridge University Press, pp. 179–202.

Pocock, J. G. A. 1999. *Barbarism and Religion, II: Narratives of Civil Government*. Cambridge: Cambridge University Press.

Proust, Marcel. [1921] 1954. *À la recherche du temps perdu, t. II. Le côté de Guermantes, II*. Paris: Bibliothèque La Pléiade.

Putnam, Robert. 2000. *Bowling Alone: The Collapse and Revival of American Community*. New York: Touchstone.

Raczymov, Henri. 2005. *Le Paris retrouvé de Marcel Proust*. Paris: Parigrame.

Rae, John. [1895] 2005. *Life of Adam Smith*. Liberty Fund, Inc. The Online Library of Liberty. http://oll.libertyfund.org/Home3/index.php.

Randeria, Shalini. 2006. 'Entangled Histories: Civil Society, Caste Solidarities and Legal Pluralism in Post-colonial India', in *Civil Society: Berlin Perspectives*, ed. John Keane. New York: Berghahn Books, pp. 213–241.

Rawls, John. 1996. *Political Liberalism*. New York: Columbia University Press.

Ricoeur, Paul. 1981. 'The Model of the Text: Meaningful Action Considered as a Text', in *Hermeneutics and the Human Sciences*, ed. John B. Thompson. Cambridge: Cambridge University Press, pp. 197–221.

Rilke, Rainer Maria. [1907] 1984. *Cartas sobre Cézanne*. Trans. Nicanor Ancochea and Kim Vilar. Barcelona: Paidós.

Robertson, John. 1983. 'The Scottish Enlightenment at the Limits of the Civic Tradition', in *Wealth and Virtue: The Shaping of Political Economy in the Scottish Enlightenment*, ed. Istvan Hont and Michael Ignatieff. Cambridge: Cambridge University Press, pp. 137–178.

Rojas, Mauricio. 2001. *Beyond the Welfare State*. Stockholm: Timbro.

Rothbard, Murray N. 1970. *Man, Economy and the State*. Los Angeles, CA: Nash.

Rothschild, Emma. 2001. *Economic Sentiments: Adam Smith, Condorcet and the Enlightenment*. Cambridge, MA: Harvard University Press.

Sandel, Michael. 1982. *Liberalism and the Limits of Justice*. Cambridge: Cambridge University Press.

Schama, Simon. 1988. *The Embarrassment of Riches: An Interpretation of Dutch Culture in the Golden Age*. Berkeley: California University Press.

Schmitt, Carl. [1927–1932] 1996. *The Concept of the Political*. Trans. George Schwab. Chicago, IL: University of Chicago Press.

Schudson, Michael. 1999a. 'Good Citizens and Bad History: Today's Political Ideals in Historical Perspective'. Keynote lecture at the conference 'The Transformation of Civic Life', Nashville, TN, 12 November.

_____. 1999b. *The Good Citizen: A History of American Civic Life*. Cambridge, MA: Harvard University Press.

Shalamov, Varlam. 1994. *Kolyma Tales*. Trans. John Glad. London: Penguin Books.

Shleifer, Andrei. 2000. *Inefficient Markets: An Introduction to Behavioral Finance*. Oxford: Oxford University Press.

Shleifer, Andrei, and Daniel Treisman. 2005. 'A Normal Country: Russia after Communism', *Journal of Economic Perspectives* 19, no. 1: 151–174.

Simmel, Georg. [1917] 1964. 'The Metropolis and Mental Life', in *The Sociology of Georg Simmel*, ed. Kurt Wolff. New York: Free Press, pp. 409–426.

Smith, Philip D. 2002. *The Virtue of Civility in the Practice of Politics*. Lanham, MD: University Press of America.

Swedberg, Richard. 2005a. 'The Economic Sociology of Capitalism: An Introduction and Agenda', in Victor Nee and Richard Swedberg, *The Economic Sociology of Capitalism*. Princeton, NJ: Princeton University Press, pp. 3–34.

_____. 2005b. 'Markets in Society', in *The Handbook of Economic Sociology*, 2nd ed., ed. Neil Smelser and Richard Swedberg. Princeton, NJ: Princeton University Press, pp. 233–253.

Swift, Jonathan. [1758] 1977. 'Hints towards an Essay on Conversation', in *The Portable Swift*, ed. Carl van Doren. London: Penguin, pp. 89–99.

Taylor, Charles. 1995. *Philosophical Arguments*. Cambridge, MA: Harvard University Press.

Trollope, Anthony. [1855] 1994. *The Warden*. London: Penguin.

Whyte, Morton, and Lucia Whyte. 1962. *The Intellectual versus the City*. New York: New American Library.

Williams, Walter. 2004. 'The Argument for Free Markets: Morality versus Efficiency', in *Economy and Virtue: Essays on the Theme of Markets and Morality*, ed. Dennis O'Keeffe. London: Institute of Economic Affairs, pp. 34–51.

Zelizer, Viviana. 2005. *The Purchase of Intimacy*. Princeton, NJ: Princeton University Press.

Chapter 2

AN ENTREPRENEURIAL THEORY OF SOCIAL AND CULTURAL CHANGE

Peter J. Boettke and Christopher J. Coyne

On a daily basis, each and every individual faces a multitude of scenarios containing coordination aspects. Etiquette, marriage, fashion, eating and drinking habits are but a few examples of situations that possess coordination characteristics. To illustrate this, consider Thomas Schelling's (1960: 54–58) famous example of picking a meeting place in New York City. If the individuals in this situation can coordinate their activities and meet at the same location at the same time, both will be better off. However, if they fail to coordinate on the same location or the same time, both fail to gain some positive payoff. Schelling asked, in the absence of full information as to a specific meeting time and place, how will individuals choose to act?

Schelling introduced the notion of focal points to explain how individuals coordinate with one another in the absence of full information. They do so by relying on information that is salient to them. Knowing how others will act helps people coordinate on a superior focal point equilibrium by forming a cooperation-inducing set of expectations. In Schelling's example, the participants chose the clock at Grand Central Station at 12 PM as the meeting location.

There are two central questions driving our endeavor. First, how did meeting at the clock at Grand Central Station at 12 PM become focal? As Schelling notes (1960: 144): 'Where there is no apparent focal point for agreement, he [the individual] can create one by his power to make dramatic suggestion ... coordination requires the common acceptance of some source of suggestion.' More generally, we seek to understand the agent (Schelling's 'he') who creates new focal points or shifts existing focal points

---

Notes for this chapter begin on page 98.

and makes these changes salient. It is our contention that the activities of these change agents are the essence of social and cultural change. Our notion of social and cultural change involves shifting the formal and infor-mal institutions which are currently focal. Social change can occur on many different margins, from minor changes within a set of political, economic and social institutions to major changes involving changes in those funda-mental institutions. Fads in clothing styles or the introduction of health care or education would be examples of the former point, while revolutions that overthrow political regimes and institutions would be an example of the latter. Across all margins of potential change, we contend that social change involves both an act of creation and one of convergence. In other words, the process of change entails not just creating a new focal point but also developing common knowledge to make it focal on a larger scale. As such, we argue that the notion of focal points is critical to any discussion of social and cultural transformation.

While others have focused on learning and the emergence of conven-tions and norms within games (see Sugden 1998; Young 1998), we focus on understanding the agents of change. Stated differently, instead of focusing on how players passively learn about the various strategies available to them and others, we focus on how new conjectures are actively created and how common knowledge is created around those conjectures.

We place the entrepreneur at the center of our analysis as the agent of change.[1] The notion of entrepreneurship underlying our analysis entails alertness to previously unrecognized opportunities for mutually beneficial exchange. Entrepreneurship involves a wishful conjecture; these conjectures represent 'bets' that individuals place on the potential of the underlying con-jecture. The entrepreneur sees things differently and acts upon that vision to affect change. This alertness transcends any one specific contextual setting and therefore requires a detailed consideration across various settings.

We initially consider the entrepreneur in the market setting. Given that he acts in the context of property, prices and profit/loss, he is able to engage in economic calculation. We then seek to extend the notion of entrepre-neurship to non-market and political settings. Clearly, social and cultural change can take place via interaction in the market setting as well as in non-market settings characterized by the absence of a price structure and the profit and loss mechanism.

In extending the application of entrepreneurship to non-market set-tings, the second issue that we seek to understand is the transferability of the desirable consequences of entrepreneurship in market settings to these non-market and political settings. In other words, how much confidence can we have that wishful conjectures of entrepreneurs will be sorted in a manner which matches them to the demands and desires of others as well as to the underlying technological possibilities and resource availability while acting outside the context of a price and profit/loss system? To answer this, we need to understand how entrepreneurs in various settings deal with the issue of economic calculation.[2]

Our core thesis is that in addition to being the catalyst of economic change, the entrepreneur is also the driver of social and cultural change. It is our contention that the desirable aspects of entrepreneurship in economic settings are transferable to non-market and political settings only to the extent that there are proxies for prices and profit/loss. We argue that while reputation serves as a soft disciplinary mechanism in non-market settings, there is a complete absence of a disciplinary device in political settings.

The existence of disciplinary devices is critical to guide actors in their allocation of resources. While the reputation mechanism is clearly imperfect, in the absence of any mechanism, actors will have no way of knowing if they are engaged in activities that allocate resources to their most highly valued uses. Therefore, an imperfect mechanism is preferable to no mechanism.

Entrepreneurs as the Agents of Social and Cultural Change

The Market Setting

In economic life, the entrepreneur is the agent of change. In this role, the entrepreneur serves a dual purpose. Via the recognition and exploitation of previously unexploited profit opportunities, the entrepreneur pushes the economy from an economically and technologically inefficient point inside the production possibility frontier towards the economically and technologically efficient point on the frontier. Moreover, in discovering and innovating new technology and new production methods which use resources in a more efficient manner, the entrepreneurial process shifts the entire production possibility frontier outward.

According to Kirzner (1992: 38–56), we can conceive of the market process as follows. There are two sets of variables in economic life: underlying variables of tastes, technology and endowment of natural resources; and induced variables of prices and profit and loss. In the context of imperfect information and knowledge, a lagged relationship exists between the two sets of variables.[3] To the extent that the induced variables of the market do not reflect the underlying variables, there will exist opportunities for pure profit for those that move in that direction (see Kirzner 1973). The entrepreneur is the economic agent who is alert to these opportunities and exploits them. However, acting in a world of uncertainty and imperfect information, it is also possible for the entrepreneur to make errors. The question then becomes how the entrepreneur knows if he is allocating resources correctly or making an error.

In the market setting, entrepreneurs are guided and disciplined by three key institutions. A well-defined set of property rights provides the incentive for entrepreneurs to allocate resources to their most highly valued use. A subsequent effect of private property is the evolution of markets and prices. Prices serve to convey knowledge and information to market participants. Current inefficiencies in economic relations are quickly translated through the informational mechanisms of the price system into profit opportunities for those entrepreneurs who can eliminate those inefficiencies and realize the gains from exchange that were previously unexploited. In short, the price system allows the entrepreneur to engage in economic calculation. Interconnected with the price system is the profit and loss mechanism.

In the market setting, the entrepreneur faces a hard constraint of real resources. Entrepreneurial efforts that serve to align the underlying and induced variables yield a profit. Likewise activities that divorce the two sets of variables yield a loss. The market disciplines the entrepreneur who engages in erroneous activities in that he incurs a real loss. The market adjusts to ensure over time that prices and profit/loss statements accurately reflect these underlying variables. The disciplinary devices inherent in the market system serve as learning tools not only for the acting entrepreneur but also for other agents in the economic setting. An activity that earns a loss signals the undesirability of that activity to both the entrepreneur who undertakes it and society at large.

Clearly, entrepreneurs in the economic setting contribute to social and cultural change. By introducing new goods and services, these entrepreneurs impact and shape the social setting and provide the tools for others to effect change as well. Consider, for instance, that almost all countries now have access to personal computers and Internet connections. While the introductions of the personal computer and Internet can themselves be seen as types of social and cultural change (see Putnam 2000: 169–180), these same technologies have also presented new opportunities for further social and cultural change through their use by those in non-market settings. As a result of the Internet, for example, one can access images of artwork from museums around the world in the comfort of one's home. Likewise, one can participate in online discussion groups with others from around the world focusing on topics ranging from specific ethnic groups to politics and sports to art and entertainment. In short, the Internet has lowered the cost of experiencing culture from around the world.[4]

This does not mean that every activity undertaken by an entrepreneur is an act of creating or shifting focal points. One can envision a distinction between activities taken within a set of focal institutions and activities causing a shift in the underlying focal points. The car market is an example of this. Within the car market, producers have established specific, well-known brands but are constantly seeking to shift their product lines within their focal brand. The recent introduction of hybrid cars by several dealers (including Honda, Toyota and Ford) serves to illustrate this point. While each car maker continues to produce its 'best sellers', each also introduces new products to market, for example, hybrid cars.

This example illustrates the state of most markets – some entrepreneurs are engaged in activities within the existing market structure while others are alert to potential means of shifting the overall makeup of the market. In other words, one can envision some activities which strengthen certain aspects of existing focal points and other, simultaneous activities which shift or create anew certain aspects of those same points of saliency.

In an attempt to make their products focal, entrepreneurs create convergence around them in a number of ways. Advertising is perhaps the most common form of developing common knowledge.[5] Closely related, both reputation and branding efforts serve to establish common knowledge around a set of products. Such efforts serve to lower information costs and create common knowledge around a good or service.

Non-market Settings

We limit the non-market setting to private agents (i.e. those outside the political setting) whose activities take place in civic society. This means that they act outside of the context of economic calculation grounded in prices and the profit/loss mechanism. In non-market settings, it has become fashionable to refer to entrepreneurship as 'social entrepreneurship'. The idea of social entrepreneurship has become an increasingly popular topic in the last decade, as the subject of the non-market component of civil society has become increasingly discussed.[6] How can civic enterprises succeed in such things as helping the needy or increasing human welfare when the state bureaucracy and the vagaries of the market have failed? New initiative is required and these new ideas of community activism are termed social entrepreneurship. Analogous to entrepreneurship in market settings, social entrepreneurship entails alertness to an opportunity for societal change and interest in betting on a wishful conjecture.

Acting within the market setting of prices and profit and loss, the entrepreneur is desirable because, engaged in economic calculation, he constantly reallocates resources to their most highly valued uses. The central question is: how transferable are the desirable consequences of entrepreneurship to settings outside the market context? While economic calculation cannot exist in the absence of monetary prices, we need to ask if any alternative disciplinary mechanisms are present to guide entrepreneurs. It is our contention that the transferability of the desirable consequences of entrepreneurship in market settings to non-market settings is directly contingent on the existence of proxies for prices and profit and loss in alternative settings.

We wish to postulate that face-to-face civic interaction and the related reputation market serve as a disciplinary mechanism for entrepreneurial activities in non-market settings. Admittedly, this mechanism is not nearly as effective as the price and profit/loss system in allowing entrepreneurs to engage in economic calculation. Reputation is a soft constraint as compared to the hard constraint of real resources faced by entrepreneurs in the market setting. However imperfect, we contend that it is preferable to the complete absence of a disciplinary device in guiding activities.

To understand our reasoning, it is important to note that the key aspect of civic interactions is that they are voluntary.[7] Those that support the activities of the entrepreneur – either monetarily, as in the case of privately funded non-profits, or through approbation – can voluntarily choose to sever the relationship at any point in time. When one undertakes an activity in a non-market setting, whether it is starting a political movement or a wearing a new style of clothing, the outcome will impact how others view him or her. If others approve of the activities they will voluntarily maintain the current level of support, and hence reputation, or increase their support of the entrepreneur. If they are unhappy with the course of action, they will likely curtail their support for the entrepreneur undertaking the activity. In other words, entrepreneurs in a non-market setting who satisfy the wants of consumers gain a 'profit' via increased reputation capital, and those who fail to meet consumer needs incur a 'loss' via decreased reputation capital.

For the reputation market to serve as an effective disciplinary mechanism, it requires intricate knowledge of the trustworthiness of the acting entrepreneur.[8] The issue becomes one of the 'span of control'. Only those who have strong ties with the entrepreneur will be in a position to have or maintain intricate knowledge of the entrepreneur's stock of reputation capital. To the extent that the reputation market relies on direct interaction, it will necessarily be limited to small social networks. In other words, entrepreneurship in non-market settings is, at least in its earliest stages, a local phenomenon. Beyond these small social networks the span of control breaks down as it becomes increasingly difficult to have intricate knowledge of the reputation of others. In short, the effectiveness of the reputation mechanism is directly dependent on the span of control.[9]

Consider, for instance, the case of micro-finance. In the standard case, members of a society who are denied access to normal financial markets can be aided through a micro-lending program to start small businesses that improve their situations. Since the individuals seeking loans do not have access to traditional forms of collateral, a substitute must be found. In many cases, in order to secure a loan, an individual must put up his or her reputation capital as collateral. For example, a specific number of non-family members from the community must vouch for the person and be willing to shoulder his or her debt if default occurs. The transaction is based on a small social network and is grounded in the existence of reputation capital.

The importance of a close social network in non-market settings is supported by work in cognitive psychology and anthropology. The anthropologist Robin Dunbar has argued that through evolution, the brains of humans have grown larger in order to deal with the complexities brought about by larger social groups. Dunbar has developed a neo-cortex ratio which compares the size of the neo-cortex to the size of the brain for a particular species. The ratio is meant to provide the maximum expected group size for the species under consideration. For humans, Dunbar has found the number to be 147.8, or approximately 150. In other words, 150 represents the maximum number of people that humans can have a close relationship with; this is the extent of their the span of control. Dunbar (1992) has applied this theory to a range of historical groups from hunter-gatherer societies to the military and has found that the number 150 holds in these various settings.

This realization of the importance of one's close social network also finds collaboration in diffusion theory as developed by sociologists. This theory considers how an idea, innovation or product moves through society. Many of the studies that employ diffusion theory have found that it takes only a small number of individuals, referred to as 'change agents', to adopt an idea, innovation or product that is eventually accepted by a larger number of people.[10]

In the framework developed here, the idea, innovation or product is first put to use by a few focal individuals whose reputation is established and well known. As those with established reputation capital adopt the idea, innovation or product, others within his or social network observe that person's actions. Risk and uncertainty begin to diminish and the number of willing participants increases.

It is critical to note that although many diffusion studies are focused on products, innovations or ideas that are linked to the market, this need not be the case. Many activities undertaken by social entrepreneurs are entirely outside the market context. What we wish to establish is that outside the market setting, reputation capital works as a soft constraint providing the entrepreneur with some guidance in his or her actions. By the very nature of reputation capital – namely, the need for face-to-face interaction – social entrepreneurship is a local phenomenon. As the idea or activity is rewarded in that local context, and as reputation capital increases, it is then possible for it to graduate to a broader context, although it need not do so.

The change agents in diffusion theory possess many of the same attributes as the entrepreneur in the economic and philanthropic literature – namely, their role as catalysts of change. These individuals create new focal points or shift existing ones. Further, they create convergence around the change because their social network looks to see what actions they are undertaking. These individuals are focal in their role as change agents; the actions they take are focal as well. In short, in non-market settings, the stock of reputation capital not only serves as a soft constraint on entrepreneurs but also as a convergence mechanism. Others will converge around the activities of those that have a well-established stock of reputation capital.

What is missing in the sociology literature is how these agents of change, to the extent that they act outside the market setting, are disciplined if they are not allocating resources to their proper uses. We have offered a potential solution here, with the reputation market as a proxy for the discipline mechanisms found in market contexts. The key aspects of the non-market disciplinary mechanism are the face-to-face nature of relationships and the fact that relationships are voluntary and can be ended if one of the parties is unhappy with the activities undertaken by the other.

Given that the reputation capital of entrepreneurs serves as collateral, they have strong incentives to accomplish the tasks for which they have received support. Indeed, it is our contention that the necessity of reputation as the main self-governing mechanism makes social entrepreneurship a function of betting on people, not on projects. Projects can be attractive, but unless the disciplinary feedback loops are well established, even the most promising project can be poorly executed.

The Political Setting

In order to gain tractability in our analysis, we limit the political setting to democracies where political agents are elected via majority voting. We adopt the standard Ferejohn political marketplace model where voters are 'owners' and politicians are the 'agents'. Political agents are self-interested vote maximizers and the owners hire or fire the agent based on economic performance (Ferejohn 1986). Again, we focus on the same questions as in the prior subsections. We seek to understand how agents in political settings create or shift focal points and how, if at all, they are guided and disciplined.

Clearly, political agents create and shift focal points in a number of ways. To the extent that the populace accepts and coordinates around a set of political institutions, the institutions themselves are focal. Acting within these institutions, political agents create and influence existing focal points. Political agents can encourage or prohibit certain types of activities through the creation of laws, rules and regulations. If, for instance, political agents want to encourage a certain line of activity, they will subsidize it. If they want to discourage the activity, they will tax it. It is common for political agents to attempt to create convergence around a certain issue by investing resources in raising awareness of the issue. Given the clear influence of political agents in social and cultural change, the question then turns to the existence or absence of suitable disciplinary devices in political settings.

We saw that in the market setting, entrepreneurs are disciplined by the profit/loss mechanism. Entrepreneurs acting in the market context face the hard constraint of real resources. In non-market settings, face-to-face interaction and the market for reputation serves as a soft constraint. On the surface, it may seem that the vote mechanism is a suitable disciplinary device in political settings. It is our contention that this is not the case. We argue that there is no direct proxy in political settings to discipline activities.

The voting mechanism is governed by the logic of concentrated benefits and dispersed costs. The interaction in democratic politics is one characterized by rationally ignorant voters, specially interested voters and vote-seeking politicians.[11] Given this, the bias is for politicians to concentrate benefits on the well-organized, well-informed special interest voters and to disperse the costs on the unorganized and ill-informed mass of voters. It is this basic examination of the logic of democratic discipline that underlies the argument for government failure theory, which is juxtaposed with market failure theory in modern political economy. In short, it is our contention that the voting booth is not an effective disciplinary mechanism.[12]

Given that there is a small probability of an individual voter influencing the outcome of an election, voters often participate in social institutions that allow them to engage with others in public discourse and debate. There are a variety of institutions in society that allows for discourse and debate. These institutions can range from the media to religious and political organizations such as unions. These institutions allow individuals to develop and coordinate their beliefs and ideas with others. For instance, many individuals join religious and political organizations because other members share similar views.

To situate this in terms of our framework, these social institutions allow for discourse which results in certain ideas becoming focal among their members. Where the individual voice is weak, larger groups of like-minded individuals may be able to generate sustainable social change. In economic terms, these social institutions may overcome collective action problems.

Although mechanisms may exist for individuals to participate in debate and discourse, this still does not means that the public sphere will generate the efficient distribution of resources. Political actors will respond to concentrated special interest groups, but the costs will be dispersed among the unorganized. In short, those who are effective in forming a special interest group will benefit while those who are ineffective in participating in such groups will suffer. To provide an example, consider farm subsidies. Farmers are able to effectively form a special interest group and lobby political agents for subsidies. The costs of these subsidies are borne by taxpayers who are not part of a special interest group and who have no recourse since they cannot, by themselves, change the political outcome.

While the key characteristic of civic relations in non-market settings is the voluntary nature of the interaction, interactions in the political setting are characterized by an enforced order grounded in coercion. While individuals in non-market settings voluntarily choose to interact and can sever that interaction if they are dissatisfied, individuals in political settings are forced to accept the terms dictated by political agents. This is not to say that reputation is absent in democratic settings, but rather to indicate that it is not nearly as effective as in non-market settings where private agents interact. The face-to-face interaction necessary to build the appropriate reputation capital is lacking. Further, where reputation capital does exist, there is no effective means of communicating satisfaction or a lack thereof to the agent.

It is not our claim that government activities fail to influence existing focal points or create new focal points. Instead, our claim is that the desirable effects of entrepreneurship in the market and in non-market settings are not transferable to the political setting. This is due primarily to the absence of a disciplinary mechanism to guide activities. Stated differently, there is no way for political agents to gauge whether they should adjust their activities to realize mutually beneficial exchanges which have been previously unexploited.

Overlap of Settings and the Implications for Entrepreneurs

In the previous sub-sections, we considered the entrepreneur in various settings in isolation. In reality, agents in different settings often interact in undertaking a certain activity. Moreover, we often observe one entrepreneur undertaking activities which overlap more than one setting. For instance, we often observe individuals in a market setting developing a unique image or reputation in order to differentiate themselves from others and make themselves focal. They are subject to the profit/loss mechanism in market settings, but the realized profit/loss is directly linked to their reputation capital. In connection with the profit/loss mechanism, it serves to inform entrepreneurs whether their efforts have been misallocated.[13]

We often observe entrepreneurs in market settings employing others who have established reputation capital to endorse their product or service and make it focal. In other words, these entrepreneurs are purchasing the use of the reputation capital of others to certify their product or service. Linking the product or service to a focal individual greatly eases the process of convergence around the good or service. Some have developed reputation capital in one setting and carried that capital over to another setting market. For instance, politicians often author books at the end of their political careers and are paid well to appear at speaking engagements.[14] In the framework developed here, they are able to carry over the reputation capital developed during their time in political settings to capitalize on their stock of capital in the market setting.

We also observe direct interaction between agents in political settings and those in market and non-market settings. As already indicated, the activities of political agents in terms of legislation and regulation directly influence, and in some cases limit, the type and extent of activities that entrepreneurs in market and non-market settings can undertake. Stated differently, political actors set the 'rules of the game' within which private individuals in both the market and non-market settings act. For instance, political agents can choose to protect property rights or engage in predation of private individuals. Further, political agents can choose to protect civil liberties or to violate these liberties. In terms of achieving economic efficiency, the role of government is enforcing general rules that allow private actors to utilize the disciplinary mechanisms present in market and non-market settings in allocate resources. These rules should be stable, predictable and general, meaning that they apply to all individuals equally. Given imperfect knowledge and information, individuals must constantly learn how to allocate resources to their most highly valued use. Acting within an environment characterized by stable and predictable rules allows them to do so. This requires constitutional constraints on government which prevents the erosion of the stability, predictability and generality of a society's rules.

As discussed above, the importance of social institutions that allow for public discourse are critical for public discourse. The public sphere also plays a critical role in establishing rules that allow these institutions to operate. For instance, in order to allow for public discourse, political agents must establish rules that allow for freedom of association, freedom of press, etc.[15] If private individuals are censored from engaging in such activities, public discourse cannot take place. In such cases, government through the threat of coercion seeks to maintain the status quo by preventing the legal discussion of political, social and economic issues that may be critical of its performance.

This interaction between entrepreneurs in the political and non-political settings creates an interesting dynamic in terms of the disciplinary mechanisms which should be addressed. We know that there is an inherent disciplinary device for entrepreneurs in market and non-market settings. We also know that a disciplinary device is lacking for entrepreneurs in political settings. What does this mean when agents in the various settings interact?

When entrepreneurs in market settings or non-market settings interact with political agents, the same disciplinary devices that guide them in the absence of the interaction with political agents are still present. For instance, if political agents subsidize the start-up costs of a business, that business will still be subject to market forces absent additional subsidies to keep it in business. Likewise, if political agents fund an entrepreneur in a non-market setting, that entrepreneur is still subject to voluntary face-to-face interactions with his or her social network. There is no guarantee that the entrepreneur's activities will be accepted by society at large.

This does not overcome the fundamental issue: political agents have no way of determining if they are, from an economic standpoint, effectively allocating resources. It does mean, however, that when agents from different settings interact, the disciplinary mechanisms that are present in isolation are still present. It is possible that the activities of agents in political settings can distort these disciplinary devices. For example, a firm that received continued subsidies would not respond to the profit/loss mechanism as it would in the absence of the subsidy.

Considering the overlap of settings also raises an important issue for political agents who wish to undertake activities aimed at creating social change which requires acceptance by groups within society at large. As diffusion theory in sociology and the two-step flow of communication hypothesis in communications theory indicate, it is critical for indigenous change agents to support the endeavor. These individuals have well-established credibility and legitimize the information they transfer. For instance, well-established indigenous individuals are more likely to generate sustainable change, as they are already well known and legitimate in the eyes of the public. This will be illustrated when we consider the post–World War II reconstruction of Germany below.

Applications

We find historical support for the general categories outlined above across a wide range of applications. Let us first consider the case of non-profits and, more specifically, apply the framework developed above to the case of Ashoka: Innovators for the Public.[16] This case illustrates entrepreneurship in a non-market setting relying on face-to-face interactions as outlined above. We will then consider, the post–World War II reconstruction of Germany.

Our focus is on the role of the cinema in crafting new focal social and cultural institutions in the wake of World War II. Finally, we consider the role of media in economic transition and development.[17] These cases illustrate the interaction of entrepreneurs across the various settings.

Ashoka: Innovators for the Public

Ashoka: Innovators for the Public is a non-profit organization whose mission is to 'develop the profession of social entrepreneurship'.[18] Founded in 1982 by Bill Drayton, the current CEO, Ashoka provides funding for social entrepreneurs in forty-eight countries across Africa, Asia, Central Europe, Latin America and North America. The organization's history illustrates many of the main points discussed above regarding entrepreneurs in non-market settings. Although it is sizeable now, Ashoka began as a small operation based on the reputation capital of Drayton.

Bill Drayton attended Harvard College, Oxford University and Yale Law School before working at the consulting firm, McKinsey & Company, and the U.S. Environmental Protection Agency (EPA). To begin Ashoka, Drayton turned to his network from his various schools as well as his close contacts from McKinsey and the EPA. With three former classmates and two former colleagues, Drayton traveled to India, Indonesia and Venezuela in 1978 and 1979. Their goal was to design a program which effectively identified and funded social entrepreneurs. India was selected as the first location for Ashoka, mainly for political reasons. Operations began in 1982 with a staff of local volunteers and $50,000, donated by three friends and Drayton himself.

The founding of Ashoka illustrates our framework of entrepreneurship in the non-market setting discussed above. The organization began in the context of a small social network in which the reputation capital of each member was well known via face-to-face interactions. That network provided not only the original members of the organization but also the necessary operating funds. As Drayton's organization has continued to grow, he has continually accumulated reputation capital. Ashoka now has approximately 1,400 'fellows' (i.e. funded social entrepreneurs) in forty-eight countries and has provided them with over $40 million in funding. Its operations are entirely funded by private means; it receives donations from individuals, corporations, foundations and other business entrepreneurs.[19]

Ashoka provides an interesting case study because it originated in a non-market setting and its main purpose is to fund other social entrepreneurs. As such, it faces the difficulties of attracting funds for its own operations and also identifying worthwhile projects. While Ashoka accepts applications from any potential 'fellow', most applicants come from a network of 'nominators' who recommend potential social entrepreneurs for funding. These nominators are located throughout the countries of operation and have an 'on-the-ground' perspective and knowledge of the potential social entrepreneur and his or her area of operation. They serve as middlemen in that they have a stock of reputation capital established with Ashoka and can also identify social entrepreneurs in their various countries because they have intricate knowledge of the potential entrepreneur's stock of reputation capital. In other words, face-to-face interactions take place on two levels – between the nominator and the potential social entrepreneur and between the nominator and Ashoka.

A multi-step, detailed selection process is undertaken to select fellows. After receiving an application, a 'country representative' reviews the application and engages in a detailed background check including personal references and a site visit. The country representative presents the information to a 'second opinion reviewer' and the 'selection panel' along with a recommendation as to the viability of the project. The second opinion reviewer is from outside the country where the potential fellow is located and serves as an external check. The final step is a series of face-to-face interviews with the selection panel before a final decision is made.[20]

The implications of this case study are critical to our thesis. The problem of attempting to determine and assess proxies for prices and profit/loss is that social entrepreneurs face the challenge of acquiring capital through reputation collateral. This requires face-to-face knowledge of the donors and of the needs and desires of the communities the social entrepreneur strives to help. The problem of dispersed knowledge necessarily makes social entrepreneurship a local phenomenon both in terms of convergence and efficiency. To accurately assess the needs of the community and have knowledge of the reputation market, the donor must be connected at the local level. The case of Ashoka illustrates the local, face-to-face nature of social entrepreneurship and the importance of reputation collateral in allowing activity in the non-market setting to be allocated to its most highly valued use.

While the founding and operation of Ashoka serves as an illustration of our framework, the activities of Ashoka fellows have, and continue to, generate fundamental social change around the world. For instance, one of Ashoka's key initiatives is the 'Full Economic Citizenship' initiative. Under this initiative, fellows will work with companies seeking to reach low-income markets. The fellows work with the companies to establish cost effective means of brining their goods and services to markets. Other specific examples of social change stemming from the work of Ashoka include the provision of reproductive health care in India, working to raise awareness of AIDS in Brazil and lobbying for human rights in Bolivia.

Cinema and the Post–World War II Reconstruction of Germany

Post-war reconstruction is one of the most difficult policy achievements. On the one hand, it involves the restoration of physical infrastructure and facilities, minimal social services, and structural reform in the political, economic, social and security sectors. On the other hand, it involves a shift in the social and cultural makeup of the country. Focal points need to be created around a new social and political order, and the populace needs to be coordinated on the conjectures underlying those focal points. Given this, a complete understanding of the reconstruction process requires an understanding of these agents of social and cultural change who create the 'dramatic suggestion' of a new set of conjectures. Hence, the framework developed here is applicable. Here we focus specifically on the role that the cinema played in the reconstruction of Germany, for reasons addressed below.

In general, while films provide entertainment and are linked to prices and profit/loss, they can also provide a social message (i.e. 'dramatic suggestion') and hence contribute to social and cultural change. Cinema played a critical role in the cultural and social reconstruction of Germany. As the film historian Sabine Hake (2002: 104) writes, 'In the Western zone, the cinema after 1945 emerged as the driving force behind the ongoing self-transformation of postwar culture and society.' Moreover, cinema involved change agents in all three settings discussed in the previous section. From its earliest beginnings in the early 1900s through 1942, when the Nazi regime nationalized the industry, the cinema industry was operated on a profit/loss basis. As a result, entrepreneurs in the cinema industry were guided by prices and the profit/loss mechanism.

The claim that cinema played an important role in the reconstruction of Germany is supported by three facts. The first is that the cinema was a well-established medium of entertainment and information dissemination. The second is that consumer demand for film is measured through film attendance. The third and final fact of note is the amount of resources invested by political leaders to control and influence the cinema industry.

A brief look at the history of the cinema industry in Germany indicates that it was a well-established medium. Introduced in the early 1900s, film was a well-known source of information and entertainment among the German populace in both the pre- and post-war periods.[21] The second indicator is attendance trends which generally increased over time (see Fehrenbach 1995: 43; Hake 1993: 72; 2002: 64–65; Welch 1983: 12; Wollenberg 1972: 36–38). This supports the fact that the populace viewed cinema as a source of entertainment and information. There was a steep increase in the early 1930s primarily due to heavy subsidization from the Nazi government. Cinema and media were at the center of Hitler's propaganda program, and the sharp increase in attendance illustrates this (Hake 2002: 59). Attendance decreased after the war due to the physical destruction and also to the end of Nazi subsidies and to occupation laws related to the cinema that slowed production. However, cinema attendance steadily increased as the film industry began to grow in the post-war period, with an attendance record reached in 1956.

Finally, political agents expended a great amount of resources in the pre- and post-war periods to control and influence the cinema. Assuming that political agents aim to maximize revenues, we would only expect them to expend resources if there was some return to be had. In this case, the return was the ability to control and influence a key medium for developing and disseminating common knowledge.

Political agents and cultural elites were involved in cinema in its earliest stages, mainly attempting to influence content along moral lines. With the beginning of World War I, censorship laws manipulated the cinema content to increase nationalism among the populace. The Weimar Republic (1918–1933) removed many of the censorship laws, allowing the cinema industry to develop in a largely unhampered environment. With the rise of Hitler in 1933, the cinema industry came under increasing state control until it was ultimately nationalized in 1942.

The U.S. government studied the German cinema industry prior to the end of World War II. Realizing the popularity of cinema and its importance in disseminating information and influencing culture, a well-developed plan for German cinema in the post-war period was critical. American government officials realized that cinema could coordinate the populace around the aims of the reconstruction. Moreover, it would enable the establishment of a national identity that would carry over into the post-occupation period.

In the immediate post-war period, the film industry was shut down. Soon thereafter, in November 1945, production of films was allowed under a set of strict guidelines. Domestic producers were required to be licensed by the U.S. Information Control Division (ICD). All personnel involved in the film industry and the content of films were screened. In order to receive a license, films were required to communicate a message consistent with the end goals of reconstruction. Films were reviewed throughout their production and a final review was undertaken before they were released.

The critical element of the occupation film laws is that they allowed indigenous agents to participate in the film industry. These individuals had intricate knowledge of German culture and ways of life, and were able to effectively make 'dramatic suggestions' to the populace. For instance, Wolfgang Staudte, Helmut Käutner and Kurt Hoffman were all directors in the pre-war period who continued their work in the post-war period.

Another link between the public and those in the film industry was the German film clubs. In general, film critics play an important role in the reputation market linking participants in the film industry and the populace.[22] Film clubs were groups of ten to twenty moviegoers – artists, journalists, writers, directors, movie-going intellectuals, etc. – who met once a week to screen a movie and discuss its artistic and cultural aspects.[23] The first film clubs were founded and subsidized by the French in their zone of occupation. The first film clubs in the U.S. zone were completely private. The first club in the U.S. zone began in Frankfurt in the summer of 1945 without the knowledge of the American occupying forces. This initial club was followed by the creation of subsequent clubs throughout the U.S. zone in various towns and universities (Fehrenbach 1995: 178–180).

These clubs were not profit driven and their main purpose was a 'cultural exchange', involving critical viewings and discussions of the latest releases.[24] In the early occupation period, the opinions of the clubs were spread to the local populace largely through word of mouth. The influence of these clubs on public opinion was directly dependent on their reputation capital. Although beginning as a local phenomenon, the clubs quickly grew in number. In 1949, the various independent clubs joined together to form the Association of German Film Clubs and thereafter had a more widespread public voice, holding annual meetings and contributing to various publications.

In general, post-war films in Germany provided widespread legitimacy for the new political and social order and also helped define the break from Germany's past. Films dealt with a wide range of topics, from anti-Semitism – *Affäre Blum* (*The Blum Affair*, 1948), *Morituri* (1948) and *Der Ruf* (*The Appointment*, 1949) – to pacifism – *Die Brücke* (*The Bridge*, 1959) – to military life – *Hunde, wollt ihr ewig leben* (*Dogs, Do you Want to Live Forever*, 1959) – to the role of women in society – *Die Sünderin* (*The Sinner*, 1951), *Mädchen hinter Gittern* (*Girl Behind Bars*, 1949), *Liebe kann wie Giftsein* (*Love Can Be Like Poison*, 1958) and *Anders als du und ich* (*Different from You and Me*, 1957).[25]

Cinema clearly played a role in shaping the social order and culture of post-war Germany. Indigenous agents with local knowledge of the pre-war German culture were effectively able to disseminate information and ideas through their films. This allowed for the creation of a political and cultural heritage separate from the Nazi past. The agents of change consisted not only of movie personnel (writers, directors, actors, etc.), but also of members of film clubs who influenced public opinion towards the film industry. The films themselves were subject to the profit/loss mechanism, and those who participated in the film industry were able to shape the cultural identity of Germany through the messages communicated in their films. Many who participated in the film industry had some stock of reputation capital from their previous films in the pre-war period. The films produced contributed to convergence around the reconstructed social order.

The members of the film clubs served as informal middlemen between the film industry and the Germany populace. Of course, these indigenous agents were acting within a set of constraints set forth by the occupying forces but nonetheless were able to contribute to crafting German culture. Clearly, many other forces were at work in the reconstruction of Germany but entrepreneurs, through the cinema industry, played an important role in shifting and creating convergence around the focal points underlying the reconstructed society. Working within the context of prices, profit/loss and reputation markets, these entrepreneurs were guided in their activities. To the extent that the Allies contributed finances to the rebuilding of the industry, it weakened the ability of these mechanisms to discipline entrepreneurs, but they were still present nonetheless. One critical implication from this case study is that attempts at social change must involve at a minimum an understanding of the already established change agents. These change agents should be included in the process to the greatest extent possible, for they are well-established and relatively low-cost means of coordinating individuals around a specific set of conjectures.

The Role of Media in Political, Economic and Social Transition

While the reconstruction process involves rebuilding social, political and economic institutions, often from scratch, the transition process involves working within a given set of institutions to bring about change. In short, the process involves transitioning to a liberal economic order. The importance of a well-functioning media in maintaining a liberal order can be traced back to Alexis de Tocqueville. In *Democracy in America*, Tocqueville ([1835–1840] 1988: 517) emphasized how newspapers 'maintain civilization'.[26] Although the role of media has been largely overlooked in the economic development community, lately one observes a shift in that trend.[27]

The media is critical for economic transition because it is in the business of making 'dramatic suggestions'. To the extent that these suggestions deal with transition efforts, they serve to coordinate the populace around. A free media is important for two reasons. First it can be seen as a signal that certain institutions have been adopted allowing the media industry to operate effectively. Second, the media serves to reinforce institutions already established as well as creating convergence around other institutions necessary for a successful transition. In equilibrium, the basic institutions are strong enough to support a free media and, at the same time, the media plays a role in shaping existing focal points and creating new ones.

A similar situation exists with consumer demand. In equilibrium, consumer demand influences what media outlets cover while the specific content of the media outlets influence consumer taste and preferences (Tullock 1968: 1265). The media profits from reporting, but part of what makes a certain media outlet attractive to consumers is the ability to provide a unique viewpoint that creates a 'dramatic suggestion'. As such, media can be seen as a key aspect of social and cultural change in terms of shifting focal points and creating convergence. Tocqueville ([1835–1840] 1988: 517–518) recognized the role of media in this context when he wrote, 'Only a newspaper can put the same thought at the same time before a thousand readers.... A newspaper is not only able to suggest a common plan to many men; it provides them with the means of carrying out in common the plans that they have thought of for themselves.'

To the extent that media is autonomous, entrepreneurs will operate in the context of the market setting as they will be subject to prices and the profit and loss mechanism.[28] The image of the media outlet itself as well as those that work for it will also be tied into the reputation market. For instance, media outlets and journalists will develop a reputation over time which is directly tied to the economic performance of the outlet. For instance, the *New York Times*, *Wall Street Journal* and *Financial Times* all have well-established, worldwide reputations as reliable news sources which benefit their overall sales and profitability. Moreover, the media does not just report on the news but influences public opinion and hence plays a role in social change. In other words, while acting within the general market context, media outlets provide employees the opportunity to be entrepreneurial and provide 'dramatic suggestion' through their work.[29] The key point is that in an environment characterized by media autonomy, entrepreneurs will have guideposts – an interconnection of the profit/loss mechanism and the reputation market – to direct their activities. In the case of a state run or influenced media, political actors will have no way to know if they are directing resources towards the 'right' ends from an economic standpoint.

Consider, for instance, the case of Poland. In 1989, Poland became the first of the Eastern European countries to overthrow its Communist regime. Although it still has problems – high unemployment, low incomes and some government corruption – Poland is considered a success relative to other Eastern European transition countries.[30] Prior to 1989, the media industry – radio, television, newspapers and magazines – in Poland was owned and operated by the state. However, Poland has since developed a strong print media industry with relatively favorable privatization, legal structures and journalistic practices (Carrington and Nelson 2002: 232). Today there are about 5,500 newspapers and periodicals on the Polish market, many of which are local or regional.[31] Moreover, a wide variety of topics are covered including general

news (*Gazeta Wyborcza* and *Rzeczpospolita*), 'light papers' providing entertainment news (*Detektyw, Skandale, Sensacje, Kobra*, etc.), magazines aimed
at shoppers (*Top, Kontakt*, etc.) and music papers (*Magazyn Muzyczny, Rock
'n Roll*, etc.). The major independent media sources are the daily papers, the
Gazeta Wyborcza and *Rzeczpospolita*, which have established reputations as
being credible and have maintained demand for their product. *Gazeta Wyborcza* has an average daily circulation of 536,000 copies, while *Rzeczpospolita* has
a circulation of 306,742.[32] Both publications have overcome the barriers of
the economic environment and lack of training through foreign investment
(Carrington and Nelson 2002: 232–235; Goban-Klas 1997: 25–26).

The newspapers in Poland have established reputation capital as credible
news sources and have played a key role as coordination-enhancing mechanisms reinforcing these institutions as well as other transition efforts. For
example, the *Rzeczpospolita* expanded its economic and political coverage
and created the 'green pages', which focus specifically on Poland's economic
development in terms of the policies adopted as well as their progress. The
paper serves as an information source on the mass privatization, allowing
readers to realize the benefits and track the progress of political efforts (Carrington and Nelson 2002: 235). In short, the media in Poland assisted in the
generation of common knowledge, allowing the government and populace
to coordinate on a set of conjectures aligning with the aims of transition.
The populace was (and continues to be) better able to understand the benefits of privatization. Further, decision makers are aware that their progress
towards privatization is being monitored.[33] This is a perfect example where
the media is able to operate because of the adoption of some foundational
institutions and also where it assists in strengthening existing convergence
and creating convergence around other institutions.

The spread of print and electronic media will also have implications for
social change in the Middle East. Discussing the impact of satellite television in the Arab world, a recent *Economist* article noted: 'Across the Arab
world, the impact of the satellite dish has been profound. It has not merely
broken the isolation of ... towns and villages ... [it] has created a sense of
belonging to and participating in, a kind of virtual Arab metropolis. It has
begun to make real a dream that 50 years of politicians' speeches and gestures have failed to achieve: Arab unity.'[34] With increasing media technologies available around the world at decreasing costs, one should only expect
the importance of media in social change to continue to grow. Media serves
to connect individuals both within societies and across societies and as
such serves as a form of association. In addition to introducing new ideas,
media increases transparency and allows for debate of fundamental social
and political issues. As such, media is a key mechanism for generating initial
social change and coordination around that change.

From a purely economic standpoint, in the absence of media autonomy, there is no way to ensure that resources are being allocated to their most highly valued use. If media autonomy does exist, entrepreneurs in the media industry will be guided by a combination of prices, profit/loss and the reputation market, all of which are driven by consumer demand.[35] Given a stable institutional environment, resources will be allocated to their most highly valued use over time. These mechanisms are absent or greatly hampered in the cases of state run or influenced media.

Conclusion

Two central issues motivated this chapter. The first was understanding how new focal points are created and how existing focal points are shifted. We postulated that the entrepreneur, who is the driver of economic change, is also the catalyst of social and cultural change. By being alert to and betting on wishful conjectures across various settings, the entrepreneur creates new focal points.

The second and related issue that we addressed was the transferability of the desirable consequences of entrepreneurship in market settings to non-market and political settings. We contended that entrepreneurship in non-market settings is initially a local phenomenon guided by reputation capital. We developed a framework for framing entrepreneurial activities in non-market settings.

Our argument is that, from an economic standpoint, non-market activity is most effective when initially limited to local actions where the reputation collateral of the entrepreneur is on the line. If we want resources to be effectively allocated to their most highly valued use, large-scale efforts at social and cultural change must be coordinated through various impersonal forces that serve as an imperfect proxy of monetary prices in the market setting. Granted, the reputation mechanism is not nearly as effective as monetary calculation, but it does provide some check on entrepreneurs in non-market settings. Small-scale efforts can be coordinated through face-to-face forces of reputation, either directly with the entrepreneur or through middlemen who possess the necessary local knowledge.[36]

Finally, in political settings, we concluded that there is no disciplinary device to guide the actions of political agents. In other words, there is no way for these agents to know if they are allocating resources towards the 'right' ends. Political interference can create social and cultural change, but will be coupled with waste and ineffectiveness because of the lack of a viable disciplinary mechanism to bring to identify errors. The main policy implication is that entrepreneurial efforts outside the market context should be undertaken at the local level where the disciplinary devices of face-to-face interaction and the reputation market can be most effective. This is especially true in underdeveloped and war-torn countries lacking well-developed social networks. Moreover, our case studies indicate the importance of identifying and involving change agents in the change process given that these individuals have an established stock of reputation capital.

Notes

1. The entrepreneur as the agent of change in market settings has received attention in the economic literature. See Baumol (1990), Boettke and Coyne (2003), Kirzner (1973) and Leff (1979). We seek to extend and explore this realization in the context of non-market settings.
2. Economic calculation is a sorting mechanism that allows actors to allocate resources to their most efficient or highly valued use. The issue is one of information and more specifically how individual know how to allocate their resources. We argue that private property and the resulting price system allows individuals to allocate resources efficiently. This price system is necessarily absent in the non-market and political settings. The implications will be discussed further in the next section.
3. This is in contrast to competitive equilibrium where the induced variables of the market correspond perfectly to the underlying variables such that all resources are utilized in their highest valued use and all least cost technologies are employed. When the market is in competitive equilibrium production efficiency, exchange efficiency and product-mix efficiency are simultaneously realized. In short, given the conditions of the world, affairs could not be arranged any better even if an omnipotent being wanted to do so.
4. The spread of the Internet has potentially interesting implications for civic society and social capital. On the one hand, an increasing number of individuals are connected. However, this could potentially lead to a decrease in face-to-face interaction and direct participation in civic society.
5. On the economics of advertising, see Ekelund and Saurman (1988).
6. Bornstein (2004: 4) indicates that 'between 1995 and 1999, 100,000 citizen groups opened shop in the former communist countries of Central Europe. In France, during the 1990s, an average of 70,000 new citizen groups were established each year, quadruple the figure for the 1960s. In Canada, the number of registered citizen groups has grown by more than 50 percent since 1987, reaching close to 200,000.... In the United States, between 1989 and 1998, the number of public service groups registered with the Internal Revenue Service jumped from 164,000 to 734,000'.
7. As Hayek (1948: 97) writes, 'In actual life the fact that our inadequate knowledge of the available commodities or services is made up by our experience with the persons or firms supplying them – that competition is in large measure competition for reputation or good will – is one of the most important facts which enables us to solve our daily problems.'
8. One can see a connection here with the work of Fukuyama (1999: 52, 88–91) in the area of social capital, and specifically with his notion of the 'radius of trust'. Our claim is that the intricate knowledge of the acting entrepreneur is initially available only to a small social network or within a small trust radius.
9. As Adam Smith wrote ([1776] 1971: 18): 'In civilized society he stands at all times in need of the cooperation and assistance of great multitudes, while his whole life is scarce sufficient to gain the friendship of a few persons.'

10. Perhaps the most well known study in this area is Ryan and Gross's (1943) study of the diffusion of hybrid corn in Iowa. Other notable diffusion studies include Hagerstrand's (1967) study of the diffusion of TB tests in Sweden and Coleman et al.'s (1966) study of the diffusion of tetracycline among Midwestern doctors.

11. The logic behind the rational ignorance of voters is that there is some positive cost to gathering information related to political actors and public policy issue. At the same time, the benefit to obtaining such information is miniscule, if not non-existent, because each voter realizes that the probability of his or her vote influencing the outcome is non-existent. As such, voters choose (i.e. rationally) to remain ignorant.

12. In contrast to this claim, Stigler (1982) and Wittman (1995) argue that inefficient policies are an illusion. Their argument is that rational individuals are no more likely to leave potential gains unexploited in political markets than in economic markets. Therefore, democratic markets must be efficient. For criticisms of Wittman, see Boudreaux (1996) and Rowley (1997). Caplan (2001) provides a defense of Wittman's logic and offers his own answer as to why political markets are inefficient. Specifically, he argues that political markets are inefficient because individuals do not pay individually for their beliefs. Given that they do not incur the cost of their beliefs, it is more likely that individuals will hold irrational beliefs. Another argument against the view that political markets are efficient is that political agents lack perfect information and therefore are subject to errors just like participants in the market setting (Boettke and Lopez 2002: 114–116, 117n6; Holcombe 2002: 143–159; Sutter 2002: 199–209). Government actions, based on coercion, force people to participate in activities where they lack information, and the incentive to gather the relevant information, and hence where they are unable to effectively determine costs and benefits. Given this, those who are informed can take advantage of the uniformed the result being an inefficient outcome (Holcombe, 2002: 156).

13. Cowen (2000: 14–16) discusses the 'snowball effect' in which fame is achieved or lost very quickly as fans accept or reject a star as long as others are willing to as well. The snowball effect itself requires the existence of common knowledge.

14. Examples include Bill Clinton, who received an advance of $10 million for his autobiography, *My Life*.

15. On the role of media in economic development and the political process, see Coyne (2005) and Coyne and Leeson (2004).

16. For an economic analysis of non-profits and a criticism of the work of Lester Salamon, see Boettke and Prychitko (2004).

17. Although we focus on the cinema and media as mediums for generating convergence around new or shifting focal points, one can also see a connection with the social capital literature. For instance, Putnam (2000: 96–97, 195–196, 218–220) considers cinema and newspaper readerships as two social connectors allowing individuals to be civically engaged with others building and/or strengthening social capital.

18. Ashoka's official website is http://www.ashoka.org/home/index.cfm.

19. See http://www.ashoka.org/what_is/endowment.cfm for a listing of Ashoka's endowments.

20. See http://www.ashoka.org/fellows/search_procedure.cfm for more details on this process.

21. Although we focus on cinema here, media was also a well-established medium which played a significant role in the reconstruction process. See Gienow-Hecht (1999) and Humphreys (1990).

22. For more on the role of critics, see Cowen (2000: 72–3) and Cowen and Tabarrok (2000).

23. For a more detailed history of the film clubs, see Fehrenbach (1995: 169–210).

24. It should be noted that some clubs did lobby the government for subsidies and some of the club leaders had relationships with members of the government. For example, in 1950 the Federal Interior Ministry placed Johannes Eckardt, who was a founder and leader of one of the clubs, on the selection committee in charge of awarding the Federal Film Prize.

25. For more on social relationships, national identity and specific films in the post-war period, see Fehrenbach (1995: 93–101).
26. A free media can be seen as a necessary condition for economic development. All of the G-7 members (Canada, France, Germany, Italy, Japan, the United Kingdom and the United States), which account for approximately two-thirds of the world's economic output, have a free media, as determined by a press survey by Freedom House (2003). Moreover, those countries that are considered transition 'successes' – Estonia, Hungary, Botswana and the Czech Republic – all have a relatively free media. However, it is critical to note that while a free media is a necessary condition for economic development, it is not a sufficient condition. One observes many countries that have a free media but remain relatively poor – Costa Rica, Benin, Bolivia, Fiji, Ghana, the Philippines, etc. This indicates that there are other key factors in addition to a free media that are requisites for development. Among these other factors are political stability, a stable economic environment outside of the media industry, quality of the media, education, ideology and interest in political, social and economic issues.
27. The role of media has recently been studied in terms of its impact on government transparency, accountability (Stiglitz 2002), solving the principal (citizens)-agent (government) problem (Besley and Burgess 2001; Besley et al. 2002), public policy (Spitzer 1993) and corporate governance (Dyck and Zingales 2002). Djankov et al. (2002) discuss how theories of media have historically fallen into one of two opposing camps: public interest theory and public choice theory. A small but growing literature theoretically addresses how state owned media prevents the adoption of growth enhancing policy reforms (Besley and Burgess 2002; Besley et al. 2002; Coyne and Leeson 2004; Sen 1984, 1999). Additionally, many case studies address the state of the media industry in specific countries (e.g. Gross 1996; Lent 1980; McAnany 1980; O'Neil 1997; Paletz et al. 1995).
28. Coyne (2005) and Coyne and Leeson (2004) consider the factors necessary for media to serve as an effective coordination-enhancing mechanism. One of these factors is media autonomy. Djankov et al. (2002) have found that state ownership of the media is higher in countries that are relatively poor, have more autocratic regimes and have higher levels of state ownership in other areas in the economy.
29. It should be noted that the claim is not that each and every media report is an instance of dramatic suggestion. Rather, those in the media industry have the opportunity to make dramatic suggestion through their reporting.
30. For instance, during the first decade of transition from communism to democracy, Poland's economy had the quickest turnaround, experiencing economic growth in 1992.
31. The number of periodicals is from Osrodek Badan Prasoznawczych Uniwersytetu Jagiellonskiego w Krakowie (Press Research Center at Jagiellonian University in Krakow), which keeps the electronic database available at http://www.media.onet.pl.
32. The source for the circulation of *Gazeta Wyborcza* is http://www.agora.pl/gw_advertising2/1,44368,1268408.html. The source for the circulation of *Rzeczpospolita* is http://www.mercury-publicity.com/germany.html.
33. It should be noted that there is still some state pressure on the media in Poland. For instance, there are still state-owned television stations (Telewizja Polska [which operates two stations, TVP1 and TVP2] and TV Polonia) and radio stations (Channels 1 and 2). Moreover, the state still exerts pressure on those media sources which are critical of the government, as evidenced by the increased number of defamation lawsuits brought by political agents (Freedom House 2003: 126).
34. 'The World through Their Eyes', *Economist*, 26 February 2005, pp. 23–25.
35. Of course, an autonomous media does not guarantee that information supporting transition efforts will be provided. Consumers must have an interest in these issues and demand coverage of certain topics from the media outlets (see Coyne and Leeson 2004: 32–34).
36. For examples of local solutions to local problems, see Ostrom (1992).

References

Baumol, W. J. 1990. 'Entrepreneurship: Productive, Unproductive, and Destructive', *Journal of Political Economy* 98: 893–921.

Besley, Timothy, and Robin Burgess. 2001. 'Political Agency, Government Responsiveness, and the Role of Media', *European Economic Review* 45: 639–640.

Besley, Timothy, Robin Burgess and Andrea Prat. 2002. 'Mass Media and Political Accountability', in *The Right to Tell: The Role of Mass Media in Economic Development*, ed. Alisa Clapp-Itnyre, Roumeen Islam and Caralee McLiesh. Washington, DC: World Bank, pp. 45–60.

Boettke, Peter J., and Christopher J. Coyne. 2003. 'Entrepreneurship and Development: Cause or Consequence?', *Advances in Austrian Economics* 6: 67–88.

Boettke, Peter J., and Edward J. Lopez. 2002. 'Austrian Economics and Public Choice', *The Review of Austrian Economics* 15, no. 2–3: 111–120.

Boettke, Peter J., and David L. Prychitko. 2004. 'Is an Independent Nonprofit Sector Prone to Failure? An Austrian School Analysis of the Salamon Paradigm and the Lohmann Challenge'. http://www.mercatus.org/pdf/materials/447.pdf.

Bornstein, David. 2004. *How to Change the World: Social Entrepreneurs and the Power of New Ideas*. New York: Oxford University Press.

Boudreaux, Donald J. 1996. 'Was Your High School Civics Teacher Right After All? Donald Wittman's *The Myth of Democratic Failure*', *The Independent Review* 1, no. 1: 111–128.

Caplan, Bryan. 2001. 'Rational Irrationality and the Microfoundations of Political Failure', *Public Choice* 107, no. 3–4: 311–331.

Carrington, Tim, and Mark Nelson. 2002. 'Media in Transition: The Hegemony of Economics', in *The Right to Tell: The Role of Mass Media in Economic Development*, ed. Alisa Clapp-Itnyre, Roumeen Islam and Caralee McLiesh. Washington, DC: World Bank, pp. 225–248.

Coleman, James S., Elihu Katz and Herbert Menzel. 1966. *Medical Innovation: A Diffusion Study*. New York: Bobbs Merrill.

Cowen, Tyler. 2000. *What Price Fame?* Cambridge, MA: Harvard University Press.

Cowen, Tyler, and Alexander Tabarrok. 2000. 'An Economic Theory of Avant-Garde and Popular Art, or High and Low Culture', *Southern Economic Journal* 67, no. 2: 232–253.

Coyne, Christopher J. 2005. 'The Role of Media as a Supporting Institution: Implications for Development Policy', *Mercatus Center Policy Series*, Policy Primer No. 3. http://www.mercatus.org/PublicationDetails.aspx?id=21244.

Coyne, Christopher J., and Peter T. Leeson. 2004. 'Read All About It! Understanding the Role of Media in Economic Development', *Kyklos* 57: 21–44.

Djankov, Simon, Caralee McLiesh, Tatiana Nenova and Andrei Shleifer. 2002. 'Media Ownership and Prosperity', in *The Right to Tell: The Role of Mass Media in Economic Development*, ed. Alisa Clapp-Itnyre, Roumeen Islam and Caralee McLiesh. Washington, DC: World Bank, pp. 141–166.

Dunbar, Robin. 1992. 'Neocortex Size as a Constraint on Group Size in Primates', *Journal of Human Evolution* 20: 469–493.

Dyck, Alexander, and Luigi Zingales. 2002. 'The Corporate Governance Role of the Media', in *The Right to Tell: The Role of Mass Media in Economic Development*, ed. Alisa Clapp-Itnyre, Roumeen Islam and Caralee McLiesh. Washington, DC: World Bank, pp. 107–140.

Ekelund, Robert B., and David S. Saurman. 1988. *Advertising and the Market Process*. San Francisco, CA: Pacific Research Institute for Public Policy.

Fehrenbach, Heide. 1995. *Cinema in Democratizing Germany: Reconstructing National Identity after Hitler*. Chapel Hill: University of North Carolina Press.

Ferejohn, John. 1986. 'Incumbent Performance and Electoral Control', *Public Choice* 50: 5–26.

Freedom House. 2003. *Freedom of the Press*. Washington, DC.

Fukuyama, Francis. 1999. *The Great Disruption: Human Nature and the Reconstitution of Social Order*. New York: Free Press.

Gienow-Hecht, Jessica C. E. 1999. *Transmission Impossible: American Journalism as Cultural Diplomacy in Post-war Germany 1945–1955*. Baton Rouge: Louisiana State University.

Goban-Klas, Tomasz. 1997. 'Politics versus the Media in Poland: A Game without Rules', in *Post-Communism and the Media in Eastern Europe*, ed. Patrick H. O'Neil. London: Frank Cass, pp. 24–41.

Gross, Peter. 1996. *Mass Media in Revolution and National Development: The Romanian Laboratory*. Ames: Iowa State University Press.

Hagerstrand, Torsten. 1967. *Innovation Diffusion as a Spatial Process*. Chicago, IL: University of Chicago Press.

Hake, Sabine. 1993. *The Cinema's Third Machine: Writing on Film in Germany, 1907–1933*. Lincoln: University of Nebraska Press.

_____. 2002. *German National Cinema*. New York: Routledge.

Hayek, Friedrich. 1948. *Individualism and Economic Order*. Chicago, IL: University of Chicago Press.

Holcombe, Randall G. 2002. 'Political Entrepreneurship and the Democratic Allocation of Economic Resources', *The Review of Austrian Economics* 15, no. 2–3: 143–160.

Humphreys, Peter J. 1990. *Media and Media Policy in West Germany*. New York: Berg Publishers.

Kirzner, Israel. 1973. *Competition and Entrepreneurship*. Chicago, IL: University of Chicago Press.

_____. 1992. *The Meaning of the Market Process*. New York: Routledge.

Leff, Nathaniel. 1979. 'Entrepreneurship and Economic Development: The Problem Revisited', *Journal of Economic Literature* 17: 46–64.

Lent, John A., ed. 1980. *Case Studies of Mass Media in the Third World*. Williamsburg, VA: College of William and Mary.

McAnany, Emile G. 1980. *Communications in the Rural Third World: The Role of Information in Development*. New York: Praeger Publishers.

O'Neil, Patrick H., ed. 1997. *Post-Communism and the Media in Eastern Europe*. London: Frank Cass.

Ostrom, Elinor. 1992. *Crafting Institutions for Self-Governing Irrigation Systems*. San Francisco, CA: ICS Press.

Paletz, David L., Karol Jakubowicz and Pavao Novosel, eds. 1995. *Glasnost and After: Media and Change in Central and Eastern Europe*. Cresskill, NJ: Hampton Press.

Putnam, Robert. 2000. *Bowling Alone: The Collapse and Revival of American Community*. New York: Touchstone.

Rowley, Charles. 1997. 'Donald Wittman's *The Myth of Democratic Failure*', *Public Choice* 92, no. 1–2: 15–26

Ryan, Bryce, and Neal C. Gross. 1943. 'The Diffusion of Hybrid Seed Corn in Two Iowa Communities', *Rural Sociology* 8: 15–24.

Schelling, Thomas C. 1960. *The Strategy of Conflict*. New York: Oxford University Press.

Sen, Amartya. 1984. *Poverty and Famines: An Essay on Entitlements and Deprivation*. Oxford: Oxford University Press.

_____. 1999. *Development as Freedom*. New York: Alfred A. Knopf.

Smith, Adam. [1776] 1971. *The Wealth of Nations*. Chicago, IL: University of Chicago Press.

Spitzer, Robert J., ed. 1993. *Media and Public Policy*. New York: Praeger Publishers.

Stigler, George. 1982. *The Economist as Preacher*. Chicago, IL: University of Chicago Press.

Stiglitz, Joseph. 2002. 'Transparency in Government', in *The Right to Tell: The Role of Mass Media in Economic Development*, ed. Alisa Clapp-Itnyre, Roumeen Islam and Caralee McLiesh. Washington, DC: World Bank, pp. 27–44.

Sugden, Robert. 1989. 'Spontaneous Order', *Journal of Economic Perspectives* 3, no. 4: 85–97.

Sutter, Daniel. 2002. 'The Democratic Efficiency Debate and Definitions of Political Equilibrium', *The Review of Austrian Economics* 15, no. 2–3: 199–210.

Tocqueville, Alexis de. [1835–1840] 1988. *Democracy in America.* New York: Harper Perennial.

Tullock, Gordon. 1968. 'A Note on Censorship', *American Political Science Review* 62, no. 4: 1265–1267.

Welch, David. 1983. *Propaganda and the German Cinema, 1933–1945.* New York: Oxford University Press.

Wittman, Donald. 1995. *The Myth of Democratic Failure: Why Political Institutions are Efficient.* Chicago, IL: University of Chicago Press.

Wollenberg, Hans H. 1972. *Fifty Years of German Film.* New York: Arno Press and New York Times.

Young, H. Peyton. 1998. *Individual Strategy and Social Structure: An Evolutionary Theory of Institutions.* Princeton, NJ: Princeton University Press.

Chapter 3

CIVIL SOCIETY ELEMENTS IN EUROPEAN COURT SYSTEMS
Towards a Comparative Analysis with Partial
Reference to Economic Factors

Stefan Voigt

Thus the jury, which is the most energetic means of making the people
rule, is also the most efficacious means of teaching it how to rule well.

Tocqueville, *Democracy in America*

Until the middle of the nineteenth century, England knew only one form of
trial, namely, trial by jury (Lloyd-Bostock and Thomas 2000: 55). Today, trial
by jury is the exception rather than the rule even in countries where this kind
of adjudication is part of the national heritage, such as England. All across
Europe, civil cases are hardly ever tried by jury today and the percentage of
criminal cases is often only around 1 percent of the total, if the institution of
the jury exists at all. So why bother to deal with a topic of seemingly little relevance? There are two reasons, the first drawing on the history of thought and
the second, on recent empirical developments. Let us start with the empirical developments: about ten years ago, one would indeed have had reason to
predict that juries were destined to perish because ever-fewer countries were
trying ever-fewer cases by jury. Yet around that time both Spain and Russia
(re-)introduced trial by jury and some countries created the legal foundations for trial by jury by incorporating it into their constitutions (such as
Kazakhstan, Latvia and Ukraine). Other countries are still thinking about the
re-introduction of the jury, and Japan is a case in point. It is interesting not
only to inquire into what has made these countries re-establish an institution
that seemed to be doomed but also to ask, in a more general fashion, what the
effects of trial by jury on various economic (and other) variables are.

Notes for this chapter begin on page 129.

As regards the history of thought, the inter-relationship of juries with civil society has played a prominent role within it. Both Hegel ([1821] 1963) and Tocqueville ([1835–1840] 1956) dealt with the institution of the jury and praised it not for its advantages concerning the efficacy of adjudication, but for its advantages concerning the participation of civil society in the running of an important state function. At the time when they were writing, the jury existed primarily in England and its current and former colonies. France had just implemented a modified jury model which spread from there to other countries on the continent as well as to other countries that were – directly or indirectly – influenced by the French, such as some countries in Latin America. As a result, today we have much empirical evidence concerning the functioning of juries within different economic, institutional and cultural contexts. Hence, we can deal with conjectures not only on theoretical but also on empirical grounds.

Does (voluntary) participation on a jury differ among countries, and, if so, why? In standard economics, it would be argued that the higher the opportunity costs of serving on a jury, the lower the probability that people would participate voluntarily. This would imply that one should expect people with little education and a low income to be over-represented on juries. An alternative hypothesis would be that in countries in which civil society plays an important role, the exact opposite should be the case because more people feel responsible for the *res publica*. A quantitative assessment of the various effects of trial by jury is surprisingly difficult to make as the amount of comparative work is very limited, and the amount of comparative work based on hard numbers is virtually non-existent. Consequently, this chapter is confined to dealing with the topic from a conceptual point of view.

The chapter is organized as follows: the next section deals with the functions of adjudication from an economic point of view. The third section presents the arguments that were made in favor of trial by jury on the basis of some ideal of civil society. We shall take both Hegel and Tocqueville very seriously and summarize their arguments as hypotheses that are presented in such a way as to make them, at least in principle, empirically testable. The fourth section gives an overview of the jury systems currently used in Europe. The last section brings the chapter to a conclusion.[1]

Potentially Relevant Functions of Adjudication and Civil Society from an Economic Point of View

This section begins with a description of the (economically relevant) functions of adjudication and continues with a description of the (economically relevant) functions of civil society. By considering these two areas, we will automatically establish some possible connections between lay participation in the judiciary and civil society.

Economic Functions of Adjudication

Prima facie, adjudication has different functions depending on whether penal or private law is involved. In economic terms, however, the functions are very similar. Let us begin by considering the function of adjudication in private law disputes, where its purpose is to resolve manifest conflicts. Conflicts have their origin in the incompatible expectations of the parties concerned (e.g. both parties may believe that they have the exclusive right to specific resources). This is also true for conflicts that end in a court trial: both parties expect to be better off by calling in a third party (the court) than by negotiating between themselves. This means that their expectations are incompatible, for otherwise they would not both be prepared to go to court. However, the role of courts is not merely confined to resolving conflicts after they have arisen but extends to preventing their emergence in the first place by means of the widespread publication of their decisions. If court decisions help to clarify the meaning of the law, parties can more easily build up expectations that are compatible with each other, and thus avoid having to take conflicts to court. In short, adjudication serves to prevent the emergence of conflict (*ex ante* function) and to resolve conflicts (*ex post* function).

Criminal law would appear to be different: one person causes harm to another and the state prosecutes the wrongdoer in the name of the public. On the one hand, the purpose of imprisonment is to make the offender feel guilty about his or her crime; on the other, it is to protect the public from any further harm that might be caused by the offender. Yet re-socialization is regularly claimed to be another goal of prison sentences. Just as in private law, adjudication in criminal law serves to prevent crimes being committed by making them less attractive.

Economically speaking, adjudication helps to reduce uncertainty generally as well as in specific cases with regard to both private and criminal law. The general level of uncertainty is, in turn, an important determinant for the level of investment: the more uncertain the future, the less likely it is that long-term investment will occur. This is true for investment not only in physical capital but in human capital as well. People will only specialize in specific qualifications if they can be fairly certain that these will still be in demand tomorrow. The amount and the quality, as well as the kinds of investment undertaken, are probably the most important factors determining income and growth.

On a theoretical level, this connection between uncertainty, investment and income is plausible and sound, and recent empirical evidence supports these theoretical constructs.

Economic Effects of Different Judicial Structures

It has been shown that the factual independence of the judiciary is (economically and statistically) significant for economic growth (Feld and Voigt 2003, 2006). This holds true for a sample of more than seventy countries, and the results appear to be quite reliable as the authors controlled for more than a dozen additional potentially relevant variables. Higher growth rates due to a factually independent judiciary will, all other things being equal, also lead to higher tax revenue for the state. It would thus seem to be in the rational self-interest of any ruler to establish a factually independent judiciary.[2] A potential means to keep control of the judiciary independent of the ruler – and within society – seems to be to assign the competence for adjudication to members of that society: the traditional jury approach.

It has also been shown (Voigt 2008) that judicial accountability is positively correlated with per capita income. Judicial independence can be misused: judges who are independent from the other branches of government as well as from the conflicting parties might decide to remain uninformed, follow their own ideologies or become lazy and even corrupt. It is assumed that everyone wants judges to be accountable to the law – and not (at least, not directly) to the other branches of government, the conflicting parties or even to the population at large. Again, it can be argued that juries are a potential way of making professional judges more accountable: if juries oblige judges to explain the central content of the law to them in a comprehensible manner, the possibility that judges can shield themselves behind complicated language seems to be reduced.[3]

Furthermore, the factual independence of prosecutors has been negatively correlated with the perceived degree of corruption in a society (Aaken et al. 2008). In turn, a high degree of corruption has been shown to distort economic growth and development (Mauro 1995). The reasoning behind these findings is straightforward: prosecutors are often not independent from the minister of justice, the prime minister or some other important member of the executive. This means that the likelihood of members of the executive being prosecuted for committing criminal acts will, all else equal, be less than in political systems in which the prosecutors are not dependent on the executive. The data seem to confirm this reasoning. Given that the procuracy enjoys some formal discretion concerning procedural issues, such as whether it chooses trial by jury or trial by a single judge, its factual (in)dependence from the executive might well be relevant: the greater the influence of the executive on the actions of the procuracy, the more problematic any discretion concerning procedures would seem to be.[4] If the prosecuting agencies have discretionary leeway concerning the involvement of a jury, this needs to be explicitly taken into account when analyzing the consequences of trial by jury.

The Relevance of the Jury System

We have referred to three aspects of judicial systems: namely, the independence of judges, their accountability to the law and the independence of prosecutors; and we have tried to establish some connections with the institution of the jury. In line with recent empirical research on the economic effects of various traits of judicial systems, it is thus of interest to inquire whether the existence of jury systems is conducive to higher degrees of judicial independence and judicial accountability. It is also interesting to ask whether trial by jury can substitute for some of these desirable characteristics if they are lacking. If, for example, *de facto* judicial independence cannot be created quickly (and common sense as well as the evidence suggest that it cannot) even though it is crucial for economic development, would the creation of a jury system then be an adequate step towards partially increasing *de facto* judicial independence, at least in the short and medium term?

Before turning to civil society and its possible relevance for economic performance, we need to deal with the economics of court systems. Court systems do not only have an economically relevant impact, they themselves can be organized more or less efficiently. Resources are needed to produce adjudication, and different adjudication systems require different amounts of resources. *Prima facie*, trial by jury is a resource-intensive way of producing adjudication: the number of people involved is high; they need more time to come to a decision as they are not legal experts; the judge usually has to spend quite some time explaining the issues to them; and making sure that enough jurors show up on the day of the trial requires preparation, etc. From an economic point of view, spending all these resources can only be justified if trial by jury entails some extra benefits such that the net balance between benefits and costs is positive.

Economic Effects of Civil Society

Let us now turn to civil society and its possible relevance to economically significant variables such as income and growth. First we need a definition of civil society. Following Putnam (1993), it can be argued that the higher the number of horizontally structured voluntary associations – and the higher their membership as a percentage of the entire population – the higher the degree of civil society that exists in a given country. The concept of civil society is thus one of degree and not of kind. The activities of (civil) society members can have both a direct influence on government behavior, by means of information provided by members of civil society, for example, and an indirect influence, by the provision of goods conventionally provided for by the state. (The adjudication of [private law] conflicts via Alternative Dispute Resolution is a case in point.) Here, we use a delineation of civil society that indicates the distinction between state and society. All those actors who do not receive their primary income from the state are considered to be part of civil society.

The notion of civil society is closely connected with the concept of governance. Although no generally agreed definition of the term has yet emerged, governance deals with the process of collective action in the pursuit of solving – or at least reducing – collective problems. 'Governance' is thus broader than 'government' as conventionally perceived because collective problems can also be solved by non-government members, that is, by civil society. The success of the concept of governance is an indicator of the dissatisfaction with established concepts such as (1) Weber's notion concerning the rationality of administration, (2) the dichotomy between market and state, (3) the paradigm of the sovereign nation-state and (4) the traditional notion of the separation of powers. Here, the latter concept is of particular relevance.

In many Continental European countries, democracy primarily means representative democracy and citizen participation is constrained to the election of legislators. But citizen participation can be broader and does not need to be confined to the legislature. Direct democracy can be applied to both the legislature and the executive. Trial by jury allows the direct participation of society in the judicature.[5] Election – that is, indirect participation – can mean the election of judges by the population, rather than their appointment by representatives of the other two branches. This is not the place to discuss the optimal degree of citizen participation with respect to the notion of the separation of powers. However, it is important to keep the various options in mind while discussing concepts such as civil society and governance (table 3.1 contains additional possibilities). We shall now turn to the possible effects of civil society on economically relevant variables.

Direct Effects of Civil Society

It is hypothesized that an active civil society can have a number of effects on economic outcomes. Various aspects of social security can be provided

Table 3.1 Some Examples of Citizen Participation in the Separation of Powers

	Legislature	Executive	Judiciary
Among branches	Elects executive (in parliamentary systems)	Appoints judiciary	Control by constitutional review
Indirect citizen participation	Elect legislators	Elect president Elect sheriffs Elect auditors	Elect judges
Direct citizen participation	Referenda Initiatives	Freedom of Information Act Voluntary self-commitments *Planfeststellungsverfahren* Executive referenda Local self-government Chambers of Commerce Police monitoring council	Jurors Lay assessors Expert witnesses

by civil society associations, which will reduce the necessity of the state to intervene. Organized groups such as labor unions, employers' associations and the like can signal their members' preferences to the government, which can, in turn, provide collective goods that are in tune with the preferences of many members of society. The existence of a more highly developed civil society may indicate a high general level of trust, which reduces transaction costs and therefore makes higher income and growth levels possible. These are mainly direct effects. It can also be argued, however, that an active civil society has a number of quite substantial indirect effects.

Indirect Effects of Civil Society

It is not self-evident that governments respect the constraints promulgated by constitutions. Many of the world's constitutions seem to lay down the foundations for wonderful rule-of-law states yet in reality they are often not implemented. Thus, the question is, which conditions have to be satisfied in order to prevent those in power from making themselves better off by ignoring the restrictions laid down in a constitution? We would argue here that any opposition to a government's attempts to renege upon such constraints will make these attempts less attractive and therefore less likely. Yet opposition is a public good and its production is thus rather unlikely. So one can argue that the production of the public good 'opposition' is much more likely if there are many organized groups in existence, even if their original purpose was entirely unrelated to providing opposition.

Putnam (1993) claims that in those Italian regions where there is a high number of voluntary associations with a horizontal organization structure, there is a link to the production of high quality local public goods.[6] Drawing on the concept of 'social capital', Knack and Keefer (1997) find that trust and civic cooperation are associated with stronger economic performance. Contrary to Putnam (1993), they find that associational activity is not correlated with economic performance.

Up to this point, two possible channels through which civil society can be conducive to the rule of law and to economic development have been presented. The potential costs of an active civil society should not, however, be overlooked. Every additional actor (or actor group) that needs to consent to a policy increases decision-making costs, thereby making the status quo more stable.[7] Additionally, the principle of 'one man, one vote' is often attenuated in active civil societies as people who are more active have a greater influence on collective decision making, which might lead to issues of legitimacy.

Summing up, I have argued that both the structure of the judicial system and the degree of civil society can have consequences for economic performance. In the next section, we try to connect these two concepts by asking whether there are any systematic relationships between civil society and the institution of trial by jury.

Court Systems and Civil Society

Introductory Remarks

This section serves to establish a connection between juries and civil society. Our aim is not to deal with normative statements but to put forward positive hypotheses that are, at least in principle, empirically testable. Fortunately, we do not have to establish the connection ourselves but can draw on a number of legal philosophers who did so centuries ago. Before looking at their arguments and hypotheses, we want to advance some considerations in favor of restricting our argument to the jury – and for not extending it to lay participation in general, which would include lay assessors.

If the structure of judicial systems is to be analyzed from the viewpoint of the concept of civil society, it would initially seem to make sense not to limit the argument to jurors but to include every kind of lay participation, particularly lay assessors who decide on questions of both fact and law together with a professional judge. The function of civil society is often perceived to be that of creating a link between the (powerful) state and (more or less powerless) individuals. The participation of individuals in the administration of one state function – namely, adjudication – could thus be interpreted as one way of circumscribing the power of the state in one specific area – the judiciary. However, the crucial difference between jurors and lay assessors is that juries are usually exclusively responsible for deciding whether an accused person is guilty or not, whereas lay assessors decide this issue in conjunction with one (or more) professional judges. Although lay assessors could, in principle, often out-vote the professional judge(s), as they are frequently in the majority, in practice this almost never happens. It has also been noted (Thaman 2000: 335) that lay assessors are a lot less active in court than jurors as regards asking questions, etc.[8]

On the Effects of Trial by Jury

Prima facie, relying on amateurs (jurors) rather than on professionals (judges) in order to make very important decisions seems an odd idea (in the past, jury verdicts were often a matter of life or death). But the eighteenth-century English jurist Sir William Blackstone ([1791] 1966) wrote of the jury as 'the glory of English law' and claimed that it placed 'a strong … barrier between the liberties of the people and the prerogatives of the Crown'. This has remained one of the central arguments in favor of trial by jury right up to the present day: it is the jury that protects the individual from the prerogatives of the state. The jury makes sure that individuals are not dependent upon the whim of a powerful state but that it is their peers who decide whether they have committed some crime or reneged upon a contract. This argument can, of course, also be read as an argument for the relevance of civil society. As our hypothesis #1, it reads:

> In countries with trial by jury, individual freedom is better protected than in countries without trial by jury.

It has been shown that individual freedom is conducive to economic growth (for a survey, see Berggren 2003). If individual freedom can indeed be safeguarded by means of trial by jury, such trials should therefore lead to higher income and growth.[9] Against this hypothesis, it could be argued that people who act contrary to established conventions might be *less* secure in the hands of jurors who may represent those conventions. Taking the argument one step further, one might even argue that trial by jury is an institution that could be a hindrance to innovation and, furthermore, that inherent to a trial by jury is the danger of what has been dubbed 'unlimited democracy'. A jury representing the median income earner might decide to punish someone by imposing a hefty fine simply because the person is wealthy. Trial by jury could thus lead to the exploitation of minorities by majorities.

It is clear that there are plausible but incompatible arguments on both sides. In order to ascertain their validity, we need to turn to empirical tests. This, of course, is also true of all the other hypotheses developed below.

Montesquieu ([1748] 1961) popularized the structure of the English political system on the continent. He famously described the jury as 'en quelque façon nul'. Concerning the appointment of judicial competence, he argued that it should be exercised by people who 'are chosen according to the law for specific times of the year from among the entire population. They ought to form a tribunal, which only exists as long as necessity demands' (Book XI, chap. 6). Hence, judicial competence should not be allocated to a tenured senate. This would reduce the level of concern the population felt towards the judiciary because juries were not connected either with any particular rank or profession. He then went on to advance other reasons for trial by one's peers. Hypothesis #2 can be formulated as follows:

In countries with trial by jury, fear of the judiciary is substantially lower than in countries without trial by jury.

Montesquieu evaluated his premise positively. If it turned out to be correct, its root cause could clearly be attributed to civil society. Yet it is more difficult to evaluate the economic consequences of this premise: does an absence of fear encourage people to take more cases to court? Would it, in other words, reduce the likelihood of disputes being settled out of court? Might that not even be a negative effect because more resources would have to be spent on the courts? With regard to criminal law, could absence of fear not entail the danger of more crime? Or can 'absence of fear' also be read as 'trust in the governance of the court system'? If the latter interpretation turned out to be true, then people might be more inclined to enter into contracts in the first place which could, in turn, lead to improved economic performance.

Against this hypothesis, it could be argued that non-conformists' fear of jurors might be greater than their fear of professional judges for reasons largely analogous to those already outlined in the argument against hypothesis #1.

In his *Philosophy of Law*, Hegel ([1821] 1963) also advanced a number of arguments in favor of trial by jury. He argued (ibid.: § 218) that in civil society (*bürgerlicher Gesellschaft*), a crime is an injury not only of something subjectively infinite (*subjektiv-unendlich*) but of general concern (*allgemeine*

Sache). It is the public at large that prosecutes criminals (ibid.: § 220) and the penalty is more than simply revenge but '(s)ubjectively, it is the reconciliation of the criminal with himself, that is, with the law known by him as his own and as valid for him and his protection; when this law is executed upon him, he himself finds in this process the satisfaction of justice and nothing save his own act'.

According to Hegel ([1821] 1963), this would, however, be doomed to failure when the suspect was entirely dependent on professional judges because society would have been excluded from jurisdiction. He formulates his ideas concerning the jury (ibid.: § 228; translated by Herzog 2001: 554):

> Owing to the character of the entire body of the laws, knowledge both of what is right and also of the course of legal proceedings may become, together with the capacity to prosecute an action at law, the property of a class which makes itself an exclusive clique by the use of a terminology like a foreign tongue to those whose rights are at issue. If this happens, the members of civil society … are kept strangers to the law, not only to those parts of it affecting their most personal and intimate affairs, but also to its substantive and rational basis, the right itself, and the result is that they become the wards, or even in a sense the bondsmen, of the legal profession.

Hegel thus argues that members of (civil) society ought to recognize that the administration of justice is part of their affairs. He refuses to accept the argument that professional judges could make decisions much more efficiently (ibid.):

> It may be the case that if the administration of justice were entirely in the hands of professional lawyers, and there were no lay institutions like juries, it would in theory be managed just as well, if not better. It may be so, but even if this possibility rises by general consent to probability, or even certainty, it still does not matter, for on the other side there is always the right of self-consciousness, insisting on its claims and dissatisfied if laymen play no part.

Unfortunately, it remains somewhat unclear what exactly Hegel had in mind when he wrote of the better management of justice. At least two interpretations are possible. Firstly, it could mean that professional judges and lay juries come to basically identical decisions, yet professional judges need fewer resources for their decisions. Economists would then be able to claim that the administration of justice by professionals is more efficient. This interpretation draws on a somewhat narrow definition of efficiency, and Hegel would presumably quarrel with it. For him, 'self-consciousness' is so important because he sees it as the only way to bring about a society-wide discourse on right and wrong, which is a precondition for general acceptance of the law. If the law is generally accepted in society, fewer people will violate it, fewer resources will have to be spent on the administration of the entire system and, at the end of the day, self-consciousness increases efficiency, in a much broader sense of the term. To turn this argument around, one could say that no legal system that is not generally accepted can ever be efficient. Hegel thus believes that the apparent trade-off between efficiency of the administration of justice on the one hand and self-consciousness on the other is only a superficial one. Economists would say that Hegel is stating lexicographic preferences: first, the need for self-consciousness has to be satisfied. Only then would Hegel start to think about the management of the judicial system.

A second possible interpretation is that due to the better administration of justice by professional judges, there is less likelihood that these judges will come to erroneous decisions than lay juries. If that was what Hegel had in mind, his normative statement in favor of lexicographic preferences would be highly controversial: it could mean that he would accept a falsely imposed death penalty for the sake of self-consciousness. Such an interpretation seems unlikely because it entails the danger of self-contradiction: the chances that a legal system would be generally accepted although the probability of a wrongful conviction was high appear to be rather slim.

Adopting the more plausible interpretation of Hegel, we can now present hypothesis #3:

Trial by jury gives rise to a discourse concerning right and wrong in society that will, in turn, reduce the overall number of crimes.

Tocqueville ([1835–1840] 1956) makes a distinction between the jury as (1) a political institution and (2) a judicial institution, and claims that it is much more important as a political than a legal one. Although it has a significant impact on the outcome of cases (as a judicial institution), its impact (as a political institution) on 'the destinies of society at large' is even more important. As the latter, he thinks it is an extremely valuable instrument to realize people's sovereignty, while as the former, he evaluates it more critically. This reflects on times that were far less complex than our own. Whereas Hegel's lexicographic preferences (first, self-consciousness, and only then the efficient administration of a narrowly defined justice) are relevant on the normative plane, Tocqueville's evaluation is concerned with the impact of the two functions of trial by jury and is thus relevant on the positive plane.

Nevertheless, his distinction hinges on the possibility of keeping the two functions separate. How can one attempt to ascertain the impact of the judicial function independent of the political one? It is reasonable to assume that a badly executed judicial function would spill over onto the 'destinies of society at large' and so the separation is not convincing. Tocqueville explicitly alludes to the possibility that juries will do a bad job in respect of the judicial function when he writes ([1835–1840] 1956: 179): 'I do not know whether the jury will be useful to those being subject to a trial, but I am convinced that it is very useful for those who have to decide a trial.' From an economic point of view, this evaluation is highly problematical: if a (badly administered) judicial function means that court decisions are unpredictable, the judicial function does not lead to a decrease in uncertainty. Such a decrease is, however, the single most important function of the judiciary from the viewpoint of economics.

According to Tocqueville ([1835–1840] 1956: 174), juries can be a republican or an aristocratic institution depending on the choice of jurors. In fact, juries will always be of a republican nature because they allocate the real conduct of the state to the governed not to the governing. Tocqueville further believed the jury to be just as important as general elections in letting the majority rule (ibid.: 176).[10] It is exactly this characteristic of the jury that prevents rulers from becoming the masters of their respective societies. According to Tocqueville, autocrats do not like to be constrained by their own population, which is why they would try to eliminate the jury (hypothesis #4):

Autocrats will try to abolish trial by jury as it prevents their domination of society.

Over a hundred years later, Brown (1951: 129) put forward the corresponding hypothesis that the institution of trial by jury would be introduced after regime changes towards democracy: 'We thus take as axiomatic that lay justices appear where there is an upsurge of democracy, or democratic aspirations.'

Much of Tocqueville's theory is based on the importance of habit. Laws can be changed overnight, whereas habits are much more enduring. If an institution is to last, it is essential that it be integrated into the habits of a people. If trial by jury is limited to criminal cases, the people become accustomed to the possibility of claiming their rights without having to rely on a jury. If, on the other hand, there is also trial by jury in private law cases, everybody's interests are affected and the jury thus becomes part of everyday habit. Once an institution has become an accepted part of a people's habits, it is much more difficult to eliminate. This leads directly to hypothesis #5:

The likelihood that juries will be abolished by autocrats is greater if their competence is limited to criminal cases. If jury competence includes private law cases, the jury will become part of the habits of a people – and will be more difficult to abolish.

But Tocqueville ([1835–1840] 1956: 128) also offers explicit arguments in favor of trial by jury. The jury would teach people equity; it would teach them that they cannot escape from responsibility for their own actions; it would teach everybody that they have duties vis-à-vis society, and it would subdue personal egoism, the deep-seated evil of society.

> The jury contributes powerfully to form the judgment and to increase the natural intelligence of a people; and this, in my opinion, is its greatest advantage. It may be regarded as a gratuitous public school, ever open, in which every juror learns his rights, enters into daily communication with the most learned and enlightened members of the upper classes, and becomes practically acquainted with the laws, which are brought within the reach of his capacity by the efforts of the bar, the advice of the judge, and even by the passions of the parties.

Formulated as hypothesis #6, these arguments could thus be summarized as follows:

In countries that use trial by jury, the population will be more knowledgeable concerning its legal order than in countries that do not use trial by jury.

Summing up his argument on trial by jury, Tocqueville writes that such an institution would not only be the most effective means of letting the people rule but also of teaching the people how to rule. Interpreted liberally, this could mean that the jury provides countries that have this institution with a breeding ground for future politicians,[11] although this might be stretching the original argument a little too far. Alternatively, it could mean that the existence of the jury increases the quality of government because large numbers of the population have been involved in a 'training course'. Hypothesis #7 is therefore:

Countries that use trial by jury should experience a higher general quality of governance.

It is worthwhile highlighting some of the differences between Blackstone's and Tocqueville's arguments. Whereas Blackstone – and many (probably most) others who are dealing with trial by jury – stresses the function of the jury as that of controlling state-paid judges, Tocqueville sees (American) judges as sharing a certain desirable spirit, which would be adopted by large numbers of the population. Economically speaking, it could be said that Tocqueville advances an argument in favor of a low degree of division of labor. He does not wish to rely exclusively on professional judges but wants to include other parts of society, which is one ideal within the notion of civil society: society itself is responsible for running the state, and in this case, the judiciary. Tocqueville argues that trial by jury should reduce the power of professional judges. But appearances are deceptive: by being in contact with professional judges, jurors would learn their quality and even develop a certain awe of them (hypothesis #8):

Judges in countries that use trial by jury should enjoy a higher reputation than judges in countries that do not, all else being equal.

So far we have put forward some hypotheses by drawing on legal philosophers. We now continue by presenting arguments in favor of the jury that can be found in many law books, which we shall also state as hypotheses. One argument often advanced in favor of trial by jury is that juries are better at finding out facts than judges (see, e.g., Duff 2000: 279). It is suggested that this may be so because a higher number of jurors will have a higher probability of getting the facts right (Condorcet's famous jury theorem). It may also be better because jurors originate from many walks of life and are thus people who have a lot of first-hand experience of the real world. If this were the main cause for the better fact-finding capacity of juries, it should be especially relevant in legal orders in which the position of a professional judge is taken up as one of the usual steps on the career ladder – in countries such as Japan or Germany. Career judges tend to become judges at a rather young age and have thus had less chance to experience at first hand the trustworthiness of statements, etc. Hypothesis #9 states:

In countries with trial by jury, judicial mistakes will occur less frequently than in countries without trial by jury.

We mentioned above that the independence of the judiciary has been found to be robustly correlated with economic growth (Feld and Voigt 2006). It seems plausible to assume that lay judges are unaffected by pressures from within the judiciary because jurors have no interest whatsoever in a judicial career. This means that they do not have to behave with caution for reasons unrelated to the current trial. However, jurors should also be more independent because the other two branches of government would find it difficult to pressurize them: the threat of firing them is not credible and neither is the threat of many other instruments often used vis-à-vis professional judges, such as a reduction in salary, etc. This might be particularly relevant in cases of direct interest to governments such as those involving the opposition or critical journalists, for example. It is precisely why many legal orders that rely on trial by jury have allocated such offences to juries. As regards pressure applied by the accused party (or the contracting parties in the case of private law), there has been some disquietude that jurors can be intimidated by people involved in organized crime. Intimidation of this nature cannot be overlooked, of course, but the threat appears to be no more serious than it is to professional judges. The possibility of bribery is another issue, and here it can be argued that the probability of jurors being bribed is actually lower than that of professional judges, for (1) there are more persons to be bribed; (2) it is a one-shot game, and establishing relationships thus becomes extraordinarily costly; and (3) the identity of the jurors is often known at only very short notice. From this follows hypothesis #10:

In countries with trial by jury, the judiciary should, all other things being equal, be more independent, which should lead to higher rates of economic growth.

In a less optimistic vein, one could argue that jurors have fewer incentives than do professional judges to care about the outcome of a case, precisely because it is a one-shot game. They do not strive for a career within the judiciary and therefore have no incentive to build up a reputation as informed, law-abiding and fair decision makers. This *might* lead them to pay less attention than professional judges to the outcome.

It has also been argued (see, e.g., Munday 1993: 221) that jury trials allow 'justice to be done in individual cases where the jury considers that it would be unduly harsh to adhere strictly to the letter of the law'. This is closely connected to another argument (ibid.) that stresses the higher degree of accountability of the state vis-à-vis its citizens. If laws appear to be inadequate or 'patently out-of-step with the views of "society"', the jury may interpret the law with greater flexibility and thus make it compatible with the values and norms of that society.

These arguments in favor of jury trial are ambivalent. On the one hand, legal certainty can suffer as a consequence of *some* juries being less harsh than the law permits. On the other, the non-application of rules based on values and norms that have long been outdated in a society can be an advantage if the legal order is to reflect current values and norms. However, the latter holds true only if we have good reason to assume that jurors are more in tune with current values and norms than judges and legislators. In addition, a normative argument for the desirability of legal decisions being in line with the views of society is required.[12] Nevertheless, there is another twist to the accountability argument that can make it more convincing: in trial by jury, the judge will usually have to explain the relevant law to the jurors and the decision will be taken after the jurors have answered a list of very detailed questions. These measures can be said to increase the transparency of judicial decision-making vis-à-vis the population at large. However, the process of decision making by juries remains opaque because the reasoning behind the verdict is often not published. Even so, one can hypothesize (#11) as follows:

The necessity for the professional judge to explain the valid law in simple terms to jurors increases accountability to the law.

Summing up, it could be argued that trial by jury increases the legitimacy of the judicial system. If juries are better at finding out facts, are more independent from pressures exerted by interested parties, apply the law in a manner in tune with the current 'views of society', and make judicial decision making more transparent, then this should lead to a high degree of legitimacy of the judicial system (hypothesis #12):

Judicial systems in countries with trial by jury enjoy a higher degree of legitimacy than judicial systems in countries without trial by jury, all other things being equal.

A high degree of legitimacy of state organs will reduce the amount of resources that have to be spent on monitoring citizens, which should, in turn, have a positive impact on economic performance. Whether this hypothesis holds true does, however, depend on other hypotheses being correct. Hypothesis #9 claimed that the probability of wrong decisions would be lower in legal orders that rely on juries. If this hypothesis proved to be wrong, we would expect the effects of the jury on the legitimacy of a legal order to be ambivalent. The participation of civil society as such could lead to an increase in the legitimacy of the judicial system, whereas the low quality of the decisions arrived at by jurors could lead to a decrease. The net effect would have to be subject to evaluation.

Until now, jury size has not been dealt with explicitly. However, it seems plausible to assume that it might have an impact on the perceived degree of legitimacy of the institution of trial by jury. The conventional number of twelve jurors can be interpreted as a small representation of society as a whole, and a jury's deliberations should thus take a large number of different aspects into account. The corresponding hypothesis (#13) would simply be:

The larger the number of jurors, the higher the legitimacy of the judicial system, all else being equal.

On the Preconditions for the Introduction of Trial by Jury

We now move on from hypotheses regarding the effects of trial by jury and turn to the possible preconditions that need to exist if juries are to be successful. Students of trial by jury have commented upon its re-introduction in Russia and Spain (and its announced introduction in Azerbaijan, Kazakhstan and Latvia) during the 1990s with astonishment. All the more so, as many adherents of trial by jury are convinced that it is part of the common law tradition and that its transplantation into countries with a civil-law tradition would be problematical. A very early example of this position is provided by the former Lord Chancellor of Henry VI, Sir John Fortescue, who fled to France and then described the differences between England and the Continent in 'A Learned Commentation of the Politique Laws of England' (first published in the fifteenth century). According to him, the superiority of the English system concerning wealth, happiness and the entire rule system was so evident that it was hard to understand why the whole world did not try to emulate the British law system. Fortescue's explanation was that the institution of trial by jury depended on a specific economic and social structure that was present only in England (Macfarlane 1978: 179ff.). But what are these specific economic and social preconditions?

Jeary (1960–1961) mentions three conditions that must be fulfilled if trial by jury is to function properly: (1) Society must be racially, culturally, linguistically, and religiously homogeneous; (2) members of society must be sufficiently educated to understand their responsibilities as jurors; and (3) members of juries must generally agree with the laws that they are supposed to enforce. In addition, it seems plausible to assume that (4) very high degrees of inequality could inhibit the beneficial use of a jury, as some jurors might be motivated by aspirations of redistribution.

Kiss (2000: 362ff.), who deals with the current discussions in Japan concerning the re-introduction of the jury, describes how the Japanese 'prefer trial by "those above the people" rather than by "their fellows" and that this caused the Japanese to distrust juries from the beginning'. Here we have yet another condition, which is potentially very relevant for the relationship of trial by jury and civil society: the legitimacy of the judicial system might not be improved by the introduction of jury trial in societies in which hierarchical relationships are widely accepted. Expressed differently, the absence of widely accepted hierarchical relationships in a society seems to be a precondition for the beneficial introduction of a jury system. All of the above would appear to be necessary, although not necessarily sufficient, preconditions for the success of the jury.

Civil Society Elements in European Court Systems

This section provides an overview of the jury systems currently in use in Europe. It is only an informal survey and it would not be possible to carry out rigorous empirical tests based on this information. Quantitative tests remain a desideratum.[13]

Table 3.2 contains a variety of possibilities whereby non-professionals can participate in the court system. As outlined above, we are only interested here in trial by jury. Such trials may be limited to criminal cases only, or they may also apply to civil cases, which gives us the two shaded cells in the matrix.

We go on to present and compare most European jury systems. The criteria used for the comparisons are introduced here, although the results for each country are not discussed in detail but can be found in table 3.3. The first criterion was the *legal basis for trial by jury*. If this basis is found within a country's constitution, the institution of the jury is entrenched and would be more difficult to abolish than if this were not the case, because constitutions

Table 3.2 Possibilities of Lay Participation in the Court System

	None	Criminal Only	Criminal and Civil
Professional judges only			
Mixture of professionals and jurors			
Jurors only			

can usually only be changed by huge majorities. Quite a number of European countries mention trial by jury in their constitutions.

Trial by jury is usually confined to specific cases. Historically, these include cases in which the government could have an interest, such as those involving freedom of the press, which have been delegated to juries. The most important distinction with regard to jurisdiction is the question of whether trial by jury is *limited to criminal cases* or whether civil cases are also included in a jury's competence. This is an important indicator of the degree to which the institution of the jury is firmly established within a society. Most European jury systems are confined to criminal cases with the addition of individual cases such as, for example, those referring to the freedom of the press. Among criminal cases, jurisdiction is usually confined to very serious crimes and is determined either by the minimum sentence that would apply were a suspect declared guilty or by the court before which the case is tried (and these two criteria usually go hand-in-hand).

The relevance of civil society to the administration of justice can be grasped by looking at the *percentage of all (criminal) trials* that are adjudicated by juries. This sounds straightforward, but there is no obvious common denominator: does it refer to all criminal cases, including ones with guilty pleas, or only those criminal cases tried in court, or only those criminal cases potentially eligible for jury trial? Vidmar (2000: 48) establishes a rule of thumb that states that the percentage of criminal cases is around 1 percent everywhere except in the United States, where it rises to about 8 percent. Duff (2000: 251ff.) points out that jury trial in Scotland ranges from 1 to 7 percent, depending on the denominator chosen. Russia is clearly an outlier here: in 1997, when trial by jury was confined to just nine of the Russian regions, up to 43.2 percent of all criminal trials were jury trials according to Dline and Schwartz (2002: 106).

The next criterion is the *modus used to select jurors*. On the one hand, the involvement of all groups in society would seem desirable if one wants

Table 3.3 Comparison of Selected European Jury Systems

Country	Legal Basis	Minimum Penalty	No. of Criminal Cases	Selection Modus	Prob. of Being Appointed[a]	No. of Jurors	Decision Rule	Jury Particip. in Determin. Sentence?	Reasons Given?	Appeal Possible?	Comments
Austria	Art. 91 of Con. (1929)	Must be used for >10 yrs.; may be for > 5 yrs.		One nominee per 200 inhabitants (in Vienna, 100)	0.005(65–25)/2 = 0.1 (in Vienna 20%)[b]	8					In case of absence, fine of up to 10,000 Schillings (plus costs of trial); 18.15 euros/hour
Belgium	Art. 150 Con.	In practice, limited to murder and other for > 20 yrs.	0.01% of all criminal cases	Randomly from jury pool		12	2/3[c]	Yes	No	No	Right of jury trial seen as right of the public to participate (not right of accused)
Denmark	1919 (Con. of 1953, Art. 65)	> 4 yrs.	~ 100	One nominee per 300 inhabitants (committee of local councils)	0.4	12	2/3[d]	Yes	No	No	School teachers, farmers, public employees of large firms heavily over-represented[e]
Norway		> 6 yrs.		Party members		10	7/10	No[f]	No[g]		US $35/day
France	1958					9	8/9			No	
Ireland	Art. 38.5; Con. of 1937	All except minor offences	0.4%	Random from register of Dáil electors		12	10/12				Many jurors unemployed[h]
Russia		Offences like murder, rape, treason	43.2% (in 1997)	Voter registration lists		12		No	No	Yes (and many decisions are reversed)	1/2 ave. daily pay of a trial judge; $4/day; fine of $250 (hardly ever imposed)

(continued)

Table 3.3 Comparison of Selected European Jury Systems (*cont.*)

Country	Legal Basis	Minimum Penalty	No. of Criminal Cases	Selection Modus	Prob. of Being Appointed[a]	No. of Jurors	Decision Rule	Jury Particip. in Determin. Sentence?	Reasons Given?	Appeal Possible?	Comments
England		Cases before Crown Court	~1%		~1%	12	10/12				Jury occup. closely matches occup. of population[i]
Scotland		Murder, rape, treason (cases before High Court)	7.7% of all trials (but only ~1% of all criminal cases)	Random from electoral roll; by ballot in court among those who have appeared		15	8/15			Yes (since 1926)	'Not proven' verdict; 'right to jury' as right of the accused do not exist
Spain	Art. 125 of Con.	2nd-level courts, provincial courts		Voter registration lists		9	7		Yes		
Switzerland (Geneva)		>5 years	1.76%	Voter registration lists	35% (being on the list)	12 (6)			Yes		

[a] 'Net-probability' should be even higher as we do not correct for illegibility due to profession, former sentences, etc.

[b] Probability of being mentioned on the *Jahresliste* (annual list). The ratio between *Jahresliste* and *Dienstleiste* will have to be investigated.

[c] Traest (2001: 38): 'If the answer to a question about a main fact of the case is positive by 7 or 5 votes, the three professional judges have to express their opinion about the question of guilt. They decide with a simple majority whether or not they will join the majority of the jury. If they do not, the ultimate vote is 8 to 7 in favour of the accused, which means an acquittal'.

[d] Plus two out of three professional judges (Garde 2001: 102). Garde (ibid.) calls this necessity of a double majority 'one of the most convincing arguments for (some kind of) trial by jury'.

[e] Garde (2001: 110): 'Some professions are heavily over-represented, such as schoolteachers and farmers, also employees of public or larger companies, whereas employees of smaller firms and the self-employed are under-represented, as are persons on welfare. Middle-aged persons, especially those in their fifties, are over-represented, the very young are under-represented'. Parties without influence on selection; lay judges paid 80 euros/day.

[f] But judgement pronounced by 'court' made up of judges and jurors, in which the jurors have the majority.

[g] Again, the 'court' is to give reasons for its sentence.

[h] See Quinn (2001: 206).

[i] See Lloyd-Bostock and Thomas (2000: 70).

Sources: Bundesministerium für Justiz Österreich (2002), Duff (2000), Gane (2001), Garde (2001), Munday (1993), Quinn (2001), Strandbakken (2001), Sträuli (2001), Thaman (2000), Traest (2001) and Vidmar (2000: chap. 13).

to give society at large the feeling of participation in the adjudication of justice. On the other, people who have already shown their concern for the *res publica* by participating in other public tasks might be expected to care more for the quality of the jury verdict. It is these two opposing views that are reflected in the two approaches towards jury selection in Europe. One is based on voter registration lists and should therefore lead to a fairly representative sample of society on the jury. The other prefers to pick members who have been active elsewhere, most often in political parties. The first approach is traditionally found in the Anglo-Saxon countries, the second one in Scandinavia.[14] Tocqueville clearly had the first approach in mind, and it is doubtful to what degree his arguments can be carried over to the second approach. Of course, this is also true of Blackstone's argument, namely, that juries protect individual freedom against a powerful state: if those in government have a substantial influence on the choice of jurors, it cannot be supposed that juries are safeguarding individual freedom against them.

As we have seen in the previous section, the participation argument is particularly important to Tocqueville. Another way of ascertaining its empirical relevance is to calculate the *probability that an eligible citizen is ever selected as a juror* or at least appears on a list from which jurors are then selected. Let us illustrate these calculations by reference to Austria, where one out of every two hundred citizens (and one out of every one hundred in Vienna) is chosen randomly from the voter lists (0.5 percent; 1 percent for Vienna). All voters between the ages of 25 and 65 are eligible, and the lists are produced every two years (a voter could thus be chosen 40:2 = 20 times). The probability of ever appearing on these so-called annual lists is thus 10 percent (and 20 percent in Vienna). Appearing on the annual list is not equivalent to being called for jury service, but the people who appear on the list are informed of the fact. It can be argued that this alone leads to increased awareness of lay participation in the administration of justice. Among the countries for which data are available, the probability of ever appearing on the list is lowest in Denmark (4 percent) and highest in the Swiss canton of Geneva (35 percent). It should be noted that the 'net probability' should actually be higher in all countries because certain groups of people who appear on the voter list are not eligible to be jurors. In many countries, judges, lawyers, priests, and also those convicted and given prison sentences etc. are not eligible.

It has been hypothesized that *jury size* determines the nature of deliberations among the jurors as well as the legitimacy-enhancing effect of the jury. Many legal orders still use the traditional number of twelve jurors, but jury size varies from eight, in Austria, to fifteen, in Scotland. The decision-rule used by the jury in order to reach a verdict is closely related to size and two approaches can be distinguished: unanimity (the traditional approach) versus some kind of (super) majority. Of course, the decision-rule has implications for the likelihood that a jury will find the 'correct' verdict but also for the possibility of acquittal. These issues will, however, not be dealt with here. It is noteworthy that none of the legal orders under consideration requires unanimity any longer. In Scotland, a simple majority (eight out of fifteen) is sufficient for conviction. It is also noteworthy that some legal orders require a double majority before the accused can be convicted: both the jury and the professional judge(s) have to find the accused guilty and if only one of the two does so, this leads to acquittal (as is the case in Denmark).

Traditionally, the jury system was based on the fiction that it was possible to separate 'fact finding' from the 'application of the law', that is, that the jury determined whether an accused had committed a particular crime and the judges determined the sentence. In actual fact, there are quite a few legal orders in which the jury participates in determining the sentence when the accused is found guilty.

Jurors are no experts in law, which is why, traditionally, juries have not given any reason for their verdicts: the accused were either guilty or not. However, this tradition is problematic for a number of reasons: the degree of transparency as well as the accountability of judicial decision making is obviously low unless the jury gives reasons for its decision. It is noteworthy that Spain, which only re-introduced trial by jury in 1996, does require its juries to offer reasons for their decisions.

An important aspect of the rule of law is the possibility of having court decisions reviewed. This right is, for example, part of the International Covenant on Civil and Political Rights (ICCPR, art. 14.5). Yet with regard to trial by jury, a traditional argument has been that juries cannot err (*vox populi, vox dei*). The *possibility of appeal* against a jury verdict still does not exist everywhere. Belgium and Denmark have opted for special treatment with regard to their ratification of the ICCPR.

Finally, the *socio-economic composition* of juries is of particular interest for our topic: do juries represent the average citizen or do jurors often display particular characteristics? This information is important in order to ascertain whether economic logic (the higher the opportunity costs, the lower the probability of participation) or some logic of civil society (it is a citizen's duty, and probably even an honor, to participate) prevails. Frequently, participation on a jury is not entirely voluntary: people who are called to be jurors and are unable to present a convincing excuse are often fined substantial amounts. The sums are indicated in the last column and the variations are quite substantial. In Denmark, it is mainly representatives of the groups that economists would expect to find on juries who are indeed jury-members. These include schoolteachers, public employees and employees of large firms, because their opportunity costs for participating in a trial by jury are often low. In Ireland, the unemployed are over-represented on juries, a finding also completely in line with economic reasoning as their opportunity costs can also be expected to be particularly low. In Scotland (Duff 2000: 257), 38 percent of potential jurors from the higher socio-economic group were excused compared with 18 percent and 23 percent from the two lower groups. Again, higher opportunity costs do seem to lead to less jury participation. Yet in England, jury composition seems to mirror the occupational structure of the population at large quite nicely.

Regarding *application of the law* by juries, Lloyd-Bostock and Thomas (2000: 87) point out that juries have the right to decide according to conscience and to refuse to apply the law. They consider this as 'essential to the democratic role claimed for the jury' and yet this causes huge problems concerning the homogeneity and consistency of law application. At the end of the day, a low consistency in law application might even undermine the legitimacy of the entire legal system. The institution of the 'not proven' verdict, which is special to Scotland, has apparently been used to the same effect.[15] Quinn (2001: 199) writes, referring to Ireland: 'It has been suggested that the root problem stemmed from the dual function of the system of jury trial. On the one hand it is supposed to enforce the law of the land; on the other hand, it is supposed to represent judgement by one's peers. Where, however, many of the laws are out of harmony with jurors' own convictions and where jurors have sympathy with many of their peers who are put on trial, the jury system can undermine the entire system of criminal justice.'

This aspect concludes our informal survey of trial by jury in Europe. A more formal survey – possibly with the inclusion of lay assessors – remains a desideratum as this is the precondition for testing the hypotheses developed empirically in the next section.

Outlook

Some British Euro-skeptics already claim that the EU is out to abolish trial by jury, but even if greater criminal law-making competence was transferred to the EU, abolition appears to be quite unlikely. There is no necessity to harmonize criminal procedures and correspondingly no necessity to abolish trial by jury. Whether its introduction into more EU countries, or even at the European level, is desirable is an altogether different question that can only be answered after more rigorous empirical analysis concerning both the preconditions for successfully implementing trial by jury and ascertaining its effects.

Before drawing normative conclusions, the relevant positive knowledge should be assembled. This chapter is the first step towards a comparative analysis, and there are a number of additional research strategies that suggest themselves. Russia, Switzerland and the United States are federal states and many institutional details of the jury system depend on the respective state that one is dealing with. One could use these differences and ask whether they lead to the predicted results. The advantage of doing such studies within federations is, of course, that many of the other institutional variables are identical and do not have to be explicitly controlled.

This chapter deals with the consequences of trial by jury. Lay participation broadly understood would, however, also analyze the consequences of lay assessor participation. From a U.S. point of view, lay assessor participation is often interpreted as an attempt to reverse direct citizen participation in the court system and the experiences in many formerly socialist states seem to corroborate that assumption. Yet our empirical knowledge concerning the effects of lay assessor participation is very scarce. It would thus seem in order to systematically compare the consequences of these two different forms of lay participation with each other. Furthermore, trial by jury and lay assessor courts are not the only ways to institutionalize civil society participation in the judiciary: justices of the peace and lay magistrates who are frequently brought in to adjudicate minor offenses are another institution whose effects seem worthy of analysis.

In the second section, it was pointed out that not only can an active civil society have a direct influence on government action but that some goods conventionally provided by the state can be provided by members of society themselves. For example, private law adjudication is provided to a large degree by private law subjects and often called Alternative Dispute Resolution (ADR). It would be interesting to inquire into the systematic relationship between trial by jury and ADR. *Prima facie*, they seem to complement each other, at least within many European legal orders: trial by jury deals primarily with criminal law issues, whereas ADR's main focus is private law disputes.

After these studies are carried out, our knowledge concerning the costs and benefits of trial by jury will certainly have improved. We should then be able to deal with normative questions such as whether trial by jury is still timely, etc. The broader questions regarding civil society involve the optimal degree of citizen participation not only within the judiciary but also within the other two branches of government.

Notes

The author thanks Anne van Aaken, Lorenz Blume, Michael Ebeling, Janina Satzer, Nguyen Quog Viet, Christof Voigt, and Jan Wagner for their constructive critiques. He also thanks the participants of the CisoNet Workshop 4, 'Markets and Civil Society in Europe' (in particular, Víctor Pérez-Díaz), and of the Social and Political Theory Seminar at the Research School of Social Sciences (Australian National University, Canberra) for stimulating discussions.

1. This chapter does not cover certain questions concerning the jury that have previously been dealt with by economists. These include the relevance of jury size to the probability of the jury getting the facts right, the relevance of the decision rule used by the jury, etc. Kornhauser (2000) offers a good survey of these issues.
2. More precisely, the benefits of a factually independent judiciary have to outweigh the benefits of factually dependent juries. These can arise due to better rent-extraction possibilities.
3. The United States is one of the few countries in which judges are subject to periodic elections. This creates a very special kind of accountability, namely, to a constituency rather than to the law. It also suggests a connection between the necessity of re-election and the immense importance of trial by jury in the United States: trial by jury is a good means of making professional judges accountable to the law as well. Re-election requirements are not evenly distributed throughout the country. It would be fascinating to inquire into whether the relevance of juries is negatively correlated with such requirements.
4. One of the reasons why there is discussion about the re-introduction of trial by jury in Japan is that judges follow prosecutors almost all of the time (Kiss 2000: 356ff.). The same was true for the Soviet Union.
5. It is interesting to ask whether direct participation in the judicature is systematically connected with other means of citizen participation, such as direct democracy. The degree of separation of powers is higher in presidential systems than in parliamentary systems, so it is also interesting to ask whether there are any regularities here.
6. He further argues that the Catholic Church has a vertical organization structure. La Porta et al. (1997) asked whether this result could be generalized, and went on to classify Islam and the various Orthodox churches as having hierarchical structures. They found (ibid.: 336ff.) that, while holding per capita income constant, 'countries with more dominant hierarchical religions have less efficient judiciaries, greater corruption, lower quality bureaucracies, higher rates of tax evasion, lower rates of participation in civic activities and professional associations, a lower level of importance of large firms in the economy, inferior infrastructures and higher inflation'.
7. It has been argued that the sum total of decision-making costs and external costs (the so-called interdependence costs; Buchanan and Tullock 1962) should be at their minimum in an optimal setting. This normative approach will not, however, be pursued any further here.
8. On the other hand, it has been observed that the absolute number of cases decided upon by lay assessors is almost certainly higher than that by juries (Kutnjak Ivkovic 1999: 18ff.). This is because civil-law countries do not have the institution of plea bargaining, which drastically reduces the number of cases actually decided upon by courts in many common-law countries.
9. However, it could be argued that this conjecture in favor of civil society participation in adjudication is subject to circularity: the reason for having civil society participate in the administration of justice is the result of a high degree of mistrust vis-à-vis governing bodies. Due to the participation of civil society, this mistrust should decline over time. As soon as the majority of the population puts its trust in governing bodies, the *raison d'être* of the jury ceases to exist.
10. On this, Tocqueville seems to echo Thomas Jefferson, the author of the Declaration of Independence and later president of the United States, who wrote (cited according to

Vogler 2001: 527): 'Were I called upon to decide whether the people had best be omitted in the Legislative or Judiciary departments, I would say it is better to leave them out of the Legislative. The execution of the laws is more important than making them.'

11. One could even ask whether a substantial number of professional politicians had once served as jurors.

12. It could be argued that, for example, legal orders will only be implemented as provided for in the law if they conform, at least to some degree, with the prevalent values and norms held by the members of society. This argument has been made in greater detail with regard to Latin America in Voigt (1998).

13. In the meantime, I have collected data from up to eighty countries and have tested some of the hypotheses developed in the last section of this chapter. The results can be found in Voigt (2009).

14. It could, however, be argued that the Scandinavian approach is more in line with the traditional delineation of civil society, as jurors are chosen on the basis of having been active in voluntary associations.

15. According to Duff (2000: 274), 'In essence, the not proven verdict provides the jury with a rather subtle way of "nullifying" the law instead of having to confront it directly and openly.'

References

Aaken, Anne van, Lars Feld and Stefan Voigt. 2008. 'Power over Prosecutors Corrupts Politicians: Cross Country Evidence Using a New Indicator'. http://papers.ssrn.com/sol3/papers.cfm?abstract_id=1097675.

Berggren, Niclas. 2003. 'The Benefits of Economic Freedom: A Survey', *The Independent Review* 8, no. 2: 193–211.

Blackstone, William. [1791] 1966. *Commentaries on the Laws of England*. London: Clarendon.

Brown, Alec. 1951. *The Juryman's Handbook*. London: Harvill Press.

Buchanan, James M., and Gordon Tullock. 1962. *The Calculus of Consent: Logical Foundations of Constitutional Democracy*. Ann Arbor: University of Michigan Press.

Bundesministerium für Justiz Österreich. 2002. *Das BMJ informiert: Schöffen und Geschworene in Österreich*. Vienna.

Dline, Irina, and Olga Schwartz. 2002. 'The Jury Is Still Out on the Future of Jury Trials in Russia', *East European Constitutional Review* 11, no. 1–2: 104–110.

Duff, Peter. 2000. 'The Scottish Criminal Jury: A Very Peculiar Institution', in *World Jury Systems*, ed. Neil Vidmar. Oxford: Oxford University Press, pp. 249–282.

Feld, Lars, and Stefan Voigt. 2003. 'Economic Growth and Judicial Independence: Cross Country Evidence Using a New Set of Indicators', *European Journal of Political Economy* 19, no. 3: 497–527.

———. 2006. 'Making Judges Independent: Some Proposals Regarding the Judiciary', in *Democratic Constitutional Design and Public Policy: Analysis and Evidence*, ed. R. Congleton and B. Swedenborg. Cambridge, MA: MIT Press, pp. 251–288.

Gane, Christopher. 2001. 'The Scottish Jury', *International Review of Penal Law* 72: 259–272.

Garde, Peter. 2001. 'The Danish Jury', *International Review of Penal Law* 72: 87–120. Hegel, Georg Wilhelm Friedrich. [1821] 1963. *Hegel's Philosophy of Right*. Trans. T. Knox. London: Oxford University Press.

Herzog, Felix. 2001. 'Philosophical and Social View of the Jury: Could It Have a Renaissance in Germany?', *International Review of Penal Law* 72, no. 1–2: 553–557.

Jeary, J. H. 1960–1961. 'Trial by Jury and Trial with the Aid of Assessors in the Superior Courts of British African Territories: I and II', *Journal of African Law* 4, no. 3: 133–146, and 5, no. 1: 36–47.

Kiss, Lester. 2000. 'Reviving the Criminal Jury in Japan', in *World Jury Systems*, ed. Neil Vidmar. Oxford: Oxford University Press, pp. 353–380.

Knack, Stephen, and Philip Keefer. 1997. 'Does Social Capital Have an Economic Payoff? A Cross-Country Investigation', *Quarterly Journal of Economics* 112: 1251–1288.

Kornhauser, Lewis. 2000. 'Judicial Organization and Administration', in *Encyclopedia of Law and Economics*, vol. 5, ed. Boudewijn Bouckaert and Gerrit de Geest. Cheltenham: Elgar, pp. 27–44.

Kutnjak Ivkovic, Sanja. 1999. *Lay Participation in Criminal Trials: The Case of Croatia*. Lanham, MD: Austin & Winfield.

La Porta, Rafael, Florencio Lopez-de-Silanes, Andrei Shleifer and Robert Vishny. 1997. 'Trust in Large Organizations', *American Economic Review, Papers and Proceedings* 87, no. 2: 333–338.

Lloyd-Bostock, Sally, and Cheryl Thomas. 2000. 'The Continuing Decline of the English Jury', in *World Jury Systems*, ed. N. Vidmar. Oxford: Oxford University Press, pp. 53–91.

Macfarlane, Alan. 1978. *The Origins of English Individualism*. Oxford: Basil Blackwell.

Mauro, Paolo. 1995. 'Corruption and Growth', *Quarterly Journal of Economics* 110: 681–712

Montesquieu, Charles-Louis de Secondat, Marquis de. [1748] 1961. *L'Ésprit des Lois*, II. Paris: Garnier.

Munday, Roderick. 1993. 'Jury Trial, Continental Style', *Legal Studies* 13: 204–224.

Putnam, Robert. 1993. *Making Democracy Work: Civic Traditions in Modern Italy*. Princeton, NJ: Princeton University Press.

Quinn, Katie. 2001. 'Jury Trial in the Republic of Ireland', *International Review of Penal Law* 72: 197–214.

Strandbakken, Asbjørn. 2001. 'Lay Participation in Norway', *International Review of Penal Law* 72: 225–251.

Sträuli, B. 2001. 'Le Jury Genevois', *International Review of Penal Law* 72: 317–344.

Thaman, Stephen. 2000. 'Europe's New Jury Systems: The Cases of Spain and Russia', in *World Jury Systems*, ed. Neil Vidmar. Oxford: Oxford University Press, pp. 319–351.

Tocqueville, Alexis de. [1835–1840] 1956. *Democracy in America*. New York: Mentor.

Traest, P. 2001. 'The Jury in Belgium', *International Review of Penal Law* 72: 27–50.

Vidmar, Neil, ed. 2000. *World Jury Systems*. Oxford: Oxford University Press.

Vogler, Richard. 2001. 'The International Development of the Jury: The Role of the British Empire', *International Review of Penal Law* 72: 525–551.

Voigt, Stefan. 1998. 'Making Constitutions Work: Conditions for Maintaining the Rule of Law', *Cato Journal* 18, no. 2: 191–208.

_____. 2008. 'The Economic Effects of Judicial Accountability: Cross Country Evidence', *European Journal of Law and Economics* 25, no. 2: 95–123.

_____. 2009. 'The Effects of Lay Participation in Courts: A Cross Country Analysis', forthcoming in *European Journal of Political Economy*.

Chapter 4

DISPUTE RESOLUTION SYSTEMS AND GLOBAL MARKETS
Why Arbitration?

Javier Díez-Hochleitner and Jesús Remón

The culture of civility, which values individual autonomy, encourages freedom of association and praises commitment in pursuit of general objectives, was for a long time circumscribed in most cases by a state's political boundaries. Nowadays, this civic awareness knows no boundaries whatsoever. On the contrary, states have to face a global debate[1] on new transnational[2] concerns (human rights, the environment, labor standards, etc.).

The emergence of the *international civil society*,[3] within the framework of so-called *globalization* (see *infra*), and the increase in international economic relations is causing a thorough transformation of the international society. Together with states and international organizations, 'non-state actors'[4] are playing an (increasingly) important role: in particular, non-governmental organizations (NGOs) and multinational corporations (Pérez-Prat Durbán, 2004). To date, non-state actors have not only penetrated the structures of international power (interacting with states and international organizations), but they have also put forward private regulatory schemes which did not previously exist.[5] According to a number of authors, a new 'private authority' in international relations is emerging that is parallel to state power and international organizations.[6] Examples of such authority would include the drafting of corporate codes of conduct[7] and the international standardization process[8] which certain service sectors are undergoing. A similar situation is occurring in the area of dispute resolution, where arbitration has grown dramatically within the context of international commercial transactions.

Notes for this chapter begin on page 142.

In plain language, arbitration is a private, generally informal, and non-judicial procedure for adjudicating disputes. René David, an authoritative voice in the field, defines it as 'a device whereby the settlement of a question, which is of interest for two or more persons, is entrusted to one or more persons – the arbitrator or arbitrators – who derive their powers from a private agreement, not from the authorities of a state, and who are to proceed and decide the case on the basis of such agreement' (David 1985: 5).

From this definition we can construe that recourse to arbitration is first and foremost consensual; in other words, the basis of arbitration resides in the will of the parties embodied in a contract (the 'arbitration agreement') or in an agreement within a contract (called the 'arbitration clause'). The freedom-of-contract principle governing the relationship between the parties comprises the appointment of the arbitrator or arbitral tribunal, the venue, the rules and the language of the proceedings.

The development of arbitration over the last few decades – in particular, international arbitration – has been made possible by the establishment of numerous arbitral institutions (the ICC International Arbitration Court, the London Court of International Arbitration, the American Arbitration Association, the Netherlands Arbitration Institute, etc.). These institutions not only offer operators the possibility of managing arbitration but also lay down rules concerning the appointment of arbitrators and the procedure. The advantages of institutional arbitration explain why, in practice, *ad hoc* arbitration proceedings are less frequent. However, neither arbitration nor the other self-regulatory mechanisms cited above can be conceived of unless they are accompanied not merely by acquiescence but by support on the part of states.

It should be borne in mind that arbitration is not intended to operate as a means for achieving dispute resolution directly through party agreement.[9] From this standpoint, arbitration is quite different from mediation[10] or negotiation.[11] The adjudicating power of arbitrators enables them to render a final decision which is fully enforceable. On this basis, arbitration is considered to be a jurisdictional equivalent through which the parties can reach the same objectives as in state courts, namely, the solution to a dispute with *res judicata* effects. However, except in cases of voluntary compliance, the effectiveness of an arbitral award usually requires seeking jurisdictional enforcement mechanisms.

Origins and Development of International Arbitration

One of the fields most immediately affected by the transnational phenomenon was international trade.[12] International trade covers one of the largest segments of global economic activity[13] and today, not surprisingly, a large proportion of such trade is conducted by private parties and multinational corporations.[14] Given the international scope of their transactions, most individuals and companies have traditionally resorted to international contracts to ensure a flexible, effective and neutral legal framework. Moreover, these agreements include, *inter alia*, (1) the right of the parties to choose the governing law of the transaction and, indeed, (2) the right to choose the applicable dispute settlement mechanism. Opting for arbitration as opposed to the jurisdiction of a state should be explained particularly in terms of *neutrality* and *flexibility*. In addition, it is an *effective* dispute resolution mechanism, as we shall see below.

The flexibility of arbitration is perhaps its major asset. Unlike ordinary jurisdiction, arbitration can be 'tailored' to respond to specific commercial practices and to the dynamics of commercial transactions, offering a myriad of advantages to the business community.[15] Among others, the parties have the right to choose the arbitrator(s) who will adjudicate their dispute.[16] Arbitrators commonly have a greater level of specialization than judges, which allows the former to find satisfactory solutions reflecting the general consensus in trade. Moreover, there is greater flexibility and speed in the conduct of the procedures: due to their experience in the relevant business sector, the appointed arbitrators typically have the capacity to reduce the significance of legal precedence, eliminate the need for complex rules of evidence and minimize the need for discovery, the use of experts or other informational trial procedures. Furthermore, because arbitral adjudication tends to be less adversarial than its judicial counterpart, the parties to arbitration are usually able to maintain their underlying commercial connection.

The greater degree of flexibility of arbitration is apparent in the procedure and in the freedom of the parties to even designate the *lex mercatoria* as the law applicable to the substance.[17] With regard to procedure, a simple comparison of the rules of the different arbitral institutions with the burdensome procedural rules applied by the courts is sufficient to make the benefits obvious. Moreover, arbitration normally operates as a single stage in the judicial process, without leave to appeal. Finally, arbitration is reputed to be confidential, in other words, the dispute, the proceedings and the outcome are not publicized. Arbitration, therefore, allows commercial parties to maintain a competitive position despite the appearance of transactional problems.

The appeal of arbitration has also been increasing in proportion to a growing rate of distrust associated with litigation before domestic courts. Critics have even pointed out that 'society is reluctant to continue accepting that the supreme regulator, a judicial system that used to be despised, remains a miserable, badly equipped and remunerated public service, whose lack of diligence and resources can be measured by the number of cases piled up on the courts' desks and the absurdly long extent of the proceedings'.[18]

Other commentators have spotted other problems, such as the increasing complexity of domestic judicial systems, the lack of good-quality legislation and the failure of national judges to follow the pace of globalization.

However, arbitration is not a panacea and can hardly be seen as 'a formula for universal justice' (Minc 1997: 163).[19] Like state jurisdiction, arbitration has its advantages and disadvantages. Most of the former will depend on the specific circumstances of the transaction in question. The decision to arbitrate should ideally be the result of comparing all possible gains and losses under each mechanism to achieve the maximum advantage in each circumstance. In this trade-off scenario, it is unlikely that there will be a displacement of the state judicial system by any form of alternative dispute resolution system, including arbitration, either today or in the foreseeable future. We will analyze the grounds for this opinion in the following paragraphs.

Several facts confirm that arbitration is in good health: the exponential increase in the number of arbitrations[20] and, in particular, the arbitrations administered by the main arbitration institutions,[21] the appearance of new private arbitral bodies and the enactment of new pro-arbitration laws.[22] In line with the latter, the 2003 Spanish Arbitration Act[23] – which is based on the UNCITRAL Model Law[24] – offers an ideal framework to develop domestic arbitration and for Spain to emerge as an attractive venue to international arbitration, particularly when Latin American parties are involved. In addition to its modern approach, the new Spanish law is supported by a pro-arbitration judiciary in fields such as interim measures, the taking of evidence and the enforcement of awards.

Although arbitration is primarily used in commercial transactions, use of the mechanism has been extended to new fields such as maritime transportation and air transportation. In such matters arbitration has, to a great extent, replaced state courts. Intellectual property, competition law, insurance, project finance and the construction industry must also be mentioned. Some of these fields currently have specialized arbitral institutions and rules, for instance, the Arbitration and Mediation Centre of the World Intellectual Property Organization (WIPO).[25]

The transnational phenomenon has favored the use not only of arbitration but also of other types of dispute resolution methods (ADR), such as mediation and negotiation.[26] The latter are regarded as either a prior step to arbitration or jurisdiction or as an alternative to both. The United States and the United Kingdom have been at the forefront in the application of these new methods. The European Union has recently recognized the necessity of introducing framework legislation addressing key aspects of civil procedure in order to promote further the use of mediation.[27]

If we add arbitration in its different guises (e.g. *ad hoc* or handled by an arbitral institution) as well as the other forms of ADR to the possibility of resorting to national courts, it is reasonable to refer to an effective 'market of dispute resolution mechanisms'. The choice of one mechanism over another will depend on the relevant transaction; it is one of the many factors that explain the increasing complexity and specialization of the legal profession.

The transnational effect has also led to the standardization of domestic and international arbitration rules. The content of most of the recently enacted laws on arbitration is indeed easily identifiable for the business community as it shares a single common base, namely, the UNCITRAL Model Law. As for the rules of the arbitral institutions, the 1998 ICC regulation is a good example of the generally accepted trends and standards in international arbitration.

The 'arbitral wave' – as it is often termed – shows no signs of weakening so far. In such an optimistic scenario for arbitration, the chronic evils of state jurisdiction appear even more visible to a sophisticated audience of merchants and entrepreneurs worried about concepts such as competence and efficiency.

States' Stances with Regard to Arbitration

Arbitration not only needs support from the courts but also requires a regulatory framework (in the form of state laws and/or international treaties) that allows it to fulfill its role. Thus, as stated above, in the absence of voluntary compliance with the award, its enforcement requires the intervention of the courts of the relevant state. States' assistance will also be necessary to ensure the effectiveness of any interim measures granted by the arbitrators, to obtain – if necessary – such interim measures before the arbitration proceedings begin, or to examine certain evidence. Moreover, only a state that has enacted laws supporting arbitration, ensuring that its courts do not interfere with the process, or accept appeals against the award – except for an application for setting it aside upon limited and specific grounds[28] – will be appointed as a venue for international arbitration.

Therefore, international arbitration does not intend to free itself from the state but rather to work together with it. Furthermore, arbitration and jurisdiction are not only not mutually exclusive systems, they actually complement and improve each other's roles.

In fact, it is not only the commercial community but states themselves which have been increasingly relying on arbitration, as evidenced by the enactment of municipal laws favoring arbitration and the overwhelming acceptance of the 1958 New York Convention on the Recognition and Enforcement of Foreign Arbitral Awards.[29] The Convention has more than 130 state parties and provides arbitral awards with a real 'worldwide passport'.

There is no other treaty on the recognition and enforcement of state court decisions with a similar number of member states.

Moreover, states' failure to provide a reliable adjudication system for international transactions have forced them to conclude international contracts (a.k.a. 'state contracts') with foreign private parties, envisaging international arbitration as the preferred dispute settlement mechanism. On the other hand, the desire of most countries to attract foreign investment led them to the creation of the International Centre for Settlement of Investment Disputes (ICSID)[30] (to administrate arbitrations between states and foreign investors, among other functions) and to the conclusion – in less than three decades – of more than 2,000[31] bilateral investment treaties (BITs).[32] The latter instrument requires the state party to offer certain international standards of protection to foreign investment and offers the private party the possibility of requesting arbitration (Diez-Hochleitner 2005b) (i.e. administered by the ICSID) in the event of a breach of the said standard.[33] Since the first BIT,[34] many controversies between states (usually, but not always, developing states)[35] and foreign investors have been solved by arbitral awards,[36] which have, in some cases, imposed the payment of high compensation on the state concerned.

Nevertheless, not all states have equipped themselves with laws that are favorable to arbitration, be it national or international, or that respond to internationally recognized standards.[37] Globalization and, consequently, the appearance of the *new international society* – defined as an area of markets, associations and the sphere of public debate (Pérez-Díaz 1993: 56) – are phenomena with unequal effects across the world. Concurrently, the development of alternatives to the judicial process has taken place fundamentally in the most industrialized countries (or in countries with emerging economies). In contrast, there are still many countries that maintain a negative opinion of arbitration, alleging that it leads to an assault on national sovereignty, entrenches social disadvantages between social classes, and debases domestic labor and environmental standards.

Arbitration and Globalization

The development of an international civil society has taken place together with the *globalization* process. Globalization is understood here not as an increase of transnational phenomena, but rather as that 'large and complex group of inter-related processes' among which it is possible to highlight the increasing independence of the economy from politics, the appearance of new decision structures which operate in real time and with a global scope of action, the current changes to the conditions in which companies, areas of activity, countries and regions compete, and the denationalization of rights (Farria 2001: 49).[38]

Therefore, the emphasis lies here not only in the multiplication of international phenomena and their increasing complexity, but also in the continuous retreat of the state as a single source of authority and/or regulations, both in the domestic arena and in the international system (Strange 1996). This transformation of the state resembles evolution rather than extinction. For the foreseeable future it will be very difficult to proclaim a (real) crisis of the state or – even more dramatically, as some authors have done – *the end* of the state (Ohmae 1995).[39] Nevertheless, the directive role of the state has been questioned, particularly in connection with the functioning of the market. This fact favors deregulation, that is, economic globalization or *'globalization from above'*, but we are also witnessing a *'globalization from below'* phenomenon, which can mainly be seen in the numerous NGOs safeguarding human rights (Falk 1999).

The replacement of hierarchies for networks and the migration of markets to cyberspace, both of which make geographic space meaningless, illustrate the sort of challenges that the territorially based state will have to address if it wants to live up to the emergence of the 'electronically networked world economy' (Reich 1990).

It is easy to comprehend that, in this context, both international and domestic commercial arbitration is at its best. The number of international transactions is increasing spectacularly and, in addition, there is a need to promote flexible systems that can provide solutions on the basis of costs and market tendencies as opposed to the formalistic approach of the judicial model. Furthermore, the scope of the areas which are considered to be freely decided by the parties has been widened considerably and, consequently, more matters can be subject to arbitration.[40] With regard to this latter aspect, the gradual reduction of the protective role of the national public order vis-à-vis the freedom of the parties to govern their relationships should be taken into account. As we have seen, both the increase in international trade and globalization itself have favored self-regulation by the business community as a method to promote exchanges and, consequently, the use of arbitration.

However, domestic court jurisdiction is not under threat. Arbitration is not intended to substitute but rather to coexist and cooperate with court jurisdiction. Nowadays, the problem is how to reach a balance. Voices around the globe warn of the risks of arbitration being 'out of control', which could lead to the needs of the weaker parties being neglected and the requirements of 'legal certainty' and 'predictability' demanded of any efficient dispute resolution system not being satisfied.[41] In order to reach the necessary balance, arbitration cannot neglect its consensus-based origin.

If the contract foresees arbitration at law and sets forth the application of a national legal system, the arbitrators are compelled to abide by this contractual provision. It would be a different matter if the contractors wanted to 'denationalize' their agreements by resorting to generic principles, such as the *lex mercatoria* or the UNIDROIT Principles on International Commercial Contracts (see *supra*), or if they opted for arbitration in equity.

In this field, we can refer to the efforts of some arbitrators to consolidate international 'commercial public order' principles.[42] The *Lagergren case* (ICC 1963)[43] is usually quoted as the first case where the use of public order in a foreign law led to a declaration that the prohibition of corruption is an issue of international public order. In some other cases, such as the *Reynolds case* (Cour d'appel de Paris, 1994),[44] the focus is placed on the importance of the existence of a single universal conception of the very concept of non-national public order. However, in actual fact, this single conception is still far from being reached, even in actions such as the prohibition of corruption or the exercise of undue influence.[45]

It is in any event inconceivable nowadays to see arbitration as being 'out of control'. Awards require enforcement by states' courts so that it is therefore impossible to avoid some form of (limited) scrutiny by those states. This can be done in one of three ways: action to set aside the award before the courts of the state of the venue of the arbitral tribunal; enforcement of the award by the same courts; or enforcement of the award by the courts of another state, that is, through the exequatur procedure of the 1958 New York Convention.

Arbitration and Jurisdiction: The Future

International arbitration has not yet become merely an alternative – albeit an extremely attractive one in certain cases – to jurisdiction, as is the case of domestic arbitration. It is still the only reasonable option for many transnational transactions.

However, despite the apparently bright future and long life ahead for arbitration in the current circumstances, one cannot disregard the fact that this situation could change, at least partly, as a result of two potential events: (1) the reinforcement of jurisdiction in the framework of regional integration processes; and (2) with reference to international arbitration between states and foreign economic operators, the creation of a new 'constitutional' framework for international trade (rebuilding the World Trade Organization [WTO]), which provides judicial mechanisms available to private parties.

On the creation of this new 'constitutional' framework, it is interesting to note the absence of any such discussion on the agenda of the Dispute Resolution System of the WTO which is currently underway (Díez-Hochleitner

2005a). The reason for this could be linked to the demanding transformation that reform of the WTO itself would entail, as this organization is still imbued with the GATT philosophy of 1947 aimed at opening up markets on the basis of reciprocal advantages for state parties (plus the European Union) rather than guaranteeing access to markets for economic operators. This explains not only why private parties are currently not qualified to appear before WTO panels, but also why the enforcement mechanisms of Dispute Resolution Body decisions are still based on negotiation between the parties and on the application of certain counter-measures. It is a perfect example of what John H. Jackson (1989) called the 'power-oriented method' of the dispute resolution methods. In this scenario, the parties negotiate over the application of trade countermeasures, and, in particular, the possibility of agreeing to commercial compensations for the benefit of the aggrieved party or, in the absence of an agreement, to the possibility of the latter imposing commercial 'reprisals'.[46]

We shall now examine regional integration processes. In the case of the European Union, the harmonization of the laws of the member states, as well as the creation of effective judicial cooperation mechanisms, have increased the confidence of European economic players in the courts of other member states. Therefore, the exponential rise in intra-community exchanges has not entailed a similar increase in international arbitrations. In the context of the European Union at this time, resorting to international arbitration has to be explained in terms of its comparative advantages over jurisdiction, as is the case with national arbitration.

In the course of an integration process, any attempt to replace the role of the national courts as guarantors for the application of Community law with international arbitration (or supranational courts) is unfeasible. In the European Union, national courts have actually become Community courts, which receive the assistance of the Court of Justice of the European Communities (through 'preliminary rulings'). The jurisdictional duties of the Court of Luxembourg are limited to promoting a uniform interpretation of European Community law, to exercising control over the legality of actions and omissions by European institutions, and to declaring breaches of Community law by member states.

The performance of national courts as Community courts in the European Union even applies – though not primarily – to conflicts between members states and nationals of other member states. For example, the freedom of establishment within Community territory, set out in the EC Treaty with a broad scope, is not guaranteed by arbitral mechanisms (or by investment protection bilateral agreements) but rather by national courts assuming their status as Community ones.

However, with regard to American or Asian regional integration processes, jurisdiction does not seem to be gaining any momentum for the moment.

NAFTA, ASEAN and MERCOSUR appear to be little more than free trade areas coupled with the rhetoric of integration and the need to advance in institutionalizing it. How does one explain, for example, Chapter XI of the NAFTA Treaty, concerning the protection of investments? Chapter XI contains the typical wording of a bilateral treaty for the protection of foreign investments, including the possibility of subjecting potential controversies between a member state of the NAFTA Treaty and a national investor of another member state to international arbitration (i.e. ICSID arbitration).

Concluding Remarks

The advent of the international civil society has heralded the abandonment of the adversarial paradigm between arbitration and jurisdiction. The attitude that Zweigert and Kotz (2000: 412) called 'suspicious(ness) of arbitration clauses because of their tendency to take the legal decision of legal disputes away from the courts' has now been abandoned for what Roebuck (1994) likes to call a 'comfortable symbiosis' between judges and arbitrators. The judiciary is giving up any remnants of 'judicial jealousy' (ibid.) to welcome arbitration as a means of clearing out dockets of burdensome, unwanted, and possibly unwarranted, litigation. If it is well handled, the new arrangement can lead to win-win scenarios: while arbitration provides parties with basic procedural fairness and access to adjudicatory services, society avoids the administrative breakdown of the judicial system. In the meantime, states remain intimately involved because the enforcement procedures before national courts serve to relocalize and reterritorialize the transactions removed temporarily from the public realm by the use of a private adjudicatory system.

The global marketplace demands confidence, certainty and predictability to operate. Once all the trade-offs are taken into consideration, international arbitration is generally favored by the business community. Distrust of the 'neutrality' of national jurisdictions plays a major role in this decision. International arbitrators are seen as impartial decision-makers who are not 'contaminated' with 'national' bias. The marketplace for arbitrators, on the other hand, is extremely small and competitive. Incompetent arbitrators are unlikely to be hired for subsequent arbitrations. The future of arbitration is well protected by the two virtues of the impartiality and the proficiency of the decision makers.

In some cases, large transnational companies resort to arbitration not in order to seek a rule-based decision but as an agreeable relief to the dispute. In these cases, the parties' counsels may take the lead in reaching a reasonable negotiated agreement, which takes into consideration the time, costs and market interests. Problems can arise when the parties to the conflict belong to different legal traditions or do not belong to the same area or business sector. Here, in order for the international arbitration system not to risk being perceived as a partial structure at the service of certain 'corporative circles', arbitrators must apply the decision rules set out in the contract which gives rise to the controversy.

The future of international arbitration relies on the sanctity of the negotiating freedom of the parties. Just as in national jurisdictions it is necessary to guarantee that judges are subject to the democratic legal order in order to avoid them being 'above the law', it is necessary to ensure that arbitrators are subject to the provisions governing the contract.

Notes

The present article is based on a presentation that the authors gave at the 'Markets and Civil Society in Europe' conference, organized by the European Civil Society Network (CiSoNet) in Madrid on 23–25 September 2004.

1. For a detailed discussion of the growing interconnectedness of movements, groups, networks and organizations engaged in a global or transnational debate see, *per omnia*, Kaldor (2003a, 2003b).
2. Although an authoritative definition of the term 'transnational' seems to be lacking, it is possible to acknowledge that 'transnational' – that is, 'beyond nations' – implies something distinct from the term 'international' – that is, 'among' or 'between' nations. See generally Garner (1999: 822, 1505).
3. On the concept of international civil society see, *inter alia*, Colás (2002). For a related discussion on how the concept of international society has evolved – it is no longer only a society of states – see Müllerson (2000) and Pérez-Prat Durbán (2004).
4. See Arts et al. (2001); the term 'non-state actors' also includes, but is not restricted to, private market institutions engaged in the setting of international standards, human rights and environmental non-governmental organizations, transnational religious movements and even mafias and mercenary armies, in some instances.
5. See again Pérez-Prat Durbán (2004). Private regulatory arrangements inexistent at the end of the last century are now widely used by the international business community, for example, regulation of the Internet, the international minerals industry, industrial production standards settings, regulation of intellectual property, the insurance industry and the maritime industry. Moreover, business associations such as the International Chamber of Commerce (ICC) are evolving into 'international trade legislatures', as an important source of norms and practices codified by these organizations (*lex mercatoria*) (Cutler 2003).
6. This retreat of the state, according to these authors, has been followed by the creation of some sort of legitimate authority in non-state actors to perform a specific role in particular domains. For a detailed discussion on this idea, see Cutler et al. (1999); for a more condensed approach, see Hall and Biersteker (2002).
7. For example, Reebok's 'Human Rights Production Standards' and Levi-Strauss' 'Terms of Engagement and Guidelines.' For a commentary on the current global demands for corporate responsibility, see generally, Westfield (2002).

8. A good example are the new standards for accounting and financial reporting that the majority of international accounting firms have adopted in the wake of the major fraudulent cases discovered in the past few years.

9. Often, this variant is called 'amicable dispute resolution', meaning '[a] mechanism where a third party helps the parties find a solution that is enforceable as a matter of contract, instead of a decision that is enforceable at law, for example, an arbitral award'. For an explanation of these methods as applied by the ICC, see generally Jiménez-Figueres (2004).

10. 'A method of non-binding dispute resolution involving a neutral third party who tries to help the disputing parties to reach a mutually agreeable solution' (Garner 1999).

11. 'Consensual bargaining process, in which the parties attempt to reach an agreement on a disputed or potentially disputed matter. Usually involves complete autonomy for the parties involved, without the intervention of third parties' (Garner 1999: 1059).

12. In general terms, international trade entails all exchanges of property, services and assets involving the economies of at least two countries.

13. See generally, UNCTAD (2004).

14. A multinational corporation has been characterized as 'any corporation which owns (in whole or in part), controls and manages income generating assets in more than one country.' The distinctions between the terms 'multinational corporation' and 'transnational corporation' are often blurred. See Muchlinski (1995).

15. For a review of arbitration advantages in an international context, see generally: Ehrenhaft (1977), who contends that arbitration is informal, quick, private, convenient, and inexpensive; Pearlman and Nelson (1983), who argue that arbitration minimizes problems of forum shopping, concurrent jurisdiction, and limited access to pre-trial discovery inherent in international litigation; and Shalakany (2000), who states that arbitration offers a quick settlement by experts in the field, informal and cordial dispute resolution, and a neutral forum for such resolution.

16. In the case of disagreement, parties under institutionalized arbitrations can ask the administrative body to appoint the arbitrators. Private institutions (ICC, LCIA and AAA) will usually take into account the characteristics of the relevant business to appoint the members of the arbitral tribunals. Arbitral tribunals usually consist of a sole arbitrator or of three-member panels. Under *ad hoc* international arbitrations conducted under the UNCITRAL Rules, the designation of appointing-authority is performed by the Secretary-General of the Permanent Court of Arbitration. See, generally, Gaillard and Savage (1999).

17. The expression *lex mercatoria* is used here in the traditional meaning, that is, non-national legal rules and international trade usages applicable to international contracts. For an in-depth discussion on the concept, see generally, Teubner (1997) and Pryles (2004). The *lex mercatoria* has widened its scope to encompass new commercial uses and technical developments. Thus, the 2004 edition of the UNIDROIT Principles of International Commercial Contracts now cover areas not included in the 1994 edition, namely, authority of agents, third-party rights, set-off, assignment of rights, transfer of obligations and assignment of contracts. The inclusion of these new areas has close connections with the explosion of technological innovations over the last decade (Unidroit 2004). For an analytical assessment of these innovations, see Bonell (2004).

18. It is interesting to note that this is not a new phenomenon. Roscoe Pound, one of America's brightest legal minds, had pointed out back in the early twentieth century that the public distrust of courts was indeed a result of the failure of the legal system to solve the problems of most Americans.

19. *Mitsubishi Motors Corp. v. Soler Chrysler-Plymouth, Inc.*, 473 U.S. 614 (1985).

20. For a review of statistics showing this trend, please refer to Nicholas and Luker (2004).

21. We have already referred to ICC, LCIA, AAA and NAI.

22. For instance, legislation based on the UNCITRAL (1985) Model Law on International Commercial Arbitration, with amendments as adopted in 2006, has been enacted in Ireland (2008), Mauritius (2008), New Zealand (2007), Peru (2008) and Slovenia (2008).

23. *Ley 60/2003 de 23 de diciembre, de Arbitraje.* For a detailed review of the law's salient legal features, see Uría & Menéndez (2004).

24. Legislation based on the UNCITRAL Model Law on International Commercial Arbitration has been enacted in Armenia (2006), Australia (1991), Austria (2005), Azerbaijan (1999), Bahrain (1994), Bangladesh (2001), Belarus (1999), Bulgaria (2002), Cambodia (2006), Canada (1986), Chile (2004), in China: Hong Kong Special Administrative Region (1996), Macau Special Administrative Region (1998); Croatia (2001), Cyprus (1987), Denmark (2005), Egypt (1996), Estonia (2006), Germany (1998), Greece (1999), Guatemala (1995), Hungary (1994), India (1996), Iran (1997), Ireland (1998), Japan (2003), Jordan (2001), Kenya (1995), Lithuania (1996), the former Yugoslav Republic of Macedonia (2006), Madagascar (1998), Malta (1995), Mexico (2005), New Zealand (1996), Nicaragua (2005), Nigeria (1990), Norway (2004), Oman (1997), Paraguay (2002), the Philippines (2004), Poland (2005), Republic of Korea (1999), Russian Federation (1993), Serbia (2006), Singapore (2001), Spain (2003), Sri Lanka (1995), Thailand (2002), Tunisia (1993), Turkey (2001), Ukraine (1994), within the United Kingdom of Great Britain and Northern Ireland: Scotland (1990); in Bermuda (1993); within the United States of America: California (1996), Connecticut (2000), Illinois (1998), Louisiana, Oregon and Texas; Uganda (2000), Venezuela (1998), Zambia (2000) and Zimbabwe (1996).

25. The Geneva-based World Intellectual Property Organization established what is called the WIPO Arbitration and Mediation Centre in 1994 to offer arbitration and mediation services for the resolution of international commercial disputes between private parties, particularly (but not exclusively) disputes involving intellectual property issues. The WIPO Rules are available at http://arbiter.wipo.int/arbitration/rules/.

26. Interestingly enough, the widespread use of international arbitration by companies in the sphere of international trading is taking place simultaneously with the expansion of alternative methods of dispute resolution (mediation and negotiation) in domestic markets (McGovern and Hare 1992).

27. Directive 2008/52/EC of the European Parliament and of the Council of 21 May 2008 is intended to provide such European legal framework in cross-border disputes.

28. Art. 34 of the UNCITRAL Model Law only provides the following grounds for setting aside an arbitral award: (1) incapacity of a party to the arbitration; (2) invalidity of the arbitration agreement; (3) infringement of the scope of the jurisdiction of the arbitral tribunal; (4) when a party was unable to present his case; (5) when the composition of the arbitral tribunal or when the arbitral procedure was not in accordance with the arbitration agreement; (6) when the subject matter of the dispute was not arbitrable; and (7) when the award conflicts with a public policy of the state.

29. *Convention on the Recognition and Enforcement of Foreign Arbitral Awards* in New York on 10 June 1958 (The NY Convention). The membership of the Convention is available at http://www.uncitral.org/en-index.htm.

30. The International Centre for the Settlement of Investment Disputes (ICSID) is a public international organization created under a treaty, the Convention on the Settlement of Investment Disputes between States and Nationals of other states (hereinafter, the Convention). The Convention was formulated by the Executive Directors of the International Bank for Reconstruction and Development (the World Bank). On 18 March 1965, the Executive Directors submitted the Convention, with an accompanying Report, to member governments of the World Bank for their consideration, with a view to its signature and ratification. The Convention came into force on 14 October 1966, when it had been ratified by 20 countries. More than 130 countries have ratified the Convention. The

ICSID Convention and arbitration rules are available at http://www.worldbank.org/icsid/basicdoc/57.htm. See Schreuer (2001).

31. A survey conducted by UNCTAD in 1999 estimated the existence of 1,857 BITs (UNCTAD 2000).
32. The proliferation of BITs is partly due to the absence of a multilateral framework of investment and dispute resolution; the most important (failed) attempt on the field was OECD's MAI. See, generally, Nunnenkamp and Pant (2003).
33. This includes treating the investment in a fair and equitable manner and compensating the foreign investor in the event of direct or indirect expropriation for public policy reasons. See Dolzer and Stevens (1995).
34. Germany was the first country to execute a BIT, as its investors had lost their foreign assets in many countries following the two world wars. See UNCTC (1988).
35. Awards issued under this heading include, *inter alia*, *Maffezini v. Spain* (ARB/97/7), available in ICSID Reports, vol. 5 (2002).
36. See the ICSID list of pending and concluded cases at http://www.worldbank.org/icsid/cases/pending.htm.
37. See, for instance, EBRD (2004), a report on the quality of commercial arbitration regimes in Armenia, Azerbaijan, Georgia, Moldova, the Kyrgyz Republic, Tajikistan and Uzbekistan.
38. For a round-up of definitions of globalization, refer to Waters (1995: 3) and Luard (1990: 168–169).
39. For a debate on how the state will remain a central factor shaping the international economy, see Pelagidis and Papasotiriou (2002).
40. Nowadays, the arbitrability of a dispute is not considered to be excluded merely on the basis of the existence of mandatory public laws (e.g. antitrust or securities laws). On the notion of arbitrability in general, refer to Bockstiegel (1987: 177) and Kirry (1996).
41. For a review of such claims in the context of the NAFTA arbitration, see, for example, Alvarez (2000), Brower (2001), Legum (2002) and Trakman (2001).
42. The existence of the so-called public order principles has been widely discussed in current literature. On the notion of 'international public order' in general, see McDougal et al. (1993).
43. A good analysis of the case can be found in Wetter (1994).
44. *Lebanese Traders Distributors and Consultants v. Reynolds* in *Revue de l'Arbitrage* (1994: 709). A brief commentary of the case is presented in Gaillard and Savage (1999: 857).
45. Yet some improvements are taking place in the area of enforcements of awards. See, generally, Mayer and Sheppard (2004).
46. For the black letter law of the WTO's dispute resolution system, see 'Understanding on Rules and Procedures Governing the Settlement of Disputes', *International Legal Materials* (1994): 1226.

References

Alvarez, Henri C. 2000. 'Arbitration under the North American Free Trade Agreement', *Arbitration International* 16: 393.

Arts, Bas, Math Noortmann and Bob Reinalda, eds. 2001. *Non-State Actors in International Relations*. Aldershot: Ashgate.

Bockstiegel, Karl-Heinz. 1987. 'Public Policy and Arbitrability', in *Comparative Arbitration Practice and Public Policy in Arbitration*, ICCA Congress Series, 3: 177.

Bonell, Michael Joachim. 2004. 'UNIDROIT Principles 2004: A Further Step towards a Global Contract Law', *Uniform Commercial Code Law Journal* 37: 1.

Brower, Charles H., II. 2001. 'Investor-State Disputes under NAFTA: The Empire Strikes Back', *Columbia Journal of Transnational Law* 40, no. 1: 43–88.

Colás, Alejandro. 2002. *International Civil Society*. Cambridge: Polity Press.

Cutler, A. Claire. 2003. *Private Power and Global Authority. Transnational Law and the Global Political Economy*. Cambridge: Cambridge University Press.

Cutler, A. Claire, Virginia Haufler and Tony Porter, eds. 1999. *Private Authority and International Affairs*. Albany: State University of New York Press.

David, René. 1985. *Arbitration in International Trade*. Deventer: Kluwer Law.

Díez-Hochleitner, Javier. 2005a. 'La Unión Europea ante la reforma del sistema de solución de diferencias de la OMC', in *Globalización y Comercio Internacional. Actas de las XX Jornadas de la Asociación Española de Profesores de Derecho Internacional y Relaciones Internacionales*, ed. Juan Manuel de Faramiñán Gilbert. Madrid: BOE, Universidad de Jaén y AEPDIRI.

———. 2005b. 'El arbitraje internacional como cauce de protección de los inversores extranjeros en los APPRIs', *Actualidad Jurídica Uría Menéndez* 11: 49–65.

Dolzer, Rudolf, and Margrete Stevens. 1995. *Bilateral Investment Treaties*. Dordrecht: Nijhoff Publishers.

EBRD (European Bank for Reconstruction and Development). 2004. *Arbitration Law Assessment Project: Report on the Quality of Commercial Arbitration Legal Regimes in Early Transition Countries*. London: EBRD.

Ehrenhaft, Peter D. 1977. 'Effective International Commercial Arbitration', *Law and Policy in International Business* 9, no. 4: 1191–1226.

Falk, Richard. 1999. *Predatory Globalization*. Cambridge: Polity Press.

Farria, José Eduardo. 2001. *El Derecho en la economía globalizada*. Madrid: Trotta.

Gaillard, Emmanual, and John Savage, eds. 1999. *Fouchard, Gaillard, Goldman on International Commercial Arbitration*. The Hague: Kluwer Law International.

Garner, Bryan A., ed. 1999. *Black's Law Dictionary*. 7th ed. St. Paul, MN: West Group.

Hall, Rodney Bruce, and Thomas J. Biersteker, eds. 2002. *The Emergence of Private Authority in Global Governance: Cambridge Studies in International Relations*. Cambridge: Cambridge University Press.

Jackson, John H. 1989. *The World Trade System*. Cambridge, MA: MIT Press.

Jiménez-Figueres, Dyalá. 2004. 'Amicable Means to Resolve Disputes: How the ICC ADR Rules Work', *Journal of International Arbitration* 21, no. 1: 91–101.

Kaldor, Mary. 2003a. 'The Idea of Global Civil Society', *International Affairs* 79, no. 3: 583–593.

———. 2003b. *Global Civil Society: An Answer to War*. Cambridge: Polity Press.

Kirry, Antoine. 1996. 'Arbitrability: Current Trends in Europe', *Arbitration International* 12, no. 4: 373–389.

Legum, Barton. 2002. 'The Innovation of Investor-State Arbitration under NAFTA', *Harvard International Law Journal* 43, no. 2: 531–539.

Luard, Evan. 1990. *The Globalization of Politics: The Changed Focus of Political Action in the Modern World*. London: Macmillan.

Mayer, Pierre, and Audley Sheppard. 2004. 'Recommendations of the International Law Association on Public Policy as a Ground for Refusing Recognition or Enforcement of International Arbitration Awards', in *Yearbook Commercial Arbitration*, vol. 29, ed. Albert Jan van den Berg. New York: Aspen Publishers.

McDougal, Myres S., Harold D. Lasswell and James C. Miller. 1993. *The Interpretation of International Agreements and World Public Order: Principles of Content and Procedure*. Leiden: Brill.

McGovern, Francis E., and Francis H. Hare. 1992. 'Lessons for U.S. Alternative Dispute Resolution', in *Mediation: An Alternative Method of Dispute Resolution?* Zurich: Schulthess Polygraphischer Verlag, pp. 165–175.

Minc, Alain. 1995. *La borrachera democrática: El nuevo poder de la opinión pública*. Madrid: Temas de hoy.

Muchlinski, Peter T. 1995. *Multinational Enterprises*. Oxford: Blackwell Publishers.

Müllerson, Rein. 2000. *Ordering Anarchy: International Law in International Society*. The Hague: Nijhoff Publishers.

Nicholas, Geoff, and Joanna Luker. 2004. 'Global Overview', in *Arbitration World*, ed. J. William Rowley. London: The European Lawyer.

Nunnenkamp, Peter, and Manoj Pant. 2003. 'Why the Case for a Multilateral Agreement on Investment is Weak', *Kiel Discussion Papers*, 400.

Ohmae, Kenichi. 1995. *The End of the Nation-State*. New York: Free Press.

Pearlman, Lawrence, and Steven C. Nelson. 1983. 'New Approaches to the Resolution of International Commercial Disputes', *International Law* 17: 215, 218–225.

Pelagidis, Theodore, and Harry Papasotiriou. 2002. 'Globalization or Regionalism? States, Markets and the Structure of International Trade', *Review of International Studies* 28, no. 3: 519–535.

Pérez-Díaz, Víctor. 1993. *The Return to Civil Society: The Emergence of Democratic Spain*. Cambridge, MA: Harvard University Press. First Spanish edition 1987.

Pérez-Prat Durbán, Luis. 2004. *Sociedad Civil y Derecho Internacional*. Valencia: Tirant lo Blanch.

Pryles, Michael. 2004. 'Application of the Lex Mercatoria in International Commercial Arbitration', *Australian Law Journal* 78, no. 6: 396–627.

Reich, Robert B. 1990. *The Work of Nations*. New York: New York Press.

Roebuck, Derek. 1994. 'The Myth of Judicial Jealousy', *Arbitration International* 10, no. 4: 395–406. Schreuer, Christopher H. 2001. *The ICSID Convention: A Commentary*. Cambridge: Cambridge University Press.

Shalakany, Amr A. 2000. 'Arbitration and the Third World: A Plea for Reassessing Bias under the Spectre of Neoliberalism', *Harvard International Law Journal* 41, no. 2: 419–468.

Strange, Susan. 1996. *The Retreat of the State: The Diffusion of Power in the World Economy*. Cambridge: Cambridge University Press.

Teubner, Gunther, ed. 1997. *Global Law without a State*. Aldershot: Darmouth Publishing.

Trakman, Leon E. 2001. 'Arbitrating Investment Disputes under the NAFTA', *Journal of International Arbitration* 18, no. 4: 385–415.

UNCITRAL (United Nations Commission on International Trade Law). 1985. *Uncitral Model Law on International Commercial Arbitration*. United Nations document A/40/17, Annex I. As adopted by the United Nations Commission on International Trade Law on 21 June.

UNCTAD (United Nations Conference on Trade and Development). 2000. *Bilateral Investment Treaties, 1959–1999*. New York: United Nations.

_____. 2004. *Trade and Development Report, 2004*. Geneva: United Nations and Oxford University Press.

UNCTC (United Nations Centre on Transnational Corporations). 1988. *Bilateral Investment Treaties*. London: Graham and Trotman.

Unidroit (International Institute for the Unification of Private Law). 2004. *Unidroit Principles of International Commercial Contracts, 2004*. Rome: Unidroit.

Uría & Menéndez. 2004. 'La nueva ley española de arbitraje', *Circular Informativa*, 3 (May). http://www.uria.com/esp/circulares/procesal/pro_May04esp.htm.

Waters, Malcolm. 1995. *Globalization*. London: Routledge.

Westfield, Elisa. 2002. 'Globalization, Governance and Multinational Enterprise Responsibility: Corporate Codes of Conduct in the 21st Century', *Virginia Journal of International Law* 42, no. 4: 1075–1108.

Wetter, J. Gillis. 1994. 'Issues of Corruption before International Arbitral Tribunals: The Authentic Text and True Meaning of Judge Gunnar Lagergren's 1963 Award in ICC Case No. 1110', *Arbitration International* 10, no. 3: 277–294.

Zweigert, Konrad, and Hein Kotz. 2000. *An Introduction to Comparative Law*. Oxford: Oxford University Press.

Part II

CIVIL SOCIETY IN TRANSITIONS TO MARKET ECONOMIES AND LIBERAL POLITIES

Chapter 5

CONSUMER CREDIT AND SOCIETY
IN TRANSITION COUNTRIES

Akos Rona-Tas

In much of the developed and developing world the 1990s saw a large increase in consumer credit. In OECD countries, just in the last half decade of the last millennium household debt as a ratio of household income rose from 78 percent to 96 percent (Babeau and Sbano 2003; Christensen and Mathiasen 2002). In post-communist transition countries, consumer credit is still a relative novelty but its pace of growth was even more impressive (Cottarelli et al. 2003). Between 1997 and 2001, consumer lending in Poland, Hungary and the Czech Republic grew by 26 percent annually[1] while other countries in the region with a lower starting point produced even more striking rates of growth. Banks everywhere in the post-communist world, even in less affluent China and Vietnam, are viewing consumer lending as the next new frontier in finance. Mortgages, purchase credit, credit cards, auto loans are advertised in all cities and an increasing number of people apply for them, to buy now and pay later.

While a large literature in economics is devoted to the sustainability of this expansion, there has been relatively little reflection on the way consumer credit reorganizes social relations between lenders and borrowers and in society in general. Recently, there have been several studies investigating the link between civil society and credit, but they mostly focus on public debt or the flow of credit between countries.[2] Sociological treatises on consumer credit, on the other hand, rarely go beyond exposing the supposed personal catastrophes or extolling the purported virtues of borrowing.

This chapter is based on a multinational research project comparing consumer credit markets, and credit card markets in particular, in eight transition

Notes for this chapter begin on page 174.

countries (Poland, the Czech Republic, Hungary, Bulgaria, Ukraine, Russia, China and Vietnam). While my original question guiding this research is concerned with the ways banks decide on creditworthiness of applicants, in this chapter I will gather some of the issues emerging from this research that I believe have relevance for civil society.

I will begin by developing a notion of modern consumer credit based on its emergence in a two-step process: first, credit separated from other moral obligations; then, the relationship between debtor and creditor shifted from trust mediated by personal networks to rational calculation mediated by institutions. Following this, I will discuss six mechanisms through which banks exercise their power to lend: (1) through *sorting*, banks link the fates of individuals to the fates of other strangers; (2) through *creating identities*, they determine how we are held accountable for our obligations; (3) through a system of *record keeping*, they decide how memory is structured and how reputation can be built; (4) through *quantification* and rendering us measurable they objectify and grant high visibility to certain characteristics of ours; (5) through deploying various techniques of *prediction*, they have the ability to foresee the future better than their clients; and (6) through generating complexity and withholding information, they *create uncertainty* for their customers. In each case, banks are constrained by their cultural, institutional and legal environment. Finally, I will make a few observations about some of the social consequences of the growth of consumer credit and bank power in transition countries.

From Lending and Borrowing to Credit

Credit, a special, rationalized form of lending and borrowing, reallocates economic resources over time by allowing people to use resources before they earn them for an explicit price that is often called interest.[3] By doing this, credit also redistributes resources and power among actors reconfiguring social relationships. For borrowers, credit always creates both opportunities and obligations. Both opportunity and obligation can reposition borrowers in the system of power relations. Borrowing can make one both powerful and vulnerable. For lenders, credit is always a gamble; therefore creditors carefully screen or select borrowers, try to keep them under some control and attempt to sanction them if they violate their obligation.

Lending and borrowing have always played an important role in social life. People have always engaged in transactions where one party's contribution to another's well-being was not immediately reciprocated. In a sense, parents bringing up their children are lending them resources to be repaid when the parents are too old to take care of themselves. Neighbors helping out each other in time of need is a form of lending and borrowing. Peasants working in the agricultural cycle making large investments up front and seeing their payoff only later, usually at the time of the harvest, often borrow tools, labor and other resources from their extended family. None of these are usually construed as credit because they are often not thought of as economic transactions and there is no clear price set for the early use of resources.

Consumer credit in its contemporary form developed in a two-step process from lending. For a long time, lending was submerged in and intermeshed with personal obligations and, as such, appeared first and foremost as a moral issue. Even transactions overtly economic in nature were understood not in the framework of the rational calculus of credit and debit but in that of duty, obligation and trust (Finn 2003; Muldrew 1998; Sullivan 2002). Lending as a moral, as opposed to an economic act was guided by religious norms for centuries. Treatments of lending in the Old Testament (Exodus, XXII; Deuteronomy, XXII; Leviticus, XXV) drew a crucial divide between brothers and others. Interest-bearing loans were forbidden to brothers – that is, members of one's own close community – but not necessarily to others, as some of the Church Fathers later emphasized (Gelpi and Julien-Labruyere 2000). Judaism makes the same distinction (Tenenbaum 1993). The essential idea is that helping brothers in need, whether through alms giving, as preferred by Christianity, or by interest-free lending, as favored by Judaism, is a moral obligation and should be seen as a part of a complex system of responsibilities, which among other things ensures reciprocity or repayment. Lending to others, people to whom we are not closely bound, is different. There the loan can be isolated from other commitments and can be given its own rules of conduct.[4]

This separation of lending and borrowing from the web of other personal obligations was the first step in the creation of modern credit. By lifting lending out of the immediate community, it was also lifted out of its entangled moral context and was made amenable to rational calculation. Credit, therefore, is a special understanding and particular way of handling arms-length obligations whereby a record of carefully circumscribed responsibilities are created, and the creditor can exact a price for advancing resources.[5]

The second step in the creation of modern credit, which happened as recently as the second part of the twentieth century, was the further, more radical disembedding of lending from social relationships. Earlier, extending credit was extending social networks often far beyond one's own community. The notaries public of seventeenth-century Paris, the people Parisiennes in need for a loan would turn to, were acting as go-betweens linking creditors and borrowers in an unbroken chain of personal contact (Hoffman et al. 2000). Credit reporters of the Tappan Mercantile Agency of New York in nineteenth-century America played the same role, making it possible for wealthy East Coast investors to reach out to farmers and entrepreneurs in other parts of the country in need of capital (Norris 1978). These mediated face-to-face contacts served double duty. They made the borrowers intelligible to lenders, explaining who they were and whether they should be deemed worthy of credit. At the same time, they also guaranteed some sanctioning in the event of bad behavior, thus ensuring a measure of accountability. The social ties fostered trust, and the lender's final decision was based on a more or less informed judgement as to whether the applicant should be trusted.

The second step dispenses with these social networks for the most part and replaces them with a set of institutions. Arm-length relationships become impersonal. The borrower is made intelligible by means of institutions and sets of precise categories that they provide.[6] Institutions are also the chief instruments for penalizing those who renege on their promise. The lender's decision is not necessarily any more informed, but trust in the borrower is not a consideration anymore. It is formal calculation that guides lenders.[7]

Modern Consumer Credit

The consumer credit revolution began in the United States in the 1920s (Calder 1999; Olney 1991), but it took off fully with the post–World War II economic boom. Before that, consumer credit was extended through a set of personal, face-to-face relationships. Households borrowed from family and friends – in which case it often did not count as credit – and received credit from local merchants. Extended on the basis of trust, credit was embedded in existing social networks which, on the one hand, made the economic transaction inseparably intertwined with other social relations, and on the other, enabled the lenders to nudge or punish borrowers who neglected their obligations. Until the start of the twentieth century, consumer credit was largely relegated to the form of store credit and pawning. Banks were reluctant to lend to individuals for non-productive purposes, and it was the manufacturers of the first consumer durables (e.g. sewing machines, pianos, typewriters and motorcars) who introduced consumer credit through their pioneering installment plans.

The novelty the consumer credit revolution brought was the rationalization and impersonalization of credit. The entry of banks into retailing credit was part of this revolution. Before the twentieth century, banks lent money to consumers only of great wealth, power or high social standing. The consumer credit revolution has changed all that. Today, banks are the main dispensers of consumer credit, along with a smaller number of specialized finance companies created for the sole purpose of offering loans to consumers. For simplicity, I will call all of them banks.[8]

From the beginning, there have been speculations about the social consequences of consumer credit. One can usefully sort the literature into two categories: one that focuses on the new opportunities credit opens up for consumers, and another fixated on the new obligations incurred by borrowers. Like the famous goblet illusion, where we see either a white goblet or two black faces, most treatments of the topic present exclusively either one or the other face of credit, but rarely both.

In the first category – credit as opportunity – a pessimistic, conservative stream criticizes consumer credit as a force undermining the Protestant work ethic, paving the road to decadence and the corruption of social virtues (Galbraith 1958; Lasch 1979; Tucker 1991). Capitalism, authors in this tradition complain, was built on the ability to defer gratification, and it will crack under the weight of the contradiction of necessary frugality and expanding hedonism (Bell 1976). Interestingly enough, this criticism echoes some of the concerns of the Marxist left, which castigates mass-consumption society with its individualistic materialism from a pessimistic but progressive position. Marxist critics have also insisted that crass materialism is not part of human nature but rather the result of relentless advertising and ideological manipulation.

The optimistic view of mass credit, on the other hand, points to its equalizing, democratizing effects – the way borrowing can soften class boundaries in consumption and allow a large part of the population to join the propertied middle classes (Boorstin 1973). This sanguine approach perceives the new opportunities not as sinister seductions but as the economic fulfillment of democracy. Indeed, the expansion of bank credit made basic necessities available for the first time to a large portion of the population, and commentators can be excused for seeing it as one more step in the process of democratic inclusion. However, a more critical analysis sharing the same set of optimistic assumptions points out that the equalizing potentials of credit are thwarted by discrimination in lending. The great potentials of credit to benefit society have been subverted by lenders biased against certain social groups (see, e.g., Munnell et al. 1996).

The obligations inherent in credit lie at the center of the second set of contributions (Galanoy 1980; Manning 2000; Ritzer 1995). There, authors warn of a new age of debt slavery when unscrupulous lenders rob people of their freedom by tricking them into borrowing beyond their means. From this perspective, the easy life through credit, the main concern of the optimistic approach, turns out to be a mirage, a ploy to deceive us. People work extra hard just to keep up with the next payment, and wholesome family values are neglected by overworked, inattentive parents (Medoff and Harless 1996). The critics of debt slavery emphasize the imperfect foresight of debtors, particularly their limited judgment, which is why these critics discuss the perils of over-indebtedness among the young in much detail. Imprudent borrowing then leads to a downward spiral where a small debt leads to ever-larger ones and finally to bankruptcy. Equality achieved through borrowing is a chimera. Rather than lifting the young and the poor up, borrowing pins them down to destitution. The rich, who either do not need consumer loans or can easily pay off debt, and, in general, tend to be more financially savvy, can avoid the debt trap, hence the gap between the well-heeled and the worse-off is bound to grow. The prime mover of consumer credit is the greed of financial institutions that care about nothing but their own bottom line.

The slightly patronizing tone of this literature is in unmistakable contrast to the more narrow treatment of credit by most economists, who assume that credit is given and taken on the basis of rational calculation on both sides.[9] The critical literature also readily confuses consumerism, the real culprit of their story, and credit, which is one of its instruments. Although undoubtedly an enabler in pursuing these desires, credit is as much the consequence of materialism as its cause. It is rarely mentioned in this literature that the primary obligations of debt frequently introduce secondary obligations. Some of these secondary obligations are less sinister. Taking out a mortgage on a house where one lives imposes not just the duty to pay back the loan but also all the rights and responsibilities of home ownership.

The critical arguments fixated on obligations limiting personal freedom neglect the fact that the new obligations are often replacements for old ones. Bank credit is frequently a substitute for a loan from family or friends. In some instances, borrowing from a bank might entail fewer and simpler obligations than borrowing from one's nasty but rich uncle. Moreover, one may not have a rich uncle who is able and willing to help.

What much of both literatures are missing is that it is not just that more and more people owe money to banks, but that the way banks exercise their power to lend has been changing dramatically.

Banks as Social Institutions

Is credit simply a private market transaction contingent on the discretion of the two parties involved? For centuries, lenders lent their own money to borrowers. For larger projects, rich financiers formed consortia, but each was risking his own funds in the transaction. Today, credit is extended mostly by banks. Banks are often thought of as private companies, rational, profit-driven market players that happen to be providing financial services. Banks, however, are special because they do not lend their own money but the money of their depositors. The bank is an intermediary, owning very little of value and therefore unlikely to be held financially accountable for misman-agement or outright fraud, a lesson that transition countries like Russia and Bulgaria learned the hard way a decade ago, and that is painfully clear now to the entire world mired in a global financial crisis.

Because banks are lending their depositors' money, they are better thought of as social institutions that serve the function of gathering and rechannel-ling the savings of the population. The credit cooperative movement that began in Germany and Italy in the mid-1800s explicitly defined itself in such terms. Savings and loans associations were civic association with a financial purpose (Guinnane 2002). Modern banks with tens or hundreds of thou-sand depositors, a wide variety of very complicated transactions often in far-away places and a military-style bureaucracy are far removed from the small credit unions where members formed committees, knew each other and most credit applicants, and decided important issues by membership vote. Today, even contemporary credit unions operate mostly like banks without members realizing there is a difference.

Still, banks are social institutions and for this reason are or should be highly regulated and supervised. Borrowers also must be given spe-cial rights. The idea that credit is a right of anyone who fulfills the basic requirements of creditworthiness developed in the United States in the 1970s through a series of laws.[10] In transition countries, bank regulation and oversight proceed at varying speed. The Central European countries that have joined the EU in May 2004 have a sounder regulatory system then those not under direct pressure to conform to EU rules, but in none of these countries do laws against discrimination cover lending explicitly, nor are there anti-usury laws.

The Power of Lenders

Issuing credit is a form of power, but it is a peculiar one. The lender is power-ful as long as the loan is not granted. Once it is, the borrower has the upper hand as now it is the borrower's discretion whether the loan with interest is repaid. A series of sanctions must be at the lender's disposal to deter debtors from simply taking the money and running. The increasing social – and often geographical – distance between lender and borrower that facilitated the simplification of the calculus of lending from balancing a complex system of moral demands to simple cost-benefit accounting, made enforcement more difficult and required the muscle of the state. Laws designed to deal with deadbeat borrowers are preconditions of a modern credit market.

Transition countries produced laws that are deficient in three ways. Existing laws are poorly enforced, some laws are missing, and laws created for other (often good) purposes, as it is the case with privacy laws, interfere with the functioning of the credit system. Poor law enforcement is a hallmark of post-communist states. In case of the borrower's default, the bank must have recourse to legal enforcement that is both fair and quick. In transition countries, the legal system is notoriously slow, and therefore collection is difficult. Courts are known to take over three years to process cases, which is much too long to make the effort worthwhile unless the loss to be avoided is very large. Lenders, therefore, try to stay away from the legal system if they can and use high collaterals and their own methods of collection that bypass the courts.

Moreover, the nature of consumer credit, which frequently provides relatively small amounts and thus requires that lenders extend a large number of such loans to make them profitable, makes recovering loans and punishing non-payers extremely costly. Even under the best legal system, if more then a miniscule segment of debtors decide not to pay, there is not much the bank can do. Going after clients owing a few hundred dollars each is simply not worth it, and hunting down thousands of them is simply impossible. Therefore, the key to the bank's power in consumer lending is not *ex post* punishment but its ability to select *ex ante* the clients who are less likely to require sanctioning later. This screening process is the key to appreciating the ways consumer lending is reshaping society.

The Power of Sorting

Credit requires a standardized system of sorting that makes the debtor's situation intelligible and credible to the lender. Sorting the applicant into proper categories is the way lenders comprehend applicants and decide what to do. Classification schemes provide a language, a set of categories to describe the debtor's finances (monthly salary, utility payments, ownership of residence, etc.). They also supply standardized nomenclatures to capture their social status (occupation, industry, level of authority, education, etc.) and past behavior (delinquency, missed payment, completion of financial obligations, etc.). All of these categories can be defined and understood in an unlimited number of ways. Some variations in meaning or classification will have little practical consequences, but others may make a big difference. Whether monthly salary includes all income from an employer, or whether a university professor is described as a professional, a teacher or a white-collar worker, or whether delinquency is defined as not paying for 30 or 90 or 180 days, all matter a lot.

There has been a growing literature on the power of classification. Starting with work by Foucault (1973, 1979), the power of classification has been stated and demonstrated over and over (Bowker and Star 1999; Desrosières 1998; Gandy 1993; Leyshon and Thrift 1999; Lyon 1994, 2003). There are two ways one can think about the power of categorization: instrumentalist claims emerge from a political-economy approach; substantive claims are rooted in culturalist perspectives (which is to sort those who write about sorting). The instrumentalist approach contends that powerful actors can use sorting for their own purposes. Here, sorting is the tool but not the source of power. Much of the post-Marxist literature on this topic belongs in this category. Power is generated *prior* to the act of classification. Classification then just accommodates existing power interests.

The substantive approach, on the other hand, accords power to categorization itself. Classification schemes have their own power, independent of who is using them. This independent power is best observed when its operation is not optimal for its users. It is in its inertia or path dependence where categorization reveals its true might (Rona-Tas 1998). Classification systems attain independent power through three mechanisms: (1) network externalities; (2) complementary verification; and (3) legal enforcement.

Network Externalities. The concept of network externalities describes the phenomenon where adopting widely used classification schemes (or standards, technologies, products, etc.) will be more beneficial than adopting ones with a narrow user base because part of their value comes from other adaptors (Katz and Shapiro 1986). This creates a self-reinforcing mechanism: the more people use a classificatory scheme, the more incentives there will be for others to use the same one. This creates a first-mover advantage: already established systems that already accumulated many followers pressure actors to adopt them rather than make up their own.

Network externalities emerge from compatibility; it is easier to move information across actors if it is coded in a common scheme. For instance, monthly salary must be interpreted by the bank, its clients and their employers the same way to make it a useful measure of the client's ability to pay. What is included (perquisites, premiums, etc.) or how it is counted (if the employee receives a thirteenth-month salary, should the monthly figure be multiplied by 13/12?) are guided by rules that were not designed to be optimal from the lender's perspective. The bank could give its very specific set of instructions about what monthly salary means, but it would make the loan application very cumbersome and its data incomparable with data from others.

The same compatibility issues emerge with occupation, industry, authority and education. All are taken from government statistical nomenclatures, because this way not only is there a convenient commonly understood standard; but also there is aggregate information from other sources that can be used to evaluate individuals as representatives of larger groups. For example, one can look at incidence of unemployment in the particular occupational or industry group and use that to evaluate the riskiness of the applicant but only if the applicant is sorted according to the categories of the unemployment statistics. Occupational sorting in transition countries illuminates this point further. In Hungary, as in most post-communist countries, occupational codes were developed under a state socialism famous for its proclivity towards giant companies. As a result, a very detailed nomenclature of employee positions in large, hierarchical organizations was developed and implemented. After the collapse of communism, most of these large organizations disintegrated and a big, and increasingly internally differentiated self-employed group emerged. The classification system, however, still reflects the old regime. As a result, the system retains distinctions rarely used anymore, such as the fine split between unskilled and semi-skilled workers, which had been used to set the nationwide salary scale by the socialist state. In contrast, important distinctions are missing, and very different cases are lumped together. An individual entrepreneur can be an architect or a sunflower seed peddler. A manager, for instance, used to be the director of a big work organization, but now he or she can be coordinating the work of a handful people in a small retail outlet or responsible for a special project without permanent employees. And new occupations are not covered; for instance, there is no occupational title for investor or speculator. All these pose problems in deciphering who the applicant is.

Industry codes are yet another example. The importance of industry, from the lender's perspective, is to guess the financial prospects of applicants. Private enterprises, when they register, must declare the field of their activity. Businesses are often unsure of what industry they belong to and are even more uncertain where they will fall in the years to come as they develop. Reflecting this uncertainty, they register as many fields as they can think of next to their primary industry, so if they stray into other fields, they do not have to re-license themselves. Yet their primary industry is how they identify themselves officially, even though this may only reflect their intentions at the inception of the firm. Still, banks accept these shaky industry designations because other agencies do the same. Or take the distinction between agriculture and services. Under communism, the people who maintained combines and tractors in agricultural cooperatives were listed as employed in agriculture, the same category to which those who drove that machinery belonged. With the reorganization of agriculture, mechanics were separated and began to work in their own ventures. They still do the same job, often on the same tractors and combines, but now they are service workers along with people like car mechanics, and therefore appear as more creditworthy. Working in the rapidly expanding service sector positions them more favorably for loans than those toiling in moribund agriculture. Banks would rather pay the price for this error than set up their own industry classification for reasons of compatibility.

Banks also stick with classification schemes for reasons of *internal* compatibility. Banks want to keep their own category systems comparable with their other records so they can compare over time and across products. The sorting scheme used to issue mortgage loans in the past will be used for applicants for new products (e.g. credit cards) in order to enable banks to use their experiences with mortgages to judge non-mortgage applicants.[11]

Complementary Verification. The second mechanism is complementary verification. A categorization is useless unless the information the categories convey can be believed. Each classification must be complemented by some way to verify the information it contains. Banks, for instance, could ask the applicant if she is the kind of person who keeps promises, but there is no way of telling the veracity of the response. Another piece of information lenders could use is whether the would-be borrower has any health problems. No lender asks this question, because verifying the answer – sending the applicant for a thorough medical checkup – would be too costly and intrusive, but without verification self-reported health would be useless information.

Compatibility facilitates verification, but as the above examples show, compatibility by no means guarantees verifiability (e.g. if the source is motivated to lie or verification is too expensive). Banks can verify information by direct checks, by consulting other databases or requiring authorized supporting documents, and by cross checking. Direct checking is usually very costly. As personal encounters between lenders and borrowers become less and less frequent direct checking is increasingly rare, except for confirming phone numbers.[12] For old customers, who have a history of transactions with the bank, the bank combs its own records: another form of direct checking.

There are different external sources banks can use to verify information. They can ask employers to confirm income and occupational data, they can consult public databases, such as phone, business and property registries.[13] Asking for supporting documents is a version of consulting external sources, except the information is obtained not directly from the source but through a document issued by the source and obtained by the applicant. The insertion of the applicant in the information gathering process, of course, introduces a new source of potential distortion.

One important institution that plays a key role both in establishing categories of people's finances and in providing a way to verify this information is the tax system. For most people, the annual ritual of filling out the tax return is the main occasion for reviewing one's finances. The tax form provides the main categories to organize people's financial activities. The tax authority with its power to audit and punish has the role to guarantee the veracity of these figures.

The tax system of transition countries is notoriously weak. Not having had a real individual income tax system under state socialism, the civic culture that underpins modern tax collection is abysmal. Tax evasion is rampant and employers and employees join forces in under-reporting wages and salaries to avoid payroll taxes. Employers, especially of small enterprises, to help employees acquire loans also over-report their income in response to bank inquiries. In transition countries, the counterbalancing pressures of taxation (which slants income reports downward) and credit (which tilts them upward) do not generate income estimates that converge around unique and true figures. In countries, like Russia, many banks simply dispense with income data altogether, because no one believes them anyway.[14]

Another piece of information that is similar in importance to the role income plays in lending decisions is educational achievement. It is curious that no lender ever asks for educational credentials but simply believes what applicants report. This can be partly explained by the fact that lenders try not to scare away customers with making the application process unduly burdensome. But it is also because education can be reasonably verified by cross checking. Cross checking looks for inconsistencies in the report. One's occupation is strongly tied to one's education, so checking self-reported education against a verified occupation should be sufficient. Cross checking is now routinely done by computer programs, flagging unlikely combinations of characteristics that require further acts of verification.

Legal Enforcement. Finally, legal enforcement also adds to the power of a particular classification. The law defines defaulting on a loan as 90, or 120 or 180 days of non-payment. By the same token, who counts as a domestic person as opposed to a foreigner for financial purposes is set by law and so is who is married and who is not. Because legal enforcement has consequences when some action is taken – in this case when default is declared or individual or joint liability is enforced – these categories are preferred over others.

Once people are sorted into verified categories, the resulting measures must be combined to produce the final sorting: the judgment of yes or no.[15] This is a secondary sorting, because it is based on the further sorting of sorted information. While the original categories and their verification come from the tax office, the state statistical office, various institutions of credentialing, etc., the way this information is put together, is prescribed by the internal procedures of the lending organization. This syntax can be a circumscribed process of human judgment, a set of formal rules, or a statistical algorithm.[16] These different syntaxes represent increasing levels of formalization and routinization.

The Power of Identifying

Sorting looks for commonalities among people. Its object is to put the applicant in a category where others were already observed. Then the past behavior of people who are similar to the applicant will be used to guess how the applicant will behave. Identification tries to establish the unique characteristics of an individual. It looks for a set that has only a single element: the applicant. Identification makes the individual available for surveillance and sanctioning. All modern states have some form of identification for their subjects, from passports and driver's licenses to social security cards and birth certificates (Rule et al. 1983; Torpey 1998). Before the French Revolution, people were identified by lineage, residence and status – that is, by various measures of where they belonged. Names, family and surnames also follow this approach. Modern state IDs, on the other hand, make an attempt to tie identity to biological characteristics of the body. The picture ID produces a likeness of facial features, and height, weight, eye and hair color are noted, along with age (date of birth). None is unique individually, but in combination they are likely to fit only one or very few individuals. Fingerprints, and more recently, iris and DNA recognition (features that require instrumentation to detect) have been added to the arsenal.

In contrast, lenders are less and less likely to have physical contact with borrowers; therefore bodily traits are not very useful. Today, most credit files do not even include pictures of the borrower. Credit returns to the older approach of identifying through belonging but does it in a distinctively twenty-first-century manner. For an ID system to work from the creditor's perspective, it must have three characteristics. The first one, as mentioned already, is that it must be unique to each individual. The second, and this is also shared with all other ID systems, it must be stable. Hair color, weight or facial features are all imperfect markers because they can all change, which limits their utility. The third important characteristic is findability. It is one thing to establish the identity of someone who shows up at the border, in the welfare office or gets stopped at a traffic check. Physical characteristics are helpful only once the person is present. Non-paying debtors are unlikely to show up at the bank, and the main task of the lender is to track down the non-payer.

Findability, therefore, involves pinning debtors down in some way. Thus, lenders ask for phone numbers and prefer land-lines, which are connected to a fixed physical location, over cell phones, which are not. They ask about address and prefer ownership over rental, not so much because owners are better off than renters. In fact, since most rural residences are owner occupied and rural areas are poorer than urban ones, home ownership is scarcely a sign of affluence. Home ownership is a sign of stability and gives the lender a physical point of departure to find the borrower if necessary. Applicants for consumer credit always have to provide the name and exact address of their employer. The lender then checks on the existence of the employer organization. Long-standing and large employers are better than small ones, because they are thought to be more likely to be around in the future. The same goes for length of employment with the employer; the longer one has worked there, the more probable it is that she can be found there in the future.

Lenders also often ask for the name address and phone of an acquaintance living in a separate household.[17] What the information about address, employer and friend provide is indications of stable social networks, in which the borrower is anchored (Rona-Tas and Guseva 2001). These groups are not unlike ship anchors that keep the boat from drifting away or, to use another metaphor, they are like the huge heavy balls convicts carry on their leg-irons. Unlike the social networks of the Maghrebi traders of the Mediterranean (Greif 1989) or of the Orthodox Jewish diamond merchants of New York (Bernstein 1992), these networks are inert, they are not expected to sanction bad behavior. Employers will not punish employees who go delinquent on their personal loan. The same is true for neighbors and friends. Nor are they responsible for the borrower's debt. With the exception of employers, they do not even provide information pertaining to the client's creditworthiness. The reason they are important from the lender's perspective is that they may help locate the client.

In sum, individual identity is constructed in consumer credit transactions in a way to anchor uniquely the would-be borrower in a stable social network so that she can be found and held accountable if necessary.

The Power of Record Keeping and Remembering

In any community, dealing with people with whom one has not had sufficient personal experience requires a system of reputation. Reputation systems serve two purposes. They punish bad behavior committed in the past and help others to avoid bad characters in future dealings. Historically, the information that built one's reputation was circulated through social networks (Landa 1995; Olegario 1999). In small communities, gossip, rumor, various forms of public branding (scarlet letters, pillory, special cloth, etc.) transferred information about the character of certain people. These systems always contained inconsistencies, contested, conflicting and competing information, and there was rarely full agreement on who was good and who was unworthy.

Reputation systems are always about information sharing and collective memory. The reputation system in contemporary lending is embodied in the credit registries (credit bureaus).[18] Unlike in earlier reputation systems, the information in these registries is highly consistent. Credit bureaus can collect and share solely negative information, or the full performance record of borrowers and include positive information as well. Because banks are competitors, information sharing about customers is not a simple matter. Information about clients is a valuable commodity that banks often acquire at a cost. Knowing who is low and who is high risk is the key to the bank's success in lending. Most transition countries have limited information sharing among lenders, and it is mostly restricted to negative information. Blacklists then punish past bad behavior by warning future lenders and closing off sources of credit from those who had not paid.

Because credit bureaus act as collective memory and they record the past, blacklists are an invitation for malefactors to switch identity and thus erase their record. Individuals can forge their documents or find proxy applicants for loans to cast away the burden of their history of bad conduct.[19] Blacklists make no distinction between applicants with perfect record and those with no previous experience; both are absent from the list.

Full records, on the other hand, provide a full picture of past behavior and thus encourage people to 'build' their reputation. This means that people must invest into their histories and cannot throw away their past without penalty even if their change of identity goes undetected.[20] With the blacklist, no information is good information, with the full list, no information is not much better than bad information. Full records not just impose a different relationship to history on would-be borrowers, they also push people to take on loans. Building a record means borrowing; building a *good* record means borrowing and paying promptly. So one must borrow (and pay) not just to afford a purchase but also to be able to borrow in the future. Full records also allow banks to evaluate the total debt exposure of their clients. Additionally, they can put non-payment in context by seeing whether it is the exception or the rule in the applicant's record.

Full information credit bureaus for consumers are very hard to develop in transition countries because retail banking is highly concentrated. In each country, what used to be *the* saving monobank under socialism dominates the market. Big banks, often possessing over 50 percent of the retail market have a lot to lose by sharing their vast amount of information with new, smaller banks that have very little to contribute to the credit bureau. Big banks would rather keep the information they have about clients and use it to their own advantage. Releasing information on good clients would be an invitation for the other banks to poach. Moreover, good clients could take their shining reputation and force banks to compete for their business driving the price they pay for their loans, and consequently the profits of banks, down. Information sharing about bad clients has a slightly different calculus. While there is some advantage for the big bank to withhold information about its old bad customers and see its competitors lose money lending to them,[21] there is also the benefit of punishing non-payers by shutting them out of the entire market by alerting other lenders. As a result, most transition countries have blacklists, and only a few managed to build a working full reporting system, ones where, as in Poland and the Czech Republic, for historical reasons, the concentration of retail banking has been less pronounced.

One law that has a strong effect on credit but was designed to address different concerns is the law on protecting personal data. Most, but not all, transition countries have strong laws to protect the privacy of personal information. Created in the aftermath of the collapse of Big Brother state socialism, people were eager to shelter themselves from an all-knowing state. Blanket data-protection laws thwart the creation of credit bureaus because they prohibit the release of personal credit information to any registry without the explicit permission of the client. In all these countries, banks argued successfully that non-payment is such a gross violation that it forfeits the borrower's right to data privacy. But that means that getting on the blacklist strips borrowers of all protection and makes it hard for them to contest judgments they feel unjust.

In Poland and the Czech Republic, where full-record credit bureaus operate, and where banks joining forces, were able to circumvent privacy regulations[22] the credit bureau collects not just information on payment behavior but also 'socio-demographic' data that include income, occupation, family information, etc. In fact, very soon these credit bureaus will be able to produce a detailed life history for each person who has been in their system long enough. Worse yet, these credit bureaus, just as their U.S. counterparts register the history of inquiries to each account. As this is available for others making their own inquiry, the history can influence their decisions. The general wisdom among lenders is that too many inquiries without loans extended are a warning sign. Even if the record does not contain negative information otherwise, it must indicate that previous lenders 'know' something unfavorable about the person that is not apparent in the record. This, of course discourages people to shop around with various lenders for the best deal.[23]

Personal data protection is an absolute necessity. Yet what transition countries need is a special law that is aimed specifically at the gathering and sharing of credit information and that specifies what information can be collected, how long it should be kept, who has access to it under what conditions, how individuals can monitor their own records and contest unfair information. There also should be popular oversight keeping an eye on the overall functioning of the credit bureau.

The Power of Quantifying

Lenders also marshal the power of quantification. Numbers are powerful not just because of their air of scientific objectivity but also because of their ultimate simplicity, easy communicability and instant comparability. Banks turn their assessments into numbers and both the Polish and the Czech credit bureau began to issue credit scores, a single numeric summary of a person's credit record based on statistical analysis of similar accounts. This quantification of creditworthiness has had enormous consequences in the United States and will likely run a similar career in these newer markets in the future. In the U.S., credit scores, a number between 300 and 850, are now used not just in gauging creditworthiness but as a general measure of character and reliability.[24] Would-be employers will request to see the applicant's credit score, and so do future landlords. Today, in the United States, 95 percent of car insurance premiums are calculated on the basis of the credit scores, as insurance companies claim it is a good predictor of future claims (Kellison et al. 2003). And recently, the largest utility company in Texas began to set what it charges for electricity based on the customer's credit score.[25] It is all the more disturbing that the algorithms that produce these credit scores are considered proprietary information and remain a mystery to the public.

The enormous power of quantification of one's reputation which covers up human judgment and discretion in the decision-making process, however, can cut both ways. While banks can legitimize their selection process by pointing to its scientific nature making challenges to their decisions difficult, the very same numbers can empower customers with high scores who can demand better terms from banks in a competitive marketplace. This is why U.S. credit bureaus, created for the collective convenience of and with cooperation from the banks, were reluctant to release scores to individuals unless their request was turned down; and only since 2001, following a California legislative decision, do people have the unlimited right to know their scores. The Polish and Czech credit bureaus do offer free access for individuals to their own record, but not to their credit scores.

The Power of Foresight

Overall economic stability is key for credit markets as credit is about the future. Unpredictable future prospects make both the borrower's and the lender's calculations futile. The early years of post-communism made guessing the future especially difficult. Large-scale institutional changes, the very essence of the post-communist transformation, created great instability. The necessary reforms were often aggravated by vast policy blunders such as the banking crisis of 1997 in Bulgaria, or 'Black Tuesday' in October 1994 and the financial meltdown of 1998 in Russia, further destabilizing entire economies.

By the late 1990s, most European transition countries completed the fundamental transformation of their economic systems. Inflation dropped to single digits and real incomes started to grow. Unemployment settled at a steady rate, new wage differentials developed, regional differences became entrenched. The window of great economic opportunities offered by privatization, the malfunctions left by the communist economy, and the inflow of foreign capital, are now closed. The economic system achieved a level of consolidation.

The banking system also got more stable. Each country dealt with the old, bad loans from the communist era. Each developed its central bank, a financial accounting system, standards for risk management, and system of oversight. Many transition countries sold off most of their banks to foreign financial institutions or let foreign banks establish their own independent subsidiaries. With foreign ownership also came Western know-how as well as money for investing in information technology and infrastructure. Foreign ownership also made it harder for the state to politicize lending and prop up moribund state companies. All of these development helped credit markets and consumer credit markets in particular to grow.

One consequence of greater economic stability is that it makes it possible for banks to use statistical models to predict the behavior of applicants. These statistical models work by extrapolating the past to the future in a rigid manner, and they are quite useless without a measure of stability and predictability in the economy. But even under the most settled conditions, some people's lives are more predictable than others. Banks reward people with stable lives; those who have stable employment will be preferred over those who may make more money but whose careers are more precarious.

The Power to Create Uncertainty

When banks receive an application for a loan, they find themselves in a situation of information asymmetry: clients may opportunistically withhold information crucial for the bank's decision (Stiglitz and Weiss 1981). They know more about their intentions and circumstances than lenders can learn, and they can hide or misrepresent relevant facts that lenders cannot verify.

One way banks are leveling this information asymmetry is by withholding information themselves. Disclosing the terms of the loan is mandatory everywhere, and several of the transition countries require that lenders provide not just the interest rate but the APR (annual percentage rate) that includes fees and costs. Yet banks do everything they can to make loans as confusing and as incomparable as possible. This is especially bad for open-ended (revolving) loans. For instance, credit card holders often pay extra for monthly statements they receive if they had activity on their account that month. Because the actual cost of these statements depend on usage, this is not included in the APR. There are separate rules for card purchase and cash withdrawal. Separate fees for transferring money to pay the credit card account. There are also various ways banks calculate the interest one pays. The complexity of lending contracts can be mind boggling. In transition countries, regulators are often ineffectual and consumer organizations that should supply advice to consumers are non-existent.

Consequences of Credit

What are some of the social implications of the advent of modern consumer credit in the transition countries? Are social inequalities reinforced or upended by the diffusion of retail loans? Consumer lending in the transition countries is becoming more inclusive and rigid at the same time. Competition among banks on the consumer credit market is on the rise, as foreign banks enter these markets. Domestic banks started to pay more attention to consumer lending partly because their large corporate clients began to abandon them to seek corporate loans abroad. One should not overstate the force of competition, however. Retail markets in transition countries, as mentioned earlier, are still highly concentrated and clients are reluctant to move from large, old banks they have grown to know to new, unfamiliar ones even if they are offered a better deal there. Upstarts complain about the inertia of customers who prefer the perceived security of the large banks. The difficulties of deciphering terms and conditions of loan products also counsel immobility.

Equally important, the routinization and automation of the lending decision have made consumer credit cheaper and thus affordable for a large segment of society. Banks are moving from an elite market to a mass market in consumer lending at varying speed and caution. A few smaller banks decided to stick with a limited, affluent clientele and offer them personalized and comprehensive financial service. But most split their clientele into two, a small circle of VIP customers and a much larger group of regular clients. Because there are few elite customers who are not already committed to a bank (and banks go out of their way to keep their VIPs), the only way to grow is to attract new, less affluent customers. The result is a more inclusive market.

At the same time, consumer lending is becoming more and more rigid. Banks are still learning about the new technologies of consumer lending, but the tendency is to centralize lending in a single credit processing center. This will erase the importance of local knowledge and impose a more universal and consistent system of criteria. As banks move in this direction, it will become impossible for someone who was turned down in one branch to get the loan from another.

Differences will fade not just within a single bank but also across banks. At this point, banks are still testing various submarkets. Some banks offer promotions to students, others to Internet users, others to good customers of cell phone companies, yet others to employees of their corporate clients. This creates a measure of diversity across lenders, even if these groups often overlap but there are groups, such as the elderly, who are not considered by any of the banks. However, as banks converge on a common methodology of client selection ('best practices') and as they learn from their own experience and from each other which groups are the desirable ones, there will be social groups that will find it consistently difficult to borrow throughout the entire market (or will be able to get loans only on predatory terms).

If the sorting of customers would be optimally designed to minimize non-payment,[26] there would still be two issues of concern. First, routinized sorting assigns individuals to groups and treats them not as individuals but as group members. This means that in groups where non-payment is relatively high (say 20 or 30 percent) all group members (including the other paying 80 or 70 percent) will be treated as high risk. The point is that the statistical models have large errors: they predict many people to be bad debtors who end up being good and forecast good behavior for many people who end up behaving badly.

The second concern is that because these models mechanically project past performance to the future, they are likely to lock poor groups into their unfavorable position and out of the opportunities provided by credit. Once a bad risk, always a bad risk.

There is no doubt that lenders will discriminate. After all, they must discriminate between good and bad borrowers. Unfair discrimination is in the way the judgment distributes its errors among different groups in the population. The literature argues that statistical decision making is less discriminatory than old-style human judgment. The empirical evidence given is lending to women in the United States, where the personal judgment of loan officers (who, until routinization deskilled the job, were mostly male) tended to prefer men while 'objective' statistical models actually favor women (Johnson 2004). But the lessons of gender discrimination in the United States may not generalize to other cases. It is hard to argue that quick decisions about a large number of complete strangers will be more error prone if done by fallible humans than computers (Rona-Tas forthcoming). The question then is as some of the old categories of discrimination will be supplanted by new methods of sorting, which are the new groups who will suffer unfair discrimination?

The slowly emerging system of mass consumer credit prizes stability. The system discriminates against the self-employed, who may be rejected even if they earn more than do employees simply because their income flow is less predictable and sometimes they are harder to anchor. The new system rewards people with educational credentials regardless of content or value and thus discriminates against those without formal degrees. Availability of the applicant is rewarded, so anyone who lives in an area where telephone landlines are hard to come by, such as people in the countryside, will be at a disadvantage.

New consumer credit strongly discriminates against older people. Most lenders have an upper age limit – usually between 60 and 65 – on eligibility to apply. One Czech bank decided to offer credit cards to university faculty, only to find out that many of the top professors did not qualify. They were too old. In fact, credit benefits mostly the younger age groups. For one thing, they are the ones that need it most. At the beginning of their life cycle they must invest in their household: buy a home, furnish it, purchase appliances etc.; yet they have little savings. Not surprisingly, they are the most interested in borrowing (Toth and Arvai 2001).

Credit comes with strings attached. The installments must be paid regularly. If one becomes unemployed even temporarily, debt makes job loss even more painful (just as saving can cushion its impact). Anyone who is fired, leaves a job voluntarily, or gets sick and carries a mortgage or a car payment will find it difficult not just to hang on to her house or car, but to avoid getting on some blacklist of bad debtors.[27] This increases the employer's power over his indebted employees. Employers are key to get the employee the loan, but once the loan is secured the loan acts as a disciplinary force serving the employer. The obligation to the bank increases the worker's commitment to her job, and employers' powers are enhanced.

With the ability to take bank loans, people depend less and less on the financial support of their family and friends. Bank credit, therefore, will weaken family ties and the extended family will lose one of its reasons for being. Still, borrowing from kin might be preferable as relatives are less likely to be inflexible if some difficulty arises and ask no or little interest. But because this type of lending is embedded in a complex set of obligations, one may have to pay for the loan in circuitous ways that seem completely unrelated to borrowing.

The availability of consumer credit for young people means that it takes them less time to become financially independent from their parents. With a vigorous mortgage market, young people can move out of their parental home more easily. The way to get to a house or an apartment in the old days was either to enter a hopelessly long bureaucratic queue for a flat in public housing or to build one's own house. Building a house required a tremendous amount of time and work at a young age, and a lot of help. Some of it was financial and came primarily from parents, but a lot more came in the form of labor, information, and assorted favors from friends and acquaintances. This created a dense system of reciprocity and mutual obligations (Kenedi 1980; Rona-Tas 1997; Sik 1988). In the countryside, it reinforced extended families and distant kinship ties. But even in the city, it mobilized a large social network of helpers. Borrowing others' help meant that one was obliged to pay back the debt in kind. With bank loans, much of the labor can be purchased for money from strangers. The poor will still prefer labor exchange, as they might not qualify for a mortgage loan or they still might find it cheaper to spend time and not money as their wages may be very low. But an increasing number of people will opt for credit, dispensing with the thick network of mutual help. Then their fate will be tied not to the fortunes of people they know, can communicate with and influence, but to those of strangers who are sorted into the same categories as themselves.

Credit also forces people to be more rational and calculative. They must draw up a budget and plan ahead. They must wrestle with time as money in the form of interest and depreciation (or appreciation), and meet payment schedules punctually. In transition countries, consumer credit may introduce some of the very same bourgeois values – self-discipline, rationality etc. – that Western critics accuse credit of destroying. But consumer credit indeed abets a consumer culture fixated on material goods. Credit is always advertised as the key to the glorified life style of consumption and instant gratification. Yet it would be a mistake to place the primary responsibility for consumerism on consumer credit. In transition countries, rampant materialism had been firmly in place well before consumer credit emerged. Just as elsewhere, consumer credit is as much a result of materialism as it is its cause.

Conclusion

In transition countries, the social infrastructure of modern consumer credit is still underdeveloped, although the Central European countries are more advanced than their eastern and southeastern neighbors. There are still a series of issues that require legislative attention to protect and aid both lenders and borrowers. Borrowers must be educated about debt in general.

There should be anti-usury and anti-discrimination laws and more transparency in credit conditions. Privacy of personal data should be guarded, but in such a way as to make a full-record credit bureau possible and to ensure a balance between the banks' legitimate needs for information and clients' needs for privacy. There should be more efficient methods of legal sanctioning of non-payment, including a system of voluntary arbitration that can relieve the court system.

Bankruptcy protection should be extended to individuals. Personal bankruptcy protection is still viewed by most banks as a license to default, and they do not favor such legislation. Nevertheless, a properly balanced personal bankruptcy law would protect not just the debtor but also his creditors. The temporary sheltering of the debtor makes it more likely that at least some of the debt will be paid, and that claims among various creditors will be handled in a predictable and equitable manner. Finally, a more efficient tax system is needed.

Civic action also has a role to play. Non-governmental organizations can provide information and education about credit and personal finances. These NGOs can help with consumer protection, personal data protection, debt counseling, and with setting up small credit associations. With the displacement of social networks by statistical categories, those sorted together on the basis of certain characteristics such as gender, student status, age or ethnicity, have to form their own associations to represent their cause vis-à-vis financial institutions. Banks must also have their own associations that allow them to cooperate in a politically accountable manner.

Modern consumer credit based on rationalized, impersonalized and routinized processes is at an early stage in transition countries. The global economic crisis will undoubtedly slow down the development of consumer credit and may even result in fundamental changes in lending. Yet in one form or another, consumer credit will play an important role in these societies and proper regulation through legislation and civic action will have to play a larger role to counter some of its ill-effects.

Notes

1. *The Economist,* 27 February 2003.
2. The relationship between credit and civil society has been discussed most extensively in the context of public finance (Centeno 2002; Ferguson 2001; MacDonald 2003; Mac-Donald and Gastman 2001). Public finance, as it emerged originally in renaissance Italy and became a central force in structuring the state's bond with society in late seventeenth-century England to spread to the rest of the Western world, created a new relationship between the sovereign and his subjects. The ruler engaged in war had to mobilize resources. War finance could not be based solely on savings of the treasury and therefore governments had to turn to citizens for loans. The domestic bond market built on the voluntary participation of citizen creditors required a form of government where the borrower's absolute power had to be curtailed so that repayment did not hinge solely on the borrower's whim, as few would have assented to lending to a despotic state that had the power to annul the lending contract. The contractual nature of credit required that the two parties enter their agreement as quasi-equals as the lender had to trust the borrower. Indebtedness of the state, of course, has never guaranteed democracy or even political accountability. The effect of public debt not surprisingly has always depended on who lent the money and whether the state was strong enough fiscally to return the loan. States indebted abroad, to foreign financiers, were under no obligation whatsoever to treat their own citizens with special consideration. In fact, despots, capable of squeezing their own subjects without democratic constraints often seemed to be better risks for foreign lenders than unruly democracies. The ability of the state to repay the loan is also important. Weak states that are unable to pay off debts can end up in a debt spiral and soon will find earlier debts a serious limitation on their capacity to attend to their basic tasks. Latin American states exemplify this problem that did not have the power to mobilize the resources necessary for mass wars of military conquest (Centeno 2002). They did borrow to finance limited although often very bloody clashes with other countries but then to repay their debt they were unable to build a proper system of taxation and relied on state monopoly over natural resources or custom duties instead.
3. Interest is not the only way to price credit. Dividend, when payment is set as a percentage of future profits is a different one. Islam bankers heeding to religious imperatives not to charge interest collect fees (see Maurer 2002).
4. Philosophically, the debate over interest turned on the conception of time. Interest is essentially a rent on time, and collecting rent can be justified only if time is scarce and valued. Time becomes scarce once a cyclical concept of time based on natural life cycles of the seasons and the biological world is supplanted by the idea of a linear and irreversible flow of time, a notion of history. Christianity, through its teachings on eschatology, did introduce this linear notion to the pagan world of medieval Europe: the world was moving inescapably towards the last judgment (Gurevich 1985; Le Goff 1989). Time was quickly depleting; time became scarce. But time on earth was not valuable, because it was just the prelude to or a shadow of the sacred life beyond. Only when life on this earth became revalorized during the Renaissance, and when, through Protestantism, the life beyond faded and the last judgment became postponed indefinitely, did time become valuable, thus opening the gate to guiltless interest collection (Weber [1904] 2001).
5. It is no coincidence that the earliest development of the technology of credit happened in long-distance trade.
6. These categories assume no actual connection among those who belong to them and are based on some abstract common characteristics.
7. Lenders still must trust the institutions that provide the information and the often quite technical methods they use but not always fully understand. We call this confidence because this kind of trust refers to abstract entities and not to people.

8. In transition countries, non-bank finance companies are still a novelty and in some lending is explicitly limited to banks by law.
9. For exceptions in the economics literature, see Ausubel (1991) and Prelec and Simester (2001).
10. Most important ones are the Equal Credit Opportunity Act of 1974, 1976 and the Home Mortgage Disclosure Act of 1975.
11. There is also a tremendous inertia lodged in the application form itself. Banks are very reluctant to change application forms because they have to reprint and distribute them, field questions from confused staff and correct unforeseen errors. There is also a clear limit to the length and complexity of these forms. In banks, marketing people always push for shorter, simpler forms, whereas risk managers want longer questionnaires with more sophisticated information.
12. In Argentina, banks for a certain class of high risk applicants make home visits. In transition countries, this would be very unusual.
13. Collateral is useless without clear property titles, easily accessible in well-maintained business and property registries (De Soto 2000).
14. One way of improving the tax system is to curtail cash transactions and expand the role of electronic payment. Here banks can play an important role.
15. The actual judgment can be more complex involving the terms of the loan.
16. There is also a fourth method in between rules and statistical algorithms. It is a point system, where rules are quantified and are used not in a binary, yes/no fashion, but by assigning weights to each. These weights, however, are not the products of statistical modeling, but they reflect expert opinion.
17. In some countries, like Russia, this is rarely asked. The assumption is that friends of clients will not give any information to lenders anyway, not to seem disloyal to their friends.
18. Credit bureaus can include information about corporations and/or individual borrowers. The distinction between corporation and individuals gets somewhat blurred for the individual entrepreneur, of which there are many in transition countries. Formalized reputation systems exist also at the company and state level. States (just as large companies) usually receive credit ratings from specialized international agencies that keep a registry of states (and large companies). The three largest, international credit rating agencies are Standard & Poor's, Moody's and Fitch.
19. For companies this is easier. They go out of business and resurface under new names.
20. Unless, of course, they steal someone else's identity and history with it.
21. Big banks will know about more bad customers than any smaller bank.
22. In both countries, the credit bureaus are bracing for legal challenges. The uncertainty about the legality of full-record credit bureaus is bigger in the Czech case, where some banks decided to take a wait and see attitude.
23. In the United States, there is a fourteen-day bundling rule. Inquiries within a fourteen-day period are considered as a single inquiry.
24. This expansive power of quantification is akin to what happened to IQ. A measure, originally designed to gauge learning difficulty in school became a widely used measure of cognitive ability of any kind. It is no coincidence that some companies request SAT 1 scores along with credit scores from applicants to judge ability and character.
25. 'TXU to Peg Some Customers' Rates to Credit Scores', *USA Today*, 9 September 2004.
26. Minimizing non-payment is different from maximizing profit. Sometimes non-paying customers are among the most profitable if they eventually pay up with penalty, and promptly paying customers can be loss-makers, as it happens in the U.S. with credit cards, where the main source of income from clients is interest and a client who pays fully during the interest-free grace period is a loss-maker and is free riding on those who revolve their debts.
27. Some banks offer insurance against sickness and unemployment, but it is usually expensive and debtors rarely buy it.

References

Ausubel, Lawrence M. 1991. 'The Failure of Competition in the Credit Card Market', *American Economic Review* 81, no. 1: 50–81.

Babeau, André and Teresa Sbano. 2003. 'Household Wealth in the National Accounts of Europe, the United States and Japan', *OECD Working Paper Series*, 2.

Bell, Daniel. 1976. *The Coming of Post-Industrial Society*. New York: Basic Books.

Bernstein, Lisa. 1992. 'Opting Out of the Legal System: Extralegal Contractual Relations in the Diamond Industry', *Journal of Legal Studies* 21: 115–157.

Boorstin, Daniel. 1973. *The Americans: The Democratic Experience*. New York: Random House.

Bowker, Geoffrey C., and Susan Leigh Star. 1999. *Sorting Things Out: Classification and Its Consequences*. Cambridge, MA: MIT Press.

Calder, Lendol. 1999. *Financing the American Dream: A Cultural History of Consumer Credit*. Princeton, NJ: Princeton University Press.

Centeno, Miguel Angel. 2002. *Blood and Debt: War and the Nation-State in Latin America*. University Park: Pennsylvania State University Press.

Christensen, Betina Sand, and Tue Mollerup Mathiasen. 2002. 'Household Financial Wealth: Trends, Structures and Valuation Methods'. Paper presented at the 27th General Conference of the International Association for Research in Income and Wealth, Stockholm, Sweden. August.

Cottarelli, Carlo, Giovanni Dell'Ariccia and Ivanna Vladkova-Hollar. 2003. 'Early Birds, Late Risers, and Sleeping Beauties: Bank Credit Growth to the Private Sector in Central and Eastern Europe and in the Balkans'. Paper presented at the Ninth Dubrovnik Economic Conference. June.

De Soto, Hernando. 2000. *The Mystery of Capital*. New York: Basic Books.

Desrosières, Alain. 1998. *The Politics of Large Numbers: A History of Statistical Reasoning*. Trans. Camille Naish. Cambridge, MA: Harvard University Press.

Ferguson, Niall. 2001. *The Cash Nexus: Money and Power in the Modern World, 1700–2000*. New York: Basic Books.

Finn, Margot C. 2003. *The Character of Credit: Personal Debt in English Culture, 1740–1914*. Cambridge: Cambridge University Press.

Foucault, Michel. 1973. *The Order of Things: An Archaeology of the Human Sciences*. New York: Vintage.

_____. 1979. *Discipline and Punish: The Birth of the Prison*. New York: Vintage.

Galanoy, Terry. 1980. *Charge It! Inside the Credit Card Conspiracy*. New York: Putnam.

Galbraith, John Kenneth. 1958. *The Affluent Society*. Boston, MA: Houghton Mifflin.

Gandy, Oscar H., Jr. 1993. *The Panoptic Sort: A Political Economy of Personal Information*. Boulder, CO: Westview Press.

Gelpi, Rosa-Maria, and Francois Julien-Labruyere. 2000. *The History of Consumer Credit: Doctrines and Practices*. London: Palgrave Macmillan.

Greif, Avner. 1989. 'Reputation and Coalitions in Medieval Trade: Evidence on the Maghribi Traders', *Journal of Economic History* 49, no. 4: 857–882.

Guinnane, Timothy W. 2002. 'Delegated Monitors, Large and Small: Germany's Banking System, 1800–1914', *Journal of Economic Literature* 40, no. 1: 73–124.

Gurevich, Aron Iakovlevich. 1985. *Categories of Medieval Culture*. Trans. George Campbell. Boston: Routledge & Kegan Paul.

Hoffman, Philip T., Gilles Postel-Vinay and Jean-Laurent Rosenthal. 2000. *Priceless Markets: The Political Economy of Credit in Paris, 1660–1870*. Chicago, IL: University of Chicago Press.

Johnson, R. W. 2004. 'Legal, Social, and Economic Issues in Implementing Scoring in the United States', in *Readings in Credit Scoring: Recent Developments, Advances, and Aims*, ed. Lyn C. Thomas, David B. Edelman and Jonathan N. Crook. Oxford: Oxford University Press, pp. 5–15.

Katz, Michael L., and Carl Shapiro. 1986. 'Technology Adoption in the Presence of Network Externalities', *Journal of Political Economy* 94, no. 4: 822–841.

Kellison, Bruce, Patrick Brockett, Seon-Hi Shin and Shihong Li. 2003. 'A Statistical Analysis of the Relationship between Credit History and Insurance Losses', Bureau of Business Research, University of Texas at Austin.

Kenedi, Janos. 1980. *Do It Yourself!* London: Pluto Press.

Landa, Janet Tai. 1995. *Trust, Ethnicity, and Identity: Beyond the New Institutional Economics of Ethnic Trading Networks, Contract Law, and Gift-Exchange.* Ann Arbor: University of Michigan Press.

Lasch, Christopher. 1979. *The Culture of Narcissism: American Life in an Age of Diminishing Expectations.* New York: Warner Books.

Le Goff, Jacques. 1989. *Medieval Civilization, 400–1500.* Trans. Julia Barrow. New York: Basil Blackwell.

Leyshon, Andrew, and Nigel Thrift. 1999. 'Lists Come Alive: Electronic Systems of Knowledge and the Rise of Credit-Scoring in Retail Banking', *Economy and Society* 28: 434–466.

Lyon, David. 1994. *The Electronic Eye: The Rise of Surveillance Society.* Minneapolis: Minnesota University Press.

_____, ed. 2003. *Surveillance as Social Sorting.* London: Routledge.

MacDonald, James. 2003. *The Financial Roots of Democracy.* New York: Farrar, Straus and Giroux.

MacDonald, Scott B., and Albert L. Gastman. 2001. *A History of Credit and Power in the Western World.* New Brunswick, NJ: Transaction Publishers.

Manning, Robert D. 2000. *Credit Card Nation: The Consequences of America's Addiction to Credit.* New York: Basic Books.

Maurer, Bill. 2002. 'Anthropological and Accounting Knowledge in Islamic Banking and Finance: Rethinking Critical Accounts', *Journal of the Royal Anthropological Institute* 8, no. 4: 645–667.

Medoff, James, and Andrew Harless. 1996. *The Indebted Society: Anatomy of an Ongoing Disaster.* Boston, MA: Little Brown.

Muldrew, Craig. 1998. *The Economy of Obligation: The Culture of Credit and Social Relations in Early Modern England.* London: Macmillan.

Munnell, Alicia H., Geoffrey M. B. Tootell, Lynn E. Browne and James McEneaney. 1996. 'Mortgage Lending in Boston: Interpreting HMDA Data', *The American Economic Review* 86, no. 1: 25–53.

Norris, James D. 1978. *R. G. Dun & Co., 1841–1900: The Development of Credit Reporting in the Nineteenth Century.* Westport, CT: Greenwood Press.

Olegario, Rowena. 1999. '"That Mysterious People": Jewish Merchants, Transparency, and Community in Mid-nineteenth Century America', *Business History Review* 73, no. 2: 161–189.

Olney, Martha L. 1991. *Buy Now, Pay Later: Advertising, Credit, and Consumer Durables in the 1920s.* Chapel Hill: University of North Carolina Press.

Prelec, Drazen, and Duncan Simester. 2001. 'Always Leave Home Without It: A Further Investigation of the Credit-Card Effect on Willingness to Pay', *Marketing Letters* 12, no. 1: 5–12.

Ritzer, George. 1995. *Expressing America: A Critique of the Global Credit Card Society.* Thousand Oaks, CA: Pine Forge Press.

Rona-Tas, Akos. 1997. *Great Surprise of the Small Transformation: Demise of Communism and Rise of the Private Sector in Hungary.* Ann Arbor: University of Michigan Press.

_____. 1998. 'Path-Dependence and Capital Theory: Sociology of the Post-Communist Economic Transformation', *East European Politics and Societies* 12, no. 1: 107–131.

_____. Forthcoming. 'Uncertainty and Credit Card Markets', in *Institutionalism in Economics and Sociology: Variety, Dialogue and Future Challenges*, ed. Klaus Nielsen and Carsten A. Koch. Northampton, MA: Edward Elgar.

Rona-Tas, Akos, and Alya Guseva. 2001. 'Uncertainty, Risk and Trust: Russian and American Credit Card Markets Compared', *American Sociological Review* 66, no. 5: 623–646.

Rule, James B., Douglas McAdam, Linda Stearns and David Uglow. 1983. 'Documentary Identification and Mass Surveillance in the United States', *Social Problems* 31, no. 2: 222–234.

Sik, Endre. 1988. 'Reciprocal Exchange of Labour: The Hungarian Case', in *On Work*, ed. Ray Pahl. Oxford: Basil Blackwell, pp. 527–547.

Stiglitz, Joseph E., and Andrew Weiss. 1981. 'Credit Rationing in Markets with Imperfect Information', *American Economic Review* 71, no. 3: 393–410.

Sullivan, Ceri. 2002. *The Rhetoric of Credit: Merchants in Early Modern Writing*. Madison, NJ: Fairleigh Dickinson University Press.

Tenenbaum, Shelly. 1993. *Credit to their Community: Jewish Loan Societies in the United States, 1880–1945*. Detroit, MI: Wayne State University Press.

Torpey, John. 1998. 'Coming and Going: On the State Monopolization of the Legitimate "Means of Movement"', *Sociological Theory* 16, no. 3: 239–259.

Toth, Istvan Janos, and Zsofia Arvai. 2001. 'Liquidity Constraints and Consumer Impatience', *National Bank of Hungary, Working Paper Series*, 2.

Tucker, David M. 1991. *The Decline of Thrift in America*. New York: Praeger.

Weber, Max. [1904] 2001. *The Protestant Ethic and the Spirit of Capitalism*. Trans. Talcott Parsons; with an introduction by Anthony Giddens. New York: Routledge.

Chapter 6

THE POLITICS OF CIVIC COMBINATIONS

Laszlo Bruszt and Balazs Vedres

Over the last decade, social and developmental partnerships have increasingly involved civic organizations. The emergence of these new localized developmental partnership forms originates from a previous episode of institutional experimentation.[1] Faced with the failures of various market- and state-led developmental programs, national governments, international financial institutions and multilateral development agencies search for a third way, or a new way to organize development (Evans 1997; Howell and Pearce 2002). With the goals of inducing economic growth, furthering the development of market institutions or increasing social and economic cohesion, international developmental agencies have played a major role in reviving the search for ways to capitalize on the collective problem-solving capacities of combined local stakeholders (OECD 1995; UNDP 1993, 1995; World Bank 1992, 1996). Such partnership projects, with state, business, and civic participation became one of the most contested forms of institutional experimentation. While some describe these institutional developments as democratic innovation, others see them as new forms of depoliticization and domination.

Developmental partnerships that combine civic organizations with state and market actors are viewed in two diametrically opposing ways in the literature. For those who are supportive, the combination of civic organizations with diverse state and non-state actors represents an innovative form of institutional experimentation. In their view, it allows diverse actors in local societies to combine and address problems of market and state failure.[2] These combinations represent an alternative way of governing collective action among actors from diverse organizational fields with a stake in

---

Notes for this chapter are located on page 199.

local social and economic development. The inclusion of civic organizations (COs) in such developmental programs and policy making is seen from this perspective as empowering, giving room for COs to represent interests, considerations and values that would otherwise be excluded. From this perspective, civic combination with state and market actors is seen as a mechanism that allows for decentralized social experimentation and for accommodating a greater diversity of social goals in developmental programs (Brown et al. 2001; Bruszt and Stark 2003; Gerstenberg and Sabel 2002; Sabel 1993, 1994, 1996; Stark et al. 2005).

Many others strongly reject these developmental combinations, arguing that they are nothing but merely a cost-effective way of alleviating some of the social and economic side effects of, variously, neo-liberal policies, the downsizing of the welfare state, or top-down developmental programs.[3] The combination of COs with diverse state and market actors at the domestic and supra-national levels turns them into service organizations, 'corporatizing' and depoliticizing them, leading to a loss of autonomy. In this approach, partnerships with state and business are contrasted with the *civic associationism* of a 'strong and vibrant civil society', and with *civic political activism*, the 'source of dissent, challenge and innovation, a countervailing force to government and the corporate sector' (Kaldor et al. 2003). If the political participation of COs in policy making is mentioned, it is described as a means to 'provide a semblance of democratic legitimacy' (Anderson 2000: 95). Instead of empowerment, this area within the literature presents their participation in partnerships with state and/or business as a mechanism of dis-empowerment, and depoliticization.

Our task in this chapter is to study the relationship between closeness to the state and civic autonomy. To do so, we have conducted a survey of 740 of the largest civic associations in three Hungarian regions, allowing us (1) to document the prevalence of their interactions with the state and other non-civic actors charting the varieties these interactions take, and (2) to document the prevalence of various developmental goals and diverse types of political action undertaken by these organizations, and to register changes in their goals and political activities. Most importantly, our data allow us (3) to analyze the relationship between these processes as we investigate whether interactions with the state come at the expense of the autonomy of civic organizations, their depoliticizing, or their giving up on (some of) their goals. Are Hungarian civic associations losing their autonomy just at the moment when they reach out to participate in collaborative developmental projects, or are there mechanisms at work that allow collaborative associations with state and other actors outside the civic sector to co-exist with the maintenance of civic autonomy?

These questions are especially important from the viewpoint of the evolution of fledgling civil societies in the Central European new member countries of the European Union. The introduction of new European developmental programs in these countries led to a rapid increase in the numbers of diverse local and regional developmental partnership projects. In Hungary, for example, more than twenty thousands project were submitted for consideration during the first year of the National Development Plan, with around half involving civic organizations. In our survey of the largest regional CO projects in Hungary we found that nearly two-thirds of CO projects involved collaboration with actors from diverse organizational fields (state, business, science, education, media, church, etc.). In more than half of the projects, the partners of COs included at least one (local, regional or national) state actor.[4]

Civic organizations in these countries are drawn into partnership projects within a political framework that provides central state agencies with the right to define developmental goals and 'best practice' in achieving them (Bruszt 2002). Put differently, the increasing inclusion of civic organizations in diverse partnership projects in these countries goes hand in hand with attempts at (re)centralization and the technocratic depoliticization of regional development. COs are invited primarily to compete ('tender') for the right to participate in the *implementation* of the centrally defined developmental programs. They have only a weak formal right to be consulted by planning authorities and must engage in political action if they wish to influence the formation of these developmental programs. But do they? Or do these societies face a forced choice between civic autonomy and mixing with the state?

We test several of these assumptions about the relationship between closeness to the state and autonomy of the COs below. We proceed in three steps, starting with the assumption that proximity to the state goes together with a loss of autonomy in civil society. First we analyze how the presence of a state partner in CO projects or ongoing activities affects changes in the number or mixture of goals, the loss of certain goals, and changes in political activism. Here, our assumption was that, if mixing with the state were to result in a loss of civic autonomy, we would find a narrower (less diverse) mix of goals, loss of a goal and decreased political activism by COs that enter into partnerships with the state. As we will see below, these expectations have proven to be unsupported by the data. We do find COs that give up on certain of their goals and that leave political action, but we cannot explain these changes by their closeness to the state. Rather, goal loss or political deactivation goes hand in hand with a distancing from the state.

In the second step, we test three alternative explanations for the loss of CO autonomy. None of these tests yields affirmative results. Collaborating with business works similarly to partnership with the state: it seems to hurt neither civic values nor goals. Nor do stopping collaboration with other civic organizations or getting out of public attention by cutting collaborative ties to media organizations account for loss in autonomy *per se*. It seems that civic control is maintained through different channels, not primarily through direct partnering with other NGOs or the media.

Here we are interested in the relationship between closeness to the state and the autonomy of COs. We were unable to find a positive answer to the question about the sources of declining CO autonomy. Given our measures for CO autonomy, we could 'only' establish that the idea that closeness to the state goes together with diminishing autonomy can be rejected. We find that a decline in the number and diminishing mix of goals, and waning political activism, go together with a distancing from the state. But do our indicators really measure autonomy? On the contrary, is it not possible that a presence or increase in political activism might indicate the loss or lack of autonomy? In the third step, we relax the assumption that political activism – our most important indicator – stands for civic autonomy, and instead test two hypotheses concerning political activism as a sign for lost or absent autonomy. An initial reason for political engagement might be that COs 'go for the money': thus, political activism could be predicted by prior funding from the state. A second reason may be that it is not the autonomous COs but rather the NGOs created by the (local) state which engage in political action. Around one-third of regional NGOs in Hungary were created not by civic actors but by the local state, and we might find that the state-created organizations are primarily behind political activism. We test both of these hypotheses: if loss of autonomy or the absence thereof has independent explanatory power in accounting for political action, we cannot reject the assumption, held by representatives of the pessimistic view, that closeness to the state and organizational autonomy are negatively related.

We have no reasons to assume that it is only the loss of autonomy or its absence which can stand for political activism. In our model accounting for political activism, we controlled for several alternative explanations for political activism, drawing freely on organizational theories and theories developed on the basis of the study of the political organization of business interests. We found no support for the thesis that political activity is solely about money, or that activism would be the preserve of state-made NGOs. We identify several mechanisms that make COs combine participation in partnership projects with autonomous political action.

Data

To identify the relationship between collaboration with the state and civic autonomy, we draw on data from a survey of Hungarian regional civic associations that we conducted in 2003 in three 'statistical regions'.[5] From among the seven 'statistical regions', we choose the following three: (1) Western Hungary, the most developed region in Hungary that received the largest share of the FDI from among the different regions; (2) the Northern Plain, the region most affected by the social and economic dislocations of economic transformation in Hungary; and (3) the Southern Plain, a region representing roughly the Hungarian average, both in the level of economic development and in the types of problems that it faces. Using the database of the Hungarian Statistical Office (HSO) on NGOs in these three regions, we compiled a list that ranked non-profit organizations by the size of their budgets. We excluded organizations in the field of sports (e.g. soccer leagues) and leisure-time activities (e.g. stamp collectors) as well as foundations whose sole purpose is to support a single organization (e.g. the fundraising arm of a museum, hospital, school or church). From the remaining list, one-third of the organizations are 'subsidiaries' of the local state: an NGO created by the local government. These organizations were not excluded from the list; instead, their presence in the sample allows us to compare the autonomy and political activity of COs and 'subsidiary' NGOs. We employed students of the Institute of Social and European Studies (ISES) at Daniel Berzsenyi College in Szombathely, which has a center of regional studies with a strong track record in empirical research on regional development, to administer our survey instrument of face-to-face interviews, typically with the elected president or chief executive officer of the organization, or their deputies. From an initial list of approximately 900 of the largest civic associations in these three 'regions' we were able to successfully contact 740 organizations distributed roughly equally among the three 'regions'.

We took as a unit of our analysis the projects of these organizations. We asked the representatives of these organizations to tell us how many projects they had undertaken during the last two years. If they had more than three projects we asked them to identify the three most important ones and then asked questions concerning these projects. If they had three or less, we asked questions concerning these projects. If they had none, we asked questions about their ongoing activity.

We defined closeness to the state as active collaboration with at least one type of state agency in developmental projects and/or in the ongoing activities of a CO. We measure state proximity by the presence of a state partner in projects or ongoing activity. Civil society autonomy, with reference to civic organizations, was defined as the power to make the rules that govern the internal affairs of the organization. The most important of these internal affairs is setting the goals of the organization. A CO is autonomous to the degree to which it can uphold its own values while selectively taking into account the interests of others, making use of diverse external opportunities. We measure civil society autonomy along the following dimensions:

change of goal mix (the number of goals), loss of a certain goal, and changes in political activism.

We defined a project as 'combinatory' if it had two or more different types of goals and had two or more types of collaborative partners. For the identification of goals pursued in the projects, we have used a list of twenty-two developmental goals that we took from the Regional Development Plans of these three regions.[6] For each project, we asked whether the furthering of any of these goals was among the goals pursued by the project. To identify the partners involved in these projects, we used a list of fifteen types of actors and for each project asked which had participated in the project.[7]

Political activism in general refers to intentional action to bring about social or political change. Activism might be oriented towards diverse social constituencies or towards various authorities, or might combine both. In the first case, COs might try to create change by trying to alter the way people see specific issues, or to make them act and thereby attain their active participation in collective action. In the second case, we are concerned with action by COs to alter regulations, laws and/or policies directly or indirectly at various levels of the state. Direct forms of political action include attempts to alter regulations or laws at different levels of the state, or lobbying for a policy goal. We define indirect forms of political action as attempts to change balance of forces in the CO's area of the activity.

For the first dimension of political activism, viz. that oriented towards diverse social constituencies, we asked questions about how often the organization tries to change public opinion, to induce their active participation and/or to increase bottom up initiatives in general. For political activism oriented towards authorities, we asked how often the organization tries to put issues on the political agenda, to change regulation at the level of national or local/regional government and/or alter the balance of forces in its own area of activity ('never', 'sometimes', 'often' or 'always'). To identify project-related political activity, we asked of each project separately whether it included any of the following activities: organization of a demonstration; petitioning; lobbying the parliament; lobbying the central government; lobbying country and lobbying local government. We found a strong correlation between activism oriented towards social constituencies and activism oriented towards authorities: those engaged in one of these types of activism are significantly more likely to engage in one of the activities that forms part of the other dimension. Because in this chapter we discuss the effects of closeness to the state, we focus on forms of political activism oriented towards the authorities.

As an alternative explanation for political activity, we used embedding in local society. We defined embedding as relationships of formal and informal accountability which tie a CO to diverse actors in local society. We speak of formal accountability when a local CO has to report formally to various local social actors. We speak of informal accountability when a local CO has to take into account the interests of various local actors when making decisions. We have included members, clients, other domestic NGOs, media and newspapers, trade unions and the general public among local social actors. Because of their increased local activity in Hungary, we have also added foreign NGOs to this list. For each of these types of actors, we asked how often the CO has to report to them and how often has it to take their interests into account when making decisions ('never', 'sometimes', 'often' or 'always').

State Proximity and Autonomy

The assumption in the literature on civil society is that proximity to the state goes together with a loss of autonomy in civil society. To evaluate this hypothesis we need to operationalize two concepts: state proximity and civil society autonomy. We measure state proximity by the presence of a state partner in CO projects or ongoing activity. We measure civil society autonomy along the following dimensions: change of goal mix (the number of types of goals, e.g. economic, social, environmental), loss of a goal, and change in political activism. To address the dynamics of civil society autonomy, we use only those COs that had at least one project so that we can compare with ongoing activities, assuming that ongoing activities precede that project. Since only about half of the organizations engaged in projects, we work with between 347 and 383 cases, depending on missing responses to the variable in focus.

After operationalizing state proximity and civil society autonomy, the next, and simplest, step is to create a two-by-two table: proximity to the state or no proximity, by autonomy or no autonomy (table 6.1). (Logistic regressions then provide more sophisticated versions of this simple table, including controls.)

State Proximity and Goals

In this first test, we focus on the goals of the organization. Goals represent a fundamental level of organizational autonomy. Resources, regulations, activism are aspects that are influenced by many contingencies, scarcities, or limitations in organizational capacities. Setting goals is somehow prior to these operational steps. We argue that if we find that state proximity leads to the loss of goals, then we capture a fundamental process of losing autonomy. Table 6.1 shows that with this first approach, we can reject the

Table 6.1 State Proximity and Goal Mix

			Single Goal		Total
			No	Yes	
State proximity	No	Count	76	84	160
		Row %	47.5	52.5	100.0
		Adj. Res.	–2.5	2.5	
	Yes	Count	114	73	187
		Row %	61.0	39.0	100.0
		Adj. Res.	2.5	-2.5	
Total		Count	190	157	347
		Row %	54.8	45.2	100.0

Chi-squared=6.31, p=.012

hypothesis that state proximity goes together with a narrower definition of goals. Those NGOs that are proximate to the state are more likely to have multiple goals (a more diversified goal mix).

Why go further? Because with this table we do not know if those NGOs that become proximate to the state were different from the state-less NGOs in terms of their goals *before* they became proximate to the state. There are several mechanisms that one can cite which would predict that goal diversification can lead to state proximity. For example: more diverse goals mean that there is a higher likelihood of meeting more diverse partners, and so a higher likelihood of meeting state actors. It may then be that this state partnership makes some of these diversified organizations drop their goals.

This simple model leaves many questions open. The first and most important is: does state proximity cause loss of autonomy, or does lack of autonomy cause state proximity? Moreover, state proximity and lack of autonomy can arise at the same moment, in the case of state created NGOs. This prompts a dynamic analysis: beyond measuring state proximity we should measure tendencies in state proximity (moving towards the state, or away from the state, or staying close, or staying away). We also need to measure tendencies in autonomy in the same way. This allows a temporal order to be established.

The basic table in this approach is a four-by-four table (table 6.2). This table provides further evidence to reject the hypothesis that state proximity leads to the loss of civil society autonomy. According to the hypothesis, an NGO moving towards the state (from having no state partner to having a state partner) should have decreased goal diversity (the goal mix should become less mixed). This does not happen. Moves in the direction of the state go hand in hand with a declining probability of reduced goal diversity.

Table 6.2 State Proximity Dynamics and Goal Mix Change

			Goal Mix Change				Total
			1 Stays Single Issue	2 More Mix	3 Less Mix	4 Stays Mixed	
State proximity dynamics	1 state–state	Count	26	24	26	59	135
		Row %	19.3	17.8	19.3	43.7	100.0
		Adj. Res.	−2.0	−.6	−.3	2.6	
	2 state–no state	Count	12	14	16	19	61
		Row %	19.7	23.0	26.2	31.1	100.0
		Adj. Res.	−1.1	.8	1.3	−.8	
	3 no state–state	Count	16	15	5	16	52
		Row %	30.8	28.8	9.6	30.8	100.0
		Adj. Res.	1.0	1.9	−2.1	−.8	
	4 no state–no state	Count	33	14	23	29	99
		Row %	33.3	14.1	23.2	29.3	100.0
		Adj. Res.	2.2	−1.5	.9	−1.5	
Total		Count	87	67	70	123	347
		Row %	25.1	19.3	20.2	35.4	100.0

Chi-squared=19.09, p=.024

Another expectation is that those NGOs that stay away from the state should be over-represented among those NGOs that maintain a diverse goal mix. This hypothesis is also not supported: the no state–no state sequence is negatively associated with maintaining a mixed goal portfolio (although the statistical association is not significant: the adjusted standardized Pearson residual is −1.5).

The patterns of this table suggest that different processes are at work. Those NGOs that are repeatedly proximate to the state (the state–state sequence) are the most likely to maintain a mixed goal portfolio (with an adjusted standardized residual of 2.6 this is a statistically significant association). Those NGOs that never partner with the state (no state–no state sequence) are statistically more likely to stay single-issue. Approaching the state ('no state–state') is associated with a growing (diversifying) mix of goals (adjusted residual of 1.9). While in the state leaving group (state–no state) the most over-represented category is a simplifying goal mix.

Changing state proximity is related to changing goal portfolio – but completely in the opposite direction that we expected. We also tested other aspects of autonomy. The first, still concerning goals, is whether becoming connected to the state means that an NGO drops goals that it had before.

This measure is different from the previous measure: goal diversity is more robust than any individual goals. An NGO can stay diversified in its goals yet lose one or more goals that it had before. We now test this more stringent criterion of losing autonomy (table 6.3).

Overall there is no significant relationship between state proximity dynamics and losing goals. The direction of the (weak) statistical association is opposite to what we expected. An NGO that become proximate to the state (no state–state) is slightly less likely than average to lose a goal. In the whole sample 27.1 percent of organizations lost a goal between their last two projects. Among those that become proximate to the state only 21.2 percent lost a goal. Among NGOs with stable state proximity (state–state) 24.4 percent lost a goal. NGOs that ceased to exhibit state proximity (state–no state) were the most likely category to experience goal loss: exactly one-third, 33.3 percent, of these NGOs lost a goal.

State Proximity and Political Activism

After analyzing goals, the next step is to understand actions. When discussing autonomy, the most important kind of action is political activism, involving some kind of contention. This is a critical capacity of civil society,

Table 6.3 State Proximity Dynamics and Goal Loss

			Lost a Goal		Total
			No	Yes	
State proximity dynamics	1 state–state	Count	102	33	135
		Row %	75.6	24.4	100.0
		Adj. Res.	.9	−.9	
	2 state–no state	Count	44	17	61
		Row %	72.1	27.9	100.0
		Adj. Res.	−.2	.2	
	3 no state–state	Count	41	11	52
		Row %	78.8	21.2	100.0
		Adj. Res.	1.0	−1.0	
	4 no state–no state	Count	66	33	99
		Row %	66.7	33.3	100.0
		Adj. Res.	−1.7	1.7	
Total		Count	253	94	347
		Row %	72.9	27.1	100.0

Chi-squared=3.38, p=.337

and contention is seen as involving the greatest risk when NGOs establish contacts with the state. Here again we focus on dynamics, changes in state proximity and changes in political activism.

Table 6.4 presents the results about political activism and state proximity. Overall, the statistical association is not significant. If we focus on standardized adjusted residuals, the highest deviation from expected frequencies is that those NGOs that exit state proximity (state–no state) also become more passive (active-passive sequence). This is contrary to the expectation that state proximity will decrease activism. On the other hand, when an NGO becomes proximate to the state (no state–state) then the sequence of political activation (passive-active) is over-represented. Contact with the state goes together with increasing political activism.

We have also used logistic regression models to tests the above hypotheses including controlling variables (results not shown here). They also failed to provide support for the hypothesis about the negative relationship between state proximity and autonomy. The models we used were not significant overall. In the model we tested with loss of goals as the dependent variable, the only significant coefficient we found was that approximating the state makes it significantly less likely that an organization will drop goals. In the model

Table 6.4 State Proximity Dynamics and Political Activism Change

			Political Activism Change				Total
			1 active–active	2 active–passive	3 passive–active	4 passive–passive	
State proximity dynamics	1 state–state	Count	10	10	15	106	141
		Row %	7.1	7.1	10.6	75.2	100.0
		Adj. Res.	.9	−.4	.5	−.6	
	2 state–no state	Count	3	10	3	49	65
		Row %	4.6	15.4	4.6	75.4	100.0
		Adj. Res.	−.4	2.5	−1.5	−.3	
	3 no state–state	Count	3	4	9	46	62
		Row %	4.8	6.5	14.5	74.2	100.0
		Adj. Res.	−.3	−.4	1.4	−.5	
	4 no state–no state	Count	6	6	10	93	115
		Row %	5.2	5.2	8.7	80.9	100.0
		Adj. Res.	−.3	−1.2	−.4	1.2	
Total		Count	22	30	37	294	383
		Row %	5.7	7.8	9.7	76.8	100.0

Chi-squared=10.57, p=.307

where political activism was the dependent variable, we found that organizations that leave the state are more likely to stop being politically active.

Loss of Autonomy: Alternative Explanations

We found that the dynamics of state proximity are not associated with changes in political activism in the hypothesized way. We subjected this negative finding to further scrutiny by assessing three alternative hypotheses. The lack of expected statistical association between state proximity, goal loss, and political activism can be attributed to competing forces that deactivate NGOs in the civic and political fields.

One alternative expectation is that the commodification of civil society projects leads to depoliticization. According to this expectation, as NGOs engage in partnerships with business organizations, they adopt the market regime of worth and think about their activities as marketable services. This framing might be incompatible with their previous goals, and especially political activism, so we expect NGOs to lose their political activism as they start collaborating with business organizations.

A second alternative expectation concerns the effects of losing civic control. NGOs often collaborate with other NGOs in their projects. These collaborations can be thought of as vehicles of collective monitoring, where it becomes possible to sanction divergence from civic values. Once NGOs leave such collaborative projects with other NGOs and engage in projects alone, they might loose civic control, and hence might be more likely to abandon previous goals, and less likely to engage in political activism.

A third alternative explanation for the loss of political activism concerns reduced public attention – cutting collaborative ties to media organizations. Reputation is an important currency in the NGO world. NGOs that collaborate with media organizations are probably more careful not to abandon civic goals. We expect that NGOs that move to projects without the participation of media organizations after previous projects with media partnerships will be more likely to abandon their original goals, and their political activism.

To test these alternative expectations we constructed contingency tables following the same logic that we used in testing the hypothesis about the dynamics of state proximity and change in political activism and the change in goals. Based on the Chi-square tests and Pearson standardized residuals we can reject all three alternative hypotheses.

As NGOs pick up project partnerships with businesses they become significantly more likely to pick up new goals, and thus follow more diverse goals. This is contrary to our expectations. NGOs do not drop their goals when they partner with a business; they do, however, lose goals when they exit such partnerships. Partnering with businesses does not seem to hurt civic values and goals. We found no statistical association between business partnership and political activism.

NGOs do not drop goals or become depoliticized when they leave projects with other NGOs and engage in solo projects. It seems that civic control is maintained through different channels, not primarily through co-organized projects.

The presence of media partners in NGO projects does not seem to be associated with goal loss or political deactivation. Again, we need to rethink the nature of the public in which civic projects are embedded. The absence of direct media attention does not result in NGO opportunism.

Factors of Political Action

We found no support for hypotheses about autonomy loss connected to state proximity. A declining number of goals diminishing mix of goals and waning political activism go together with a distancing from the state. But do our indicators really measure autonomy? For example, might it not be possible that, to the contrary, the presence of, or increase in, political activism indicates a loss or lack of autonomy?

We stated that the most important kind of action in the context of autonomy is political activism involving some kind of contention. This is a critical capacity of civil society, and contention is seen at the highest risk when NGOs establish contacts with the state. In previous analyses, we assumed that political action is an automatic sign of civic autonomy. Here, we relax this assumption and consider alternative explanations for political action. It might be that political activism is not about autonomy but, to the contrary, is a sign of the lost or non-existent autonomy of these organizations.

One possibility that we have considered was that political action was primarily about money: political action might have not much to do with the desire to represent local interests or increase room for decentralized experimentation. Instead, by engaging in political action COs 'go for money'. COs that have applied successfully for central government or local government funds might have strong incentives to try again and are, accordingly, more likely to enter into political action – for example, by lobbying the (local, regional or national) state to frame developmental programs in the 'right way'. To control for the effect of this factor, we used two variables: whether the CO applied successfully for central government money ('money from government') and whether the CO applied successfully for local state money ('money from local government').

A second possibility that we have considered was that it is not the autonomous COs that engage in political action but rather the NGOs created by the local state. Such 'subsidiary NGOs' might be the convenient lobbying arms of the local governments, giving a 'civic' voice to local alliances trying to influence the central state. To control for this effect, we have used questions about the founders of the NGOs and the membership of (local) state actors in the leading bodies of the NGOs. If the (local) state was among the founders of the organizations and/or it was represented on the leading body of the organization we counted the organization as a 'subsidiary NGO' ('founded by local government').

We have tested several alternative explanations for political activism, drawing freely on organizational theories and theories developed on the basis of the study of the political organization of business. One alternative might be that political activism is the effect of local accountability relations: COs deeply embedded in the local society will not lose their autonomy while combining with the state and are actually pushed into politics. The extensive networks of accountability to local actors (members, clients, other COs, the local public, etc.), while preventing regional COs from losing their autonomy, also push them to pursue their goals both by participating in partnerships and by politicizing the goals and values they represent. This hypothesis draws on and extends the 'logic of membership' argument of Schmitter and Streeck (1999): organizational behavior is the function of local roots (characteristics of the accountability to members).

Informal and formal accountability to local social actors means that COs have to take into account the interests of diverse local actors when making decisions and/or have to report to them. To assess the role of informal and formal accountability we used the following variables in the equations below: (1) the CO has to take into account the interests of members, clients, other domestic NGOs, foreign NGOs, the media/newspapers, the general public and the trade unions; (2) the CO has to formally report to members, clients, other domestic NGOs, foreign NGOs, the media/newspapers, the general public and the trade unions.

We take our second alternative explanation from a co-authored essay by Streeck and Schmitter (1985): a specific pattern of state-NGO relationship pulls NGOs into policy networks and makes them combine participation in collaborative projects with political action. State actors, according to Streeck and Schmitter, might have little incentive to work with non-autonomous COs; rather, they might need contextualized information and guarantees for both responsive policies and smooth implementation. Joint projects with COs are normal political exchanges: state actors have strong incentives to find autonomous partners and local COs need opportunities to pursue their goals. The stronger and more encompassing the collaboration between state actors and COs, the higher the likelihood that COs become part of policy networks. It is not closeness to the state *per se* but a specific pattern of interactions between the state and COs that accounts for political activism. Or, put simply, political action by COs is the effect of deep integration with the state. We test this hypothesis by using the results of a cluster analysis of the different types of interactions between the central state and the local COs (results not shown here). In the equations below we use the cluster of 'deep integration with government'. This is a pattern of interaction with government that combines direct participation of a state actor in the projects of the CO with formal and informal accountability relationships and monetary contributions to the project.

A third explanation might be the size of the CO: larger, more resourceful COs and COs that are not dependent on a small number of sources for money might be more able to afford to engage in political action. In the equations below, we used the logarithm of the size of the budget of the CO and the diversity of the sources of CO revenue (types of monetary sources) to control for this effect.

A fourth explanation might be that goal combination might push COs into political action: COs learn by combining. By pursuing more diverse goals, they are more likely to meet more diverse partners and are more likely to discover new combinations of developmental goals and face the limitations in the way developmental programs are framed by the state. This 'learning through combining' might push COs to try to alter definitions of developmental goals and/or to frame programs and policies in a more inclusive fashion. To test this hypothesis we have used 'goal mix', standing for COs that combine in their projects all three types of goals (economic, social and territorial-environmental) that we have used in questionnaire. Finally, COs in one region might have different opportunities to enter into political action than in others. We include variables for the Southern Plain and Western Hungary, omitting the Northern Plain as the reference category.

Since political activism and partnerships happen at the level of projects and ongoing activities, in this part of the analysis we use projects and activities as units of analysis. The number of cases ranges between 1,243 and 1,279 in the three models.

Political Action: Attempt to Change Regulations

In the first equation below, we used a logistic regression analysis with, as our dependent variable, whether or not attempts to change regulation at the level of central government or local government had been made (table 6.5). This model does not support the hypothesis that political activity is about money. The fact that a CO has applied successfully for central government money or for local state money does not predict attempts to change regulations. We must also reject the hypothesis that subsidiary NGOs are more likely to enter in political action.

Goal combination has a significant effect on political action: highly combinatory COs are 1.8 times more likely to try to change central or local government regulations. Accountability to local actors is another significant and independent predictor of political action: COs that must take into account the interests of their members are 1.5 times more likely to enter in this type of political action. The effect of formal reporting requirements to members

Table 6.5 Logistic Regression, Dependent Variable: Attempts to Change Regulation at the Level of Central or Local Government

	B	Exp(B)	S. E.	Wald	Sig.
Goal mix	.599	1.820	.152	15.557	.000
Taking into account:					
Members	.407	1.502	.206	3.919	.048
Clients	-.091	.913	.182	.251	.616
Domestic NGOs	.161	1.175	.183	.773	.379
Foreign NGOs	.453	1.574	.205	4.872	.027
Media organizations	.189	1.208	.183	1.068	.301
General public	.350	1.419	.199	3.079	.079
Trade unions	.383	1.467	.316	1.472	.225
Reporting to:					
Members	.397	1.488	.168	5.619	.018
Clients	.232	1.261	.203	1.298	.254
Domestic NGOs	.013	1.013	.191	.005	.946
Foreign NGOs	.038	1.038	.267	.020	.888
Media organizations	-.154	.858	.215	.509	.476
General public	.267	1.306	.200	1.790	.181
Trade unions	-.369	.691	.402	.845	.358
Logarithm of budget	.590	1.804	.102	33.125	.000
Types of monetary sources	-.040	.961	.039	1.018	.313
Money from government	.108	1.114	.157	.478	.489
Money from local gov.	.056	1.058	.166	.114	.736
Founded by local gov.	.175	1.191	.171	1.047	.306
Dependent on local gov.	.043	1.044	.176	.059	.807
Deep integration with gov.	.781	2.184	.218	12.828	.000
Southern Plain	-.167	.846	.163	1.047	.306
Western Hungary	-.482	.618	.162	8.898	.003
Constant	-3.006		.049	.466	41.638	.000

N=1243, Nagelkerke R Square .253

is similar. Whether or not COs take into account the interests of foreign NGOs and of the general public has the same effect.

The effect of the size of budget is also significant. COs with a budget one order of magnitude greater (we used base-ten logarithm here) are 1.8 times more likely to engage in this type of political action. COs that are deeply integrated in their interactions with the central government are two times more likely to enter in political action. Finally, COs in Western Hungary are significantly less likely to engage in political action.

Political Action: Trying to Change the Balance of Forces

In the second equation below, we used as our dependent variable whether or not COs had attempted to try to change the balance of forces in the CO's area of activity (table 6.6). As in the equation above, local social relations of accountability matter significantly. COs that have to take into account the interests of their members are 1.8 times more likely to try to alter the balance of forces. The effects of the need to take into account the interests of general public, the interests of trade unions and formal reporting require-ments to the general public are similar. Goal combination, on the other hand, is not a predictor of this type of political action. COs which complain of excessive dependency on local governments are 1.8 times more likely to enter into this type of political action.

This model also fails to support the hypothesis that political action is about money. The fact that a CO has applied successfully for central government money or for local state money does not predict attempts to undertake this type of political action. We must also reject the hypothesis that subsidiary NGOs are likely to enter into this type of political action. Resources matter significantly: COs with larger budget are 1.2 times more likely to try to alter the balance of forces. As above, COs from Western Hungary are less likely to act.

Political Action: Lobbying Central Government

Finally, in the third equation below we used lobbying central government as the dependent variable (table 6.7). It is in this equation that we find an independent effect of receiving money from central and local government. Both matter but in dramatically different ways. Successful applications for central government money significantly increases, successful application for local state money significantly decreases the probability of lobbying central government.

Table 6.6 Logistic Regression, Dependent Variable: Attempts to Alter the Balance of Forces

	B	Exp(B)	S. E.	Wald	Sig.
Goal mix	.216	1.242	.144	2.246	.134
Taking into account:					
Members	.597	1.817	.198	9.066	.003
Clients	.025	1.025	.177	.020	.889
Domestic NGOs	.203	1.225	.181	1.258	.262
Foreign NGOs	.203	1.225	.199	1.044	.307
Media organizations	−.328	.720	.181	3.294	.070
General public	.539	1.715	.195	7.626	.006
Trade unions	.669	1.952	.294	5.181	.023
Reporting to:					
Members	.088	1.092	.162	.293	.588
Clients	.093	1.098	.190	.241	.624
Domestic NGOs	−.087	.917	.183	.226	.635
Foreign NGOs	.179	1.196	.252	.504	.478
Media organizations	−.099	.906	.207	.228	.633
General public	.553	1.739	.192	8.289	.004
Trade unions	.548	1.730	.428	1.639	.200
Logarithm of budget	.194	1.214	.098	3.878	.049
Types of monetary sources	−.009	.991	.038	.056	.812
Money from government	.249	1.283	.155	2.578	.108
Money from local gov.	.200	1.221	.161	1.544	.214
Founded by local gov.	−.229	.796	.166	1.897	.168
Dependent on local gov.	.632	1.882	.179	12.536	.000
Deep integration with gov.	.126	1.134	.198	.405	.525
Southern Plain	.143	1.154	.159	.805	.369
Western Hungary	−.327	.721	.155	4.430	.035
Constant	−1.850	.157	.446	17.207	.000

N=1266, Nagelkerke R Square: .212

This, however, is not the full picture. High goal combination doubles the probability of lobbying the government. Also, as in the equations above, relations of local accountability are independent predictors of political action: the need to take into account the interests of members, the need to take into account the interests of trade unions and the requirement to report to other domestic NGOs all significantly increase the probability of lobbying central government. Resources also matter: more resourceful COs, or COs that have more diverse resource portfolios are somewhat more likely to lobby central government. Finally, deep collaboration of COs with central government nearly doubles the probability of this type of political action.

Table 6.7 Logistic Regression, Dependent Variable: Lobbying Central Government

	B	Exp(B)	S. E.	Wald	Sig.
Goal mix	.718	2.050	.143	25.274	.000
Taking into account:					
Members	.451	1.570	.231	3.829	.050
Clients	−.211	.810	.200	1.107	.293
Domestic NGOs	−.031	.970	.195	.025	.874
Foreign NGOs	−.105	.900	.199	.281	.596
Media organizations	−.174	.840	.186	.874	.350
General public	.173	1.188	.213	.658	.417
Trade unions	.592	1.808	.260	5.205	.023
Reporting to:					
Members	.063	1.065	.178	.125	.724
Clients	−.012	.988	.196	.004	.953
Domestic NGOs	.374	1.453	.188	3.950	.047
Foreign NGOs	.201	1.223	.234	.740	.390
Media organizations	−.048	.953	.200	.059	.808
General public	−.012	.988	.201	.004	.951
Trade unions	.090	1.095	.341	.070	.791
Logarithm of budget	.245	1.277	.105	5.468	.019
Types of monetary sources	.089	1.093	.040	4.974	.026
Money from government	.574	1.775	.170	11.457	.001
Money from local gov.	−.530	.589	.174	9.311	.002
Founded by local gov.	−.251	.778	.177	2.012	.156
Dependent on local gov.	−.346	.708	.186	3.436	.064
Deep integration with gov.	.679	1.973	.185	13.528	.000
Southern Plain	−.098	.907	.162	.368	.544
Western Hungary	−.468	.626	.167	7.869	.005
Constant	−2.954	.052	.488	36.626	.000

N=1279, Nagelkerke R Square .164

Conclusions

In this chapter we have explored the ways in which partnerships with the state within state-led developmental programs might affect the autonomy of civic organizations and their readiness to enter in political action. We did not find support for the theses that mixing with the state might undermine the autonomy of COs and lead to their political neutralization. Nor did we find support for the hypotheses that political action is solely about money or is the exclusive preserve of subsidiary NGOs. We have identified several mechanisms that allow COs to combine participation in partnership projects while maintaining political activism.

Based on the work of Schmitter and Streeck (1999), we expected that the 'logic of local embedding' will be one of the factors of pushing COs towards political action. We found that participatory COs that are accountable to their members and that are integrated in local societies are significantly more likely to engage in political action, either by trying to change regulations, by lobbying or by trying to change the balance of forces in their field of action. We also tested the 'learning by combining' hypothesis. We found that intense combinations with actors from other organizational fields including the state, far from reducing political activism, is instead an independent factor in explaining civic political activity. Finally, we tested the 'political exchange' hypothesis and found that deeper forms of collaboration with the state significantly increase the likelihood of civic political action. Using the language of the social movement studies, we can say that the changed opportunity structure (the growing possibility of combining with the state in developmental projects) alters CO's action repertoire, but does not transform activist organizations into mere service organizations.[8] The growth in collaborative developmental projects does not endanger the autonomy of integrated civil societies.

Based on our findings, we can also say that it is misleading to underestimate the transformative potential of associative civic action involving collaboration with actors from other organizational fields.[9] In forging various developmental associations, civic organizations that work together with actors from other organizational domains (business, national and local government, education, church, etc.) can contribute to the coming about of local and regional publics, thereby allowing the formulation and implementation of more inclusive policies and programs. While making alliances across groupings and integrating what had formerly been disjointed, civic organizations' projects draw connections between interests that perhaps had not been seen as compatible. They are therefore producing new frames in which dissimilar notions of the public good can be redefined and associated. In that sense, the combination of associating diversity in ever-changing developmental projects with political action might lead to the occurrence of what Fraser (1994) called 'strong publics': arenas for assembling diverse ideas, metrics of valuation and interests for joint policy formulation, not just implementation.

Notes

1. For a critical overview of the literature on developmental partnerships, see Howell and Pearce (2002) and Kaldor et al. (2003).
2. There are several roots to this approach. In economic sociology and the literature on forms of economic governance, the works of Charles Sabel (1993, 1994, 1996) and Wolfgang Streeck and Philippe C. Schmitter (1985) influenced most of the thinking about the role played by developmental associations or associative action. On linking local associative action and democratic experimentalism in the framework of the concept of 'directly deliberative poliarchy', see Sabel and Cohen (1997). Another direction that influenced thinking on different developmental partnerships came from the literature on the non-profit sector linking associative action to the production of diverse types of public goods; see the work of Anheier and Salamon (1998) and Powell and Clemens (1998). On deliberative association in post-socialist transformation, see Stark and Bruszt (1998).
3. For example, in their introductory chapter to *Global Civil Society*, Kaldor et al. (2003) subsume these combinations at the supra-national level under the rubric of 'new public management' and talk about the 'basically neo-liberal role NGOs assume in public management manifestations'. See also Chandhoke (2002), Kettl (2000) and Perrow (2001, 2002). For a more balanced critique of NGO participation in partnerships, see Howell and Pearce (2002).
4. Information based on an interview in the Ministry of Economy and Trade.
5. 'Statistical regions' were created in Hungary during the process of preparation for the reception of EU regional development funds. As the name suggests, these 'regions' do not have autonomous political representation.
6. The list consisted of various *social goals* (improving health conditions, improving social conditions, improving education, increasing employment, strengthening higher education), *economic goals* (furthering industrial development, furthering agricultural development, development of tourism, development of firm creation, strengthening economic innovation, furthering capital influx in the region), *environmental goals* (improving the quality of environment, optimal use of environmental resources, environmental education) and *general regional goals* (improve transportation within the region, improve internal cohesion in the region, improve external territorial relations of the region, further cross-territorial communication, improving the administrative, political institutions of the region).
7. The list of actors used in the questionnaire: donors, central government, county government, local government, Regional Development Council/Regional Development Agency, political party, other domestic NGO, foreign NGO, international organization, church, media, a business organization, scientific organization and trade union.
8. See Tarrow (1998) for a discussion of opportunity structures and the form and types of organizing.
9. See our paper co-authored with David Stark for further discussion of civic associative action (Stark et al. 2005).

References

Anderson, Kenneth. 2000. 'The Ottawa Convention Banning Landmines, the Role of International Nongovernmental Organizations and the Idea of International Civil Society', *European Journal of International Law* 11, no. 1: 91–120.
Anheier, Helmut K., and Lester M. Salamon, eds. 1998. *The Nonprofit Sector in the Developing World: A Comparative Analysis*. Manchester: Manchester University Press.

Brown, L. David, Sanjeev Khagram, Mark H. Moore and Peter Frumkin. 2001. 'Globalization, NGOs, and Multi-Sectoral Relations', in *Governance in a Globalizing World*, ed. Joseph S. Nye, Jr. and John D. Donohue. Washington, DC: Brookings Institution Press, pp. 271–296.

Bruszt, Laszlo. 2002. 'Making Markets and Eastern Enlargement: Diverging Convergence?', in *The Enlarged European Union: Diversity and Adaptation*, ed. Peter Mair and Jan Zielonka. London: Frank Cass, pp. 121–141.

Bruszt, Laszlo, and David Stark. 2003. 'Who Counts? Supranational Norms and Societal Needs', *East European Politics and Societies* 17, no. 1: 74–82.

Chandhoke, Neear. 2002. 'The Limits of Global Civil Society', in *Global Civil Society Yearbook*, ed. Mary Kaldor, Helmut K. Anheier and Marlies Glasius. Oxford: Oxford University Press.

Evans, Peter, ed. 1997. *State-Society Synergy: Government and Social Capital in Development*. Berkeley: University of California at Berkeley.

Fraser, Nancy. 1994. 'Rethinking the Public Sphere: A Contribution to the Critique of Actually Existing Democracy', in *Habermas and the Public Sphere*, ed. Craig Calhoun. Cambridge, MA: MIT Press.

Gerstenberg, Oliver, and Charles F. Sabel. 2002. 'Directly Deliberative Polyarchy: An Institutional Ideal for Europe?', in *Good Governance in Europe's Integrated Market*, ed. Christian Joerges and Renaud Dehousse. Oxford: Oxford University Press, pp. 289–341.

Howell, Jude, and Jenny Pearce. 2002. *Civil Society and Development: A Critical Exploration*. Boulder, CO: Lynne Rienner.

Kaldor, Mary, Helmut K. Anheier and Marlies Glasius. 2003. *Global Civil Society Yearbook 2003*. Oxford: Oxford University Press.

Kettl, Donald. 2000. *The Global Public Management Revolution: A Report on the Transformation of Governance*. Washington, DC: Brookings Institution Press.

OECD (Organization for Economic Cooperation and Development). 1995. *Participatory Development and Good Governance*. Paris: OECD.

Perrow, Charles. 2001. 'The Rise of Nonprofits and the Decline of Civil Society', in *Organizational Theory and Nonprofit Form*, ed. Helmut Anheier. London: London School of Economics, Centre for Civil Society, pp. 33–44.

_____. 2002. *Organizing America: Wealth, Power and the Origins of American Capitalism*. Princeton, NJ: Princeton University Press.

Powell, Walter W., and Elisabeth S. Clemens, eds. 1998. *Private Action and the Public Good*. New Haven, CT: Yale University Press.

Sabel, Charles. 1993. 'Studied Trust: Building New Forms of Cooperation in a Volatile Economy', *Human Relations* 46, no. 9: 214–267.

_____. 1994. 'Learning by Monitoring: The Institutions of Economic Development', in *Handbook of Economic Sociology*, ed. Neil Smelser and Richard Swedberg. Princeton, NJ: Princeton University Press and Russell Sage Foundation, pp. 137–165.

_____. 1996. *Ireland: Local Partnerships and Social Innovation*. Paris: OECD.

Sabel, Charles, and Joshua Cohen. 1997. 'Directly-Deliberative Polyarchy', *European Law Journal* 3, no. 4: 313–342.

Schmitter, Philippe C., and Wolfgang Streeck. 1999. 'The Organization of Business Interests: Studying the Associative Action of Business in Advanced Industrial Societies', *Max Planck Institut für Gesellschaftsforschung. Discussion Papers*, 99/1.

Stark, David, and Laszlo Bruszt. 1998. *Postsocialist Pathways: Transforming Politics and Property in East Central Europe*. Cambridge: Cambridge University Press.

Stark, David, Balazs Vedres and Laszlo Bruszt. 2005. 'Global Links, Local Roots? Varieties of Transnationalization and Forms of Civic Integration'. Unpublished manuscript.

Streeck, Wolfgang, and Philippe C. Schmitter. 1985. 'Community, Market, State – and Associations? The Prospective Contribution of Interest Governance to Social Order', in *Private Interest Government: Beyond Market and State*, ed. Wolfgang Streeck and Philippe C. Schmitter. London: Sage Publications, pp. 1–29.

Tarrow, Sidney. 1998. *Power in Movement: Social Movements and Contentious Politics*. Cambridge: Cambridge University Press.

UNDP (United Nations Development Programme). 1993. 'UNDP and Organizations of Civil Society: Building Sustainable Partnerships'. Mimeo.

_____. 1995. 'Proposed UNDP Regional Programme: Civil Society Empowerment for Poverty Reduction in Sub-Saharan Africa'. Mimeo.

World Bank. 1992. *Governance and Development*. Washington, DC: World Bank.

_____. 1996. *The World Bank's Partnership with Nongovernmental Organizations*. Washington, DC: World Bank.

Chapter 7

INFORMAL INTERMEDIARIES AND CIVIC ORGANIZATIONS IN STATE-BUSINESS RELATIONSHIPS IN RUSSIA

Irina Olimpieva

The development of a robust rule-of-law environment can be regarded as a key factor in Russia's transition. The rule of law will not be established either in political institutions or popular perceptions unless it is accepted in the business sphere, which represents one of the main arenas of post-socialist transformation. However, numerous studies of market economy development in post-reform Russia demonstrate the increasing role of informal rules, the 'deformalization' of economic institutions attesting to the substitution of informal rules for formal ones, and the domination of parallel informal institutions in either 'horizontal' business interactions or 'vertical' relationships between businesspeople and officials at different levels (see, e.g., Ledeneva 1999; Levin and Satarov 2000; Olimpieva 2005; Radaev 2001). This chapter seeks to explore the question of how the informal rules dominating the business sphere affect the formation of civic dialog between business and authorities in present-day Russia.[1] It addresses the problem of growing informality and corruption in the business sphere during the post-reform period and goes on to consider the formation of such a dialog through the prism of this problem. The role and specific features of the recently formed 'civic sector' in the business sphere – a variety of non-governmental and non-commercial organizations aimed at promoting the formation of a civilized business environment – are described from the perspective of anti-corruption activities. The purpose of the chapter is not

---

Notes for this chapter begin on page 219.

to summarize the extensive debates on growing corruption and civil society formation in Russia during the period of transformation,[2] but rather to analyze the empirical evidence reflecting these two interrelated processes.

The chapter uses data compiled in the course of two studies: one, a study of informal relationships between business and the authorities in St. Petersburg, and the other, a study of the role of NGOs and business associations in the development of anti-corruption policies. The first study examined the situation of small and medium-size businesses and focused primarily on the informal (corrupt) practices that SME (small and medium enterprise) businessmen use in their everyday interactions with state officials. The second study looked at civil society organizations in the business sphere, as represented by NGOs and various non-commercial associations of businessmen (which are the main object of our interest). It focused on the anti-corruption activities of civic organizations, and the role that they play as civic agents in the anti-corruption field.[3] Although both studies were focused on the St. Petersburg municipality alone, the perceived outcomes and conclusions are not specific to St. Petersburg and could reasonably be extended to the situation of small and medium-size businesses in Russia as a whole.

The development of small business is seen as one of the important preconditions of democracy building. Besides playing a special role in the development of the economy, small business is also considered to have a great impact on social-structure formation by providing the social basis for the emergence of a middle class, or, in other words, a class of independent proprietors. Many researchers stress the linkage between the development of civil society and small business. Legalization of entrepreneurial activity in the course of economic reforms in Russia was supposed to lead to (1) the emergence of a dynamic and autonomous (or at least less subject to state intervention) SME economic sector providing the economic and social basis for the formation of civil society, and (2) the emergence of various associations and organizations representing SME business interests in state-business relationships, providing businessmen with an institutionalized mechanism for overcoming the problems caused by an uncertain and unfavorable economic environment. The studies were aimed mainly at testing these assumptions.

The chapter begins by considering the growing informality and corruption as a specific feature of the post-socialist economic environment. The focus on micro-level, informal practices used by businessmen to overcome bureaucratic barriers provides explicit illustrations of how 'vertical' relationships in the business sphere are really formed. Drawing on an empirical study of corruption in the SME sector, the chapter demonstrates the emergence of new informal institutions (informal intermediaries) facilitating informal relationships between businessmen and officials. It then proceeds to an analysis of the civic sector in the business sphere by considering different ('ideological' and 'rational') groups of civic agents operating in the anti-corruption field. In the concluding part of the chapter it is argued that the institutionalization and formalization of corrupt mediating services in the state-business relationship has become a significant factor hindering both the development of a 'civic sector' in the business sphere and, consequently, the civilized lobbying mechanisms for furthering business interests. Using the empirical data, we also attempt to test some widespread expectations regarding the scale and specific features of civil society in Russia.

Businessmen and Officials: The Problem of Corruption

It would be no exaggeration to say that the majority of business activities in present-day Russia still lie under a shadow. This is particularly true for small and medium-size businesses, to the extent that they could still be described as informal or semi-formal. The data collated in the course of the study have confirmed that, for such businesses, the problem of the impracticability of formal regulations remains the main problem of doing business. A statement made quite frequently is 'You cannot conform to all the rules, it is just impossible – you would have to close your enterprise!' (a variation on this theme is 'It is impossible to pay all the taxes'). People believe that such legal problems are intentionally created and deliberately maintained by officials. The result is that people in business are always guilty – regardless of their intention to follow the rules.

> In such a situation, with the real state of things, constantly, whatever you do, you always violate the law. And you always feel yourself a criminal and, in fact, you are forced to make pay-offs. (Director of a construction firm)

The impracticability of the formal rules leads to a situation in which their violation is no longer a deviation from the social norm but rather a norm in its own right, one, moreover, providing fertile ground for bureaucratic extortion.[4]

It is worth highlighting that not all impracticable rules are considered by businessmen to be unfair. The particular category of rules that tends to be the cause of most businessmen's indignation is the regulations (not laws) of a department that are totally outdated and fail to correspond to contemporary business conditions. Although such regulations have no bearing on reality, any violation of them may lead to serious punitive measures – even including the total prohibition of business activities. This applies to a department's regulations, for instance, as regards sanitary and fire protection services. Some of these regulations date back to the 1960s and 1970s, and others go as far back as the 1930s, and are thus totally outdated and cannot be complied with in practice. Officials who conduct inspections of enterprises are well aware of this situation, and the only way to deal with the issue as a businessperson is to bribe them so that they 'close their eyes' to violations of ridiculous rules that are unfortunately still in force. This quotation from an interview with the manager of a café illustrates one such situation:

> We belong to [the economic sector of] public catering, but we don't cook anything ourselves. They insist on us having three new sinks installed, for example. We don't need them! We don't cook anything! But if they want, they can shut us down because of this. And these norms, these rules, they have not been changed practically since 1974, and now it's 2004! (Manager of a café)

Another situation that is seen as iniquitous is the contradictory nature of the rules, which makes it impossible to follow the requirements of one regulative department without infringing the requirements of another. And even if the regulations are not considered to be unreasonable by businessmen, implementing the formal requirements is often unfeasible for small enterprises. In most cases businessmen again feel obliged to employ informal or semi-formal means of solving the problem.

> An automatic prevention of ignition system is one of the requirements for production lines of this type. This system is very expensive, and we still cannot afford to buy it and set it up, therefore we needed to find another way out … we hire a fireman of a certain rank, pay him a salary, and he supervises us.… It works out somehow, at least, nobody has bothered us so far. Yes, it costs us money, but the relationship is secure and it is clear that these are relations with an official at the financial level. (Director of industrial construction firm)

These quotations demonstrate the defenselessness of business against the power of state officials. Such a situation has already been labeled 'soft terror' in Russian literature (Usyskin 2003). Businessmen can find themselves hostage to any bureaucratic structure, and a firm can be closed down at any moment. According to our informants, corruption in Russia is not only incorporated into the bureaucratic system in general but they believe that it is an integral part of it. It means that businessmen are ready to give bribes to officials *a priori*, without even trying to find legal and official ways of resolving their problems. Officials, as a matter of fact, do not impose strict sanctions on businessmen, or only do so selectively.

> In reality, when the inspectors come to your business and find problems, you understand that they have not come to shut you down as soon as possible. No, they have come in order to get some money from you. (Manager of a café)

The majority of conflicts between businessmen and the authorities are barely regulated by formal means, but rather by some 'unwritten rules' resulting from interpersonal negotiations based on conventional common sense and some shared interpretations of justice. Although both business-men and bureaucrats appeal to laws and regulations, the latter simply serve as a formal background to conflicts that are being settled by the application of informal or semi-formal procedures. Perhaps this is the reason for the surprising unawareness of our informants about the laws protecting their rights. According to the survey data, 73 percent of respondents have never heard about the law on fighting corruption, 80 percent do not know any-thing about the Civil Servant Behavior Code, and 83 percent are unaware of the Conception of the Program of Administrative Reform, which has been debated publicly for several years.

Businessmen and Civic Activism

What action can business take against the 'soft terror' of state bureaucracy? From a Western perspective, the most obvious way is to resort to civic activism in order to influence the state's legislative policy, which implies the formation of business associations, lobby groups, etc. In our study we attempted to find out about businessmen's attitudes towards different orga-nizations which could help them to protect their rights. According to the survey, 57.3 percent of respondents have never applied to anybody for help, advice or protection when they have faced corrupt situations. While 16.4 percent of them do not do so because they do not believe in the effective-ness of fighting the authorities, 30 percent believe that it is easier to pay rather than to try to change the system. The data collected in the study demonstrated a low level of trust in official institutions and their ability to protect the interests of entrepreneurs. Only 2.7 percent of respondents fac-ing bureaucratic extortion appeal to the courts; while slightly more of them (4.2 percent) turn to state power structures. At the same time, it demon-strated the huge importance of informal contacts with friends in difficult situations: about 15 percent mentioned that when extortion occurs they appeal to friends, and another 20.6 percent, to business acquaintances with experience of these issues.

When answering the questions 'Which organizations can protect entrepre-neurs from unjustified actions on the part of officials, and which organizations are you ready to cooperate with if the fight against corruption starts in Rus-sia?', 35.2 percent of respondents stated that 'no organization' could protect businessmen from bureaucratic despotism, and one quarter of respondents (25.1 percent) did not wish to cooperate with any of the listed anti-cor-ruption organizations. The following arguments were those most frequently employed to explain their refusal (in reply to an open-ended question):

> All these organizations will very soon become corrupt themselves.
> The state is able to fight corruption alone without any help.
> I don't have time to fight corruption, I have to work.

Nonetheless, the respondents who answered this question affirmatively preferred to cooperate with organizations that are independent from the state. Of these, 'organizations initiated by businessmen' received the most positive responses (38.2 percent); while NGOs were mentioned as potential partners by 27.5 percent of respondents.[5] However, the qualitative details bring out a more negative side to the quantitative picture. The general attitude towards associations of businessmen expressed in interviews is pessimistic and indicates that associations are a very good idea, but to be effective in fighting corruption they require a lot of time and money which small entrepreneurs lack.

> All the entrepreneurs can get together and sit in a room, smoking, drinking coffee and saying OK, now we start to fight. But when a single businessman is contacted by some agency, he will solve his problems by himself, because he knows very well that if he doesn't give a bribe just because he wants to stick to his principles, he will have far more to lose in the future. (Director of a wholesale firm)

Thus, on the one hand, businesspeople are dissatisfied with the situation in business-state relationships and are generally interested in changing it; do really need some entity protecting their rights, needs and interests in the dialog with the authorities; and consider business associations as the most trustworthy organizations (as compared with other organizations). But, on the other hand, they do not believe in the effectiveness of such associations even if they were set up, and they often possess no (financial or time) resources to invest in third-sector activities or infrastructure and support.

Businessmen and Informal Intermediaries

Interviews with businessmen have explicitly demonstrated the emergence of a large-scale market for informal and semi-formal services mediating relations between business and the authorities. In recent years, there has been a growth of legalized and formalized firms/mediators selling bureaucratic services. We have called this phenomenon the *intermediary boom*.

At first glance, everything looks above board: the system of official rules and regulations is so complicated that any businessman who is not experienced in dealing with the bureaucracy needs advice from a consultant in order to meet all the bureaucratic requirements. However, although functionally the intermediaries providing the links between authoritative bodies and businessmen look similar to analogous institutions in the West, the system works very differently in Russia. In the West, the main purpose of intermediaries is to process bureaucratic procedures that are highly complicated and need special skills to handle. In Russia, their services seem to function as a screen, being in fact a covert form of rewarding officials for accelerating bureaucratic procedures by means of additional payment. The interviews provided some evidence for this statement.

The difference becomes more obvious if we compare the work of *customs brokers* – a mediating institution present in both Western countries and in Russia. Complicity and the intricate nature of customs rules are inherent in every country, therefore cargo carriers always seek the assistance provided by intermediaries, namely, customs brokers. Why then do we call the services provided by customs brokers in Russia 'corrupt mediation'? In fact it becomes rather difficult to separate consulting mediation from corrupt mediation, even for businessmen themselves. In the following quotation, the respondent is speaking about relationships with customs:

> OK, as for customs ... they solve the problem in another way. They do not have ... how would you say ... these direct relationships like 'bribe-decision'. Everything is rather covert there, and, they have, say, parallel customs structures that guide all the operations with your cargo and solve the problems with customs officials. Is this bribery or not? (Director of construction firm)

The main task of customs brokers in Russia is not so much to assist businessmen in going through customs formalities as to achieve reductions in cargo costs and to accelerate the process via informal channels. A special market of informal customs services has been set up through which customs brokers offer a wide spectrum of possible customs schemes – from 'light-gray' to 'fast black' (the cheaper the scheme, the longer it takes and the lower the risk). While doing this, brokers 'take the responsibility for substantiation of the declared cost of cargo, using for this purpose an informal agreement with customs officials' (Radaev 2003: 53), that is, they reduce customs payments to the lowest possible level through negotiations with customs bodies.[6] Another function of customs brokers is to speed up the customs procedure via informal contacts with the customs service. According to our respondents, the 'do-it-yourself' variant costs money and time.

> The way through customs – it is just horrible! We were doing everything by 'a white scheme'. The system works as follows – we try to do everything fairly, paying all customs duties, etc. But the customs rules and laws are very complicated, they can cavil at anything, and won't let a commodity through. But it can be done very easily.... We tried once to go through customs procedures using a 'gray' scheme. And it turned out to be much easier and much cheaper. And now we are thinking: What for? Why have we suffered so much for five years? Every time we bring a commodity through customs it costs me four days of my life. (Shop owner)

Real estate firms serve as intermediaries between businessmen and the Department of State Property, distributing state-owned premises for rent. Renting state-owned premises is cheaper and sometimes even free for some SMEs, although access to them is limited. However, there are real estate companies connected to local administrations that help in finding appropriate state-owned premises for a low rental price on condition that a businessman will make monthly payments of additional money to the company in black cash. So real estate firms do not simply mediate in these relationships (as can be seen from the following quotation):

> Q: Did you have any problems with officials to open your shop?
>
> A: Oh yes, it was dreadful! There was a firm of lawyers at the district administration that offered us very good premises. But then it turned out.... Well, we said at the very beginning that everything was official and we completed a cashless transfer. Nonetheless, we were told that 'You need to bring $300 every month in cash anyway....' And it was impossible to reject, because this firm is at the administration and we were told: 'We will simply not allow you to work in this district!' (Shop owner)

Another issue is *licensing (and certification)*. For our informants, it is obvious that in order to get a license or certificate it is better to avoid direct contact with licensing and certification centers, which complicate the procedure deliberately, and to work through an intermediary firm, which will issue the same papers on the basis of the same documents but at a different price.

> Naturally, I have never seen anybody, but everything goes to a firm. We pay the firm, and they do everything. They collect all the necessary documents, which are simply bought, because nobody has enough time to collect all this – it would take me half a year! In reality nobody does anything but the documents are here, they are on official paper and look nice. From institutes and training centers, that somebody has attended courses, passed the exams, commission accepted, etc.... It turns out that this pyramid is specially built on an empty base. And these firms, they are created around the officials who deal with issuing licenses. There are about a dozen people involved, you know.... If *they* take in this paper – it will be accepted [by the officials], if not – well, it won't. It's amazing! (Director of a construction firm)

The study provides numerous examples demonstrating the same situation with the state monopolies providing electric power, gas or water. It takes months or even years to get permission from these organizations to start a business or to introduce some changes related to these utilities. Once again the solution is to go through an intermediary firm and then the question can be resolved in a few days, though at a higher price.

Why do businessmen prefer to deal with intermediaries? Because it is simpler (intermediaries know all the details and hidden dangers of the process), faster (it saves time and therefore money) and less stressful (not by any means the least important factor). It is possible to avoid emotional strain, which is usually a painful part of the interpersonal communication between businessmen and officials. When businesspeople go to intermediaries, the situation is different: they feel like customers who are buying a formal service.

The number of intermediaries that specialize exclusively in the informal mediation of bureaucratic extortion is not as large as the number of firms that focus on 'cutting red tape'. As a matter of fact, intermediaries combine *explicit functions* with *hidden or shadow* functions in their activities. Explicit functions include the absolutely legal services that could be found within any economic system: consultancy, equipment sales, real estate operations, etc. Therefore, on the official side (from documents and official reports), these firms appear to be ordinary business organizations running 'normal' businesses (and they actually do). At the same time, intermediaries fulfill shadow or hidden functions by promoting informal relations between businesses and the state. The main resource for accomplishing these functions is access to a bureaucratic structure (or merely a bureaucrat) that provides them with the possibility of obtaining the necessary bureaucratic service.

It can be affirmed that informal bureaucratic mediation is currently going through a process of *institutionalization*, which means that it has become a generally accepted, autonomous and profitable activity in the business sphere. This process is accompanied by the *formalization* of mediating services, which are now provided by legal, licensed firms. Apparently we are seeing the emergence of a new entrepreneurial sphere – informal mediation – parasitizing on the limits and uncertainty of the institutional environment. With good reason, these business activities can be referred to as 'unproductive entrepreneurship' (Coyne and Leeson 2004), which is flourishing in economies undergoing transformation.

Two options – the civic and the informal – are generally available for businessmen to cope with uncertain and unfavorable business environments. 'Civic activism' implies the self-organization of businesses (the creation of business associations) and cooperation with third-sector organizations in order to influence state policy on business development. The 'informal' option is to establish direct informal (or informally mediated) relationships with authoritative bodies and officials in order to solve problems. The study has shown that businessmen generally consider the informal way to be more effective and quicker. Apparently, their general distrust of official organizations and unbelief in the effectiveness of public organizations also bring businessmen to 'informal encouragement' of bureaucrats. Informal (corrupt) mediation is becoming a significant factor promoting further development of the 'informal way' in state-business relationships.

Civic Organizations and Anti-corruption Activities

We shall now go on to describe the civic organizations[7] that are involved in anti-corruption activities from two perspectives. Firstly, why do such organizations consider corruption as a problem that must be eliminated or reduced? According to their reasoning, we can distinguish two groups of 'anti-corruption agents'. The first group, which we call *ideological agents*, comprises international and local NGOs aimed at protecting human rights, the development of civil society, transparent governance and the building up of a truly democratic society. As long as corruption (including business corruption) remains an obstacle hindering democracy-building processes, 'ideological agents' will focus their activities on fighting this social evil. In our study, ideological agents are represented by NGOs working for human rights protection and control of the authorities as well as by so-called Public Policy Centers and Think Tanks (analytical centers) focusing on public policy research and development, including issues of anti-corruption and related problems.

We call our second group of civic organizations the *rational agents* in the field of anti-corruption. From the point of view of economic rationality, corruption is a negative factor that impedes true economic competition in the market by holding down foreign investment flows and hindering business development as a whole. In this respect, anti-corruption activities are supposed to increase the rationality of the system and make state regulation more effective and economic resources more accessible. Hypothetically, the main 'rational anti-corruption agents' should be represented by the various associations of businessmen interested in the creation of a favorable and robust business environment. In our study we considered the business associations in St. Petersburg and the surrounding region. Most of them declare that 'defending businessmen's rights', 'promoting business development' or 'the creation of a favorable business environment for the development of business', etc. are their main organizational purposes. If corruption is seen as one of the barriers obstructing business development, then business associations should, logically, be concerned with this problem.

Secondly, in our analysis of anti-corruption activism, we ask where the driving forces behind such activity come from. In this respect, we can distinguish three types of initiative: (1) the *bottom-up* initiative, which is supposed to be represented by grass-roots activism aiming to solve the problem of corruption; (2) the *top-down* initiative, undertaken by a variety of authoritative structures – departments, committees and commissions – at different levels of authority: federal (or national), city or district; and (3) the *lateral* initiative, promoted by different international organizations and foundations providing support for democratic development in countries in transition. With these two perspectives in mind, we consider the different groups of civic agents in the anti-corruption field.

NGOs as 'Ideological Civic Agents'

It is true that the overwhelming majority of Russian NGOs are supported by Western money coming from various international foundations, organizations and international agencies of Western governments. Russia received billions of dollars devoted to civil society assistance programs and anti-corruption measures throughout the 1990s. Some researchers of civil society in Russia consider that the Russian NGOs are a new form of public establishment that have emerged due to Western support (including financial support) of the democratization processes in changing societies. They argue that these organizations are not the result of bottom-up civic processes and have therefore failed to receive sustainable grass-roots legitimization from the population (see, e.g., Henderson 2003).[8]

NGOs working in St. Petersburg are no exception to this general rule, especially as regards anti-corruption activities. The money for the anti-corruption projects set up by these organizations comes from different international sources including USAID, IRIS, TACIS, Eurasia Foundation, the World Bank, the European Bank for Reconstruction, the National Endowment for Democracy, the Ford Foundation, the Soros Foundation, Transparency International, etc. Very few sources of money are of Russian origin and come from federal or local authorities. For example, only 5 percent of the overall financial support for one of the most advanced Centers for Public Policy in St. Petersburg (which was one object of our study) came from Russian sources. For NGOs that take a critical stance towards the authorities, there is no Russian funding at all. The prevailing role of the '*lateral* initiative' is illustrated by this opinion expressed in an interview by the director of one of the economic think tanks: 'If there was no support from Western organizations, Russian TTs would die right away.'

The fact that NGOs are financially independent from the state could be considered as a positive factor if it were complemented by constructive dialog between civic organizations and the authorities. However, in practice, there is a lack of any institutionalized mechanism through which NGOs can influence state policy. As far as can be judged from interviews, the possibility for cooperation is more often provided by personal contacts between NGO activists and representatives of the City Administration and the City Assembly. These personal relationships have mainly survived from the time of the first democratic 'wave' when members of the City Assembly and the government were recruited from the same community of active supporters of democratic change.

The current lack of dialog between NGOs and authorities is aggravated by the absence of institutional mechanisms for legislative initiatives that could deal with corruption prevention issues. There are only a few regions in Russia where the right of NGOs to initiate legislation is laid down in a city's laws. The attempts to establish this right for NGOs in the local Parliament in St. Petersburg did not succeed.[9]

Local authorities rarely provide NGOs working in the anti-corruption field with any financial support. This is particularly true for NGOs specializing in the protection of human rights and the development of democracy. While economic think tanks receive requests from the city government for their economic and social expertise from time to time, any demand from the state for anti-corruption activities is wholly lacking. Nevertheless, the state is considered by NGOs' representatives to be a most influential player in the anti-corruption field. In interviews they express the opinion that the situation cannot be changed without 'goodwill' and initiative 'from above', that is, from federal or local authorities.

> In our country nothing happens without initiative from above, especially regarding anti-corruption. (Co-director of the Center for Public Policy)

The bonds linking the NGOs involved in anti-corruption activities in St. Petersburg are rather uneven. While several leading NGOs have close (personal or organizational) relationships with each other, the ties between less powerful organizations are looser. When representatives of the latter were asked to list their partner organizations, they mentioned partners in other Russian cities, CIS countries, Western and Eastern European countries and various international organizations – but not local ones. The necessity for collaboration is acknowledged by all NGOs but, as was mentioned by representatives of one of the leading organizations, they 'really have no time' to work on local communicative activities.

The fact that 'lateral' initiatives provide the main driving force in fighting corruption does not mean that the people working in NGOs do not really strive against this social evil. However, it is clear that the fight is neither a 'bottom-up' initiative carried on by the local population nor is it part of a consistent and comprehensive social policy pursued by the state.

Business Associations as 'Rational Civic Agents'

Our description of 'rational civic agents' must begin with a brief outline of the colorful assortment of business associations in St. Petersburg. Firstly, there are the ones that exist at a federal level, which are represented by regional branches of all-Russia organizations. The best known among these are OPORA, Delovaja Rossija, the Chamber of Commerce and Industry, the All-Russia Association for SM Business Support and the Institute of Business and Investments. Secondly, there are local business associations, among which we can distinguish two groups according to the characteristics of their members. The first group includes associations encompassing businesses belonging to different industrial sectors. The largest among them is the St. Petersburg Association of Entrepreneurs (SPb AE), and another large one is the Union of Industrialists and Employers, which acts on behalf of employers in social partnership negotiations. The second group includes associations comprising businesses belonging to the same industrial sector, and professional associations like, for instance, Kupecheskij Klub (the Merchant Club), Liga Obuvschikov (the Footwear Industry League), the Association of Customs Brokers, the Association of Zoo-businesses or the Association of Accountants, etc. Lastly, there is a special type of business association set up on a territorial basis. The latter are primarily non-commercial partnerships, Centers for Entrepreneurship Development, in which we were particularly interested for our research as they are designed to support SMEs. In the following analysis, we will focus mainly on local business associations related to small and medium-size businesses.

The participation of SME businessmen in business associations is generally low, the most obvious reason being that the majority of SMEs are struggling to survive. The businessmen who join associations are generally looking for new possibilities of business development, seeking new partners, or introducing technical and economic innovations, etc. The majority, who are principally concerned with their own survival, are not really interested in becoming members. However, another important reason is the lack of information available about business associations: very few of the ones in our case study employ any coherent PR strategy in order to attract new members. According to a telephone survey of SPb AE members, the majority of them had chosen this association because they did not know of any others. Only about one-third of respondents were able to recall even one business association in St. Petersburg apart from AE.

It is somewhat confusing to classify business associations according to the initiative that led to their creation and subsequent functioning; nonetheless, the first wave can be mainly referred to as part of the 'bottom-up' initiative. The burst of entrepreneurial activity in the early 1990s was characterized by legislative and economic ignorance. The lack of information about enacting norms and regulations or keeping accounting records, and the absence of any experience of running a business among new businessmen led to the spontaneous emergence of business unions providing consulting services and other forms of support for the fledgling entrepreneurs. In the first half of the 1990s, very few associations had permanent links with authoritative structures. Later on, with the declaration of state 'support for the development of small and medium-size business', some of the most active associations preferred to link up with the city administration and get support from budgeted funds destined for the development of the SME sector. There are also some examples of 'top-down' initiatives, like the Centers for Entrepreneurship Development that were initially created by district administrations within the framework of the special program for SME support but then had to become individual business initiatives as program funds dried up.

According to the data from a telephone survey, the main benefit that businessmen get from membership of a business association is relatively cheap assistance in solving accounting, juridical and other problems. This is particularly true for 'old' members who joined an association more than six to eight years ago. Newcomers also consider an association as 'an arena for broadening professional communications', 'providing better access to business information', etc. Interestingly, none of the informants mentioned the need for protection of businessmen's rights as a reason for membership. This lack of demand for advocacy functions is certainly determined by the specificity of small business, which is more concerned with legal advice and training than with representing business interests before the authorities (Jedrzejewska 2004: 28).[10] In sum, the main services provided by the majority of business associations are relatively cheap consulting services concerned primarily with juridical and accounting issues, professional training for their members and market research and consultancy.

In fact, the personality of the association leader plays a crucial role in creating the image of the association and influencing the range of its activities. A leader can aim at setting up a real business community and providing real support for the businessmen involved in that community (we gathered some empirical evidence of the existence of this sort of association). In contrast, the term can serve merely as an 'umbrella', a legal façade, or a front for a consulting company run by the association leader, providing different kinds of services for businessmen on a commercial basis. The study has also turned up numerous examples of such 'associations'.

From the empirical data, business associations do not consider 'fighting corruption' to be among their main purposes. None of the informants mentioned either that or the protection of businessmen from bureaucratic extortion as problems which associations are urged to solve. The extreme position on this point was expressed by the director of one of the district Centers for Entrepreneurship Development (Non-Commercial Partnership):

> There is no corruption in business relations, there are some relationships involving different means and forms of conducting deals.… We entrepreneurs used to work and still work in a country where the state has created its own game rules.

> That is why it is possible to say that we have no corruption!... Everybody here knows that in order to work it is necessary to give a bribe. And we give bribes, and nothing bad happens. These are the rules.... No associations and unions are able to influence corruption. This is not their task – leave it to the state!

Although the protection of businessmen's rights is stated as being among the main purposes of business associations, they consider this protection to be mainly 'informational support' for businessmen in order for them to avoid conflict situations with the authorities. Cases of business associations helping businessmen to take an appeal to court are almost non-existent. At least two reasons for this were mentioned: first, very often businessmen are guilty (either as a result of the impracticability of the rules or their attempts to avoid additional expenses), and, second, generally a court decision does not help in resisting bureaucratic extortion because the interaction between businessmen and officials does not end with the decision.

> If a policeman comes to your place, who is able to argue with him? Or a tax inspector? Or a fireman? Even if you win in court today, they will come back tomorrow and find another reason to fine you. (Director of the Center for Entrepreneurship Development)

For business associations, the nature of their relationships with the city authorities can be considered as a crucial factor of development strategy. Some of them try to get access to the authoritative structures which control the financial resources of the city budget allocated for development of the business sector. This is generally the aim of big inter-branch associations that are operating at the city level and trying to portray themselves as representative of a social group of businessmen as a whole. Other associations keep a maximum distance from the state authorities, particularly the type that appears to be more like an individual business project based on the personal financial investments of the association's leader. These are not as big and not so concerned about increasing their membership (with from 50 to a maximum of 100 members). Unfortunately, the data collected are insufficient to make more detailed conclusions regarding the development strategies of associations.

Interaction between business associations themselves, as well as between them and NGOs is not intensive. While federal business associations and inter-branch associations at the regional level cooperate with each other, single branch or professional associations do not go beyond the boundaries of their specific professional niches. One reason for the lack of cooperation between professional associations is that they compete with each other in the market for consulting services, although they attempt, as one respondent put it, 'to focus on different purpose groups and not to bother each other'.

It is noteworthy that our informants are rather critical in assessing the efforts of some NGOs to enlist businessmen and businesses to participate in conferences and meetings. It is only the training seminars and the SME Forum that they consider to be really useful. Associations' leaders see the latter as an opportunity to demonstrate that they belong to a community of associations. For them, participation in the Forum marks a boundary between 'us' and 'them', distinguishing the 'real' associations from other merely consultative groups. Low levels of cooperation between NGOs and business associations may be explained by the fact that businesses do not consider NGOs as strong partners (by 'strong' they mean with a strong possibility of influencing the state in lobbying for business interests). Business is only ready to cooperate with the institutions of civil society when such cooperation promises to benefit them. In other words, business associations will not cooperate with the 'ideological agents' of civil society unless they themselves are weak.

Conclusions

The domination of informal rules in the business environment in Russia has led to a situation where businessmen resort to informal (or semi-formal) intermediaries in order to cope with the impracticability of the formal rules and limitations of the institutional environment. They consider 'informal' ways of solving problems as more effective and more practical than 'civic' ways, and they avoid resorting to civic mediators – that is, organizations of civil society in the business sphere. The study has revealed the emergence and rapid development in recent years of the market for informal and semi-formal mediating services facilitating relationships between businessmen and authorities. We argue that informal bureaucratic mediation is currently going through a process of *institutionalization*, which means that informal mediation has become a generally accepted practice and a profitable though 'unproductive' entrepreneurial activity. The process of institutionalization is accompanied by the *formalization* of mediating services, which means that they are undertaken by legal firms possessing licenses for a large number of services.

The situation is aggravated by the lack of effectiveness of the anti-corruption activities of civic organizations in the business sphere. *Lateral* initiatives play a dominant role among the anti-corruption activities of NGOs – the 'ideological agents' of the anti-corruption field. Business associations, which are the 'rational agents', leave the problem of corruption to the state, although the state fails to demonstrate any coherent anti-corruption policy.

In recent years, a wide variety of business associations and unions have been set up in the business sphere aimed at the support and protection of their members, the development and maintenance of professional standards, and the promotion of professional and informational exchanges. As institutions belonging to civil society, business associations work for the integration of professional communities, and the development of new institutions, professional codes of ethics and common norms and rules. However, despite the growing number of business associations, they rarely act as civil society mediators in the dialog between business and authorities. More often business associations (initially at the local level) emerge as networking projects or trust institutions, which serve to institutionalize and formalize business relationships, or as individual business projects aimed at providing consulting services. The main purpose of business associations is to assist businessmen in adjusting to an unfavorable or constantly changing institutional environment rather than to improve it.

The prevalence of 'horizontal' or parallel (Jedrzejewska 2004: 29) functions in business associations' activities seems to reflect some general peculiarities of the emerging civil society in Russia. Civil society is generally acknowledged as a necessary condition of the transformation from a totalitarian state towards a democratic society. This claim is based on a view of civil society that can be labeled a 'vertical project' (Kharkhordin 1997), stressing its political role. Civil society appears as a system of democratic institutions (or organizations) which are supposed to defend individuals and groups in the face of state oppression and its abuse of power. It is also significant that civil society should offer the possibility for individuals and groups to influence the state by providing civic mechanisms that permit lobbying in defense of the interests of different social groups, against unfair or unreasonable formal rules imposed by the state, and in defense of political rights, etc.

In contrast to this vertical projection of civil society, its 'horizontal project' emphasizes the creation and fostering of civilized relationships within communities, peaceful (not aggressive) settlement of conflicts, and the provision of information and services that the state is unable to provide (Jedrzejewska 2004: 29). Despite the significance of these 'horizontal' functions, they have been overlooked in the discourse on post-socialist transformation because overcoming the legacy of centralized and unlimited power has been considered to be the key issue here. However, as can been seen from our study, the 'civilizing' of business relationships is an urgent matter for the Russian business environment, which is still characterized by the extremely high importance of informal relations.

Using vertical and horizontal projections helps to reconcile the discrepancies in assessments of civil society in Russia provided by different experts. According to some of them, the scale of civil society in Russia is comparable to that of civil societies in some European countries. This assertion is usually based on statistical data on the number and dynamics of non-commercial organizations. It is true that in recent years Russia has seen the dynamic development of non-governmental, non-political, non-commercial organizations. Their total number amounts to around 350,000.[11] However, according to others – and it is their assessments of civic activism in Russia which are apparently prevailing – Russian civil society is weak, uncoordinated and completely dependent on Western financial support. Two projections of civil society make it possible to avoid the alternative nature of these two conclusions. Social expectations about the emergence of the 'vertical' civil society do not seem to be relevant in the case of Russia; today we are witnessing the emergence of a 'horizontal' model characterized by a general movement towards more civilized and formalized business relations.

Notes

1. It is worth mentioning that informality itself (the breaking or ignoring of formal rules, the so-called informal economy or second economy) was not always seen as a negative factor. Indeed, many researchers consider the informal economy in Soviet Russia as the source of a 'Soviet type of civil society', eroding the economic monopoly of the state and facilitating the process of individualization and decentralization (see, e.g., Alapuro 1993; Rigby 1991). Since the term 'civil society' was originally coined by Western scholars and for societies of a Western type, it appeared rather problematic to apply this term to 'non-Western' countries, especially for societies of a 'Soviet type'. Even after the collapse of the Soviet system, the 'Western model' of civil society was seen by many researchers as unachievable for the foreseeable future (Gray 1991). However, supporters of the idea of a 'Soviet type civil society' sought various forms of activities and networks, which provided an alternative to centralized, state-regulated forms. The informal economy in Soviet Russia was considered as one of the bases of civil society alongside such sources as a relatively independent and dynamic urban culture ('city air') (Starr 1988), and informal networks, friendship and family networks (Shlapentokh 1989).

2. A review of the literature on the problem of civil society formation in Russia is presented in Schmidt (2005). See also *Pro et Contra* (1997). For reflections on informality and corruption in Russia, see, for example, Glinkina (1998), Levin and Satarov (2000) and Varese (2001).

3. The project 'Prospects for Fighting Corruption in Post-Socialist Countries: Cases of Russia and Hungary' was carried out in 2003–2004 within the framework of the Think Tank Partnership Program supported by USAID, IRIS and KPMG Consulting Barents Group. Another project, 'Mobilizing Social Support to Fight Corruption: Civic Activism in Business Sphere of Russia', was conducted in 2004 with the support of the American University, Washington, DC.

4. Far be it from us to assert that, in the dialog between business and state, it is only businessmen who 'suffer'. As in any economic system, many examples could be found where businessmen break the rules in order to make better profits. However, it is true that the uncertainty of legislation and the intricacy of business regulations in post-reform Russia make businessmen (and especially those in small and medium-size businesses) an easy target for bureaucratic extortion.

5. Organizations created under the aegis of the state had the support of 22.4 percent of respondents; 14 percent were ready to cooperate with organizations created under the aegis of law enforcement agencies (Ministry of Internal Affairs, etc.). The least popular among anti-corruption organizations were political parties (3.9 percent).

6. For instance, if customs brokers declare in official documents that computers are 'green beans' (which is the cheapest product in terms of import taxes), then in most cases custom officials know about it. However, they won't inspect the real cargo to see whether it corresponds with what is declared in the documents because of informal agreements with custom brokers. This is the reason why, according to official statistics in the mid 1990s, Russia seemed to be inundated with green beans, and at the same time there was almost no importation of electronic devices – of course, the true picture was different (see Radaev 2003).

7. We deliberately use the term 'civic organizations' or 'civil society organizations' instead of the commonly used term 'non-governmental organizations' (NGOs) in order to subsume all kinds of non-commercial and non-governmental entities representing 'independent public activity' in the business sphere (see Schmidt 2003). Moreover, in the business sphere (grass-roots discourse), the term 'NGO' is used mainly to designate a certain type of civic organization related to democracy development issues.

8. Cited in Schmidt (2005).

9. The draft of a new law developed by representatives of NGOs was not accepted by the Legislative Commission of the City Assembly. The Commission agreed only to allow NGOs' representatives attending Assembly sessions to arrange for the electronic delivery of information by the Assembly Press Center through the mailing list of NGOs about the sessions' agendas and approved laws.

10. However, the size of an association's membership has no bearing on the absence of corruption issues on an association's agenda.

11. See http://www.strana.ru/print/85216.html.

References

Alapuro, Risto. 1993. 'Civil Society in Russia?', in *The Future of the Nation State in Europe*, ed. Jyrki Iivonen. Cambridge: Cambridge University Press, pp. 194–218.

Coyne, Christopher J., and Peter T. Leeson. 2004. 'The Plight of Underdeveloped Countries', *Cato Journal* 24, no. 3: 235–249.

Glinkina, Svetlana P. 1998. 'The Ominous Landscape of Russian Corruption', *Transitions* 5, no. 3: 16–23.

Gray, John. 1991. 'Post-Totalitarianism, Civil Society, and the Limits of the Western Model', in *The Reemergence of Civil Society in Eastern Europe and the Soviet Union*, ed. Zbigniew Rau. Oxford: Westview Press, pp. 145–160

Henderson, Sarah L. 2003. *Building Democracy in Contemporary Russia: Western Support for Grassroots Organisations*. Ithaca, NY: Cornell University Press.

Jedrzejewska, Sidonia. 2004. 'Report from the Field: Chambers of Commerce and Industry – Between Civil Society and Market? Comparing Poland and Sweden'. Paper presented at the Conference on Markets and Civil Society in Europe. Madrid, 23–25 September. http://www.asp-research.com/Papers%20CiSoNet/MADRIDSEPT%20(1).pdf.

Kharkhordin, Oleg. 1997. 'Proekt Dostoevskogo', *Pro et Contra* 2, no. 4: 38–60.

Ledeneva, A. 1999. 'Tenevoj barter: Povsednevnost malogo bisnesa', in *Neformalnaja economika: Rossija i mir*, ed. T. Shanin. Moscow: Logos.

Levin, Mark, and Georgy Satarov. 2000. 'Corruption and Institutions in Russia', *European Journal of Political Economy* 16, no. 1: 113–132.

Olimpieva, Irina. 2001. 'Neformal'nye ekonomicheskiye praktiki v strategiyakh vyzhivanija uchenykh I nauchnykh organizatsii V: *Problemy dejatelnosti uchjonyh I nauchnyh kollektivov'*. *Ezhegodnik*, Vyp. XVI. St. Petersburg: SPBGTU.

_____. 2005. 'Informal Character of Organizational Changes in Post-Socialist Firms', in *The End of Transformation?* ed. Rainhart Lang. Munich: Hampp Verlag, pp. 255–267.

Pro et Contra (Special Issue). 1997. *Grazhdanskoe Obshchestvo*. Moscow: Moskovskii Tsentr Karnegi.

Radaev, V. V. 2001. *Novyj institutsionalnyj podhod I deformalizatsija pravil rossijskoj ekonomiki*. Moscow: GU-VSHE.

_____. 2003. 'Tamozhnja daet dobro? Rossijskis biznes na puti k legalizatzii', in *Neformalnaja ekonomika v postsovetskom prostranstve: Problemy issledovanija I regulirovanija*, ed. Irina Olimpieva and Oleg Pachenkov. St. Petersburg: CNSI.

Rigby, Thomas Henry. 1991. 'Mono-organizational Socialism and the Civil Society', in *The Transition from Socialism: State and Civil Society in the USSR*, ed. Shandran Kukathas, David W. Lovell and Willian Maley. Melbourne: Longman Cheshire.

Schmidt, Diana. 2005. 'Grazhdanskoe obshchestvo v Rossii – problematichnoe, mifichnoe ili prosto drugoe?', *Neprikosnovennyi Zapas* 39, no. 1: 125–133.

Shlapentokh, Vladimir. 1989. *Public and Private Life of the Soviet People: Changing Values in Post-Stalin Russia*. New York: Oxford University Press.

Starr, S. Frederic. 1988. 'The Communist Thaw: The Soviet Union. A Civil Society', *Foreign Policy* 70: 26–41.

Usyskin, L. B. 2003. 'Ljudi pervyh millionov (socioekonomicheskie zametki nesociologa i neekonomista)', *Neprikosnovennyj zapas* 5, no. 31. http://magazines.russ.ru/nz/2003/5/usyskin.html.

Varese, Federico. 2001. *The Russian Mafia: Private Protection in a New Market Economy*. Oxford: Oxford University Press.

Chapter 8

ENTREPRENEURS, CONSUMERS AND CIVILITY
The Case of Poland

Andrzej Rychard

The aim of this chapter is to answer the question as to what degree economic participation in a post-communist country can contribute to the
building of civil society.[1] The point of departure for this analysis is the fact
that Poles' participation in politics is relatively weak – as it is in wider public
activity – while their participation in the market is comparatively stronger.
It is not my intention to prove that one kind of participation can replace the
other, and I am not therefore asserting that since politics is failing to build
civil society, the market can accomplish the job 'in its place'. I would, however, like to show that certain characteristics of Polish participation in the
market may have consequences 'outside the market', that is, in those areas
essential for building civil society.

I realize that political and economic participation are fundamentally
different, and will deal with this in a later section. At this point, I would
merely draw attention to the fact that political participation usually takes
the form of collective activity, while its economic counterpart tends to
have an individual character, although unfulfilled economic needs may give
rise to collective claims. Generally speaking, consumers are more individualized than citizens, and therefore we cannot talk about the substitution
of one kind of activity for the other. It is merely a question of what the
consequences of market participation can be for civil society – and this is
the basis for my analysis.

I begin my argument by demonstrating the weakness and specificity of
political participation. Then I set out the characteristic traits of economic

---

Notes for this chapter begin on page 237.

participation and their possible consequences for the building of civil society. In this economic analysis, I shall be taking into account the role of entrepreneur as well as that of consumer.

The relationship between market and civil society belongs in a classical area of interest for social thought. Nevertheless, the present text makes no attempt to argue with the classical theorists. Its ambition is the far more modest one of setting out some introductory hypotheses about the possible consequences for civil society of Poles' engagement in the market. The attempt to relate these empirical hypotheses to existing theoretical concepts will be undertaken only at the next stage of my work.

The Weakness of Political Participation

In sociology and in political science, the term 'political participation' has a well-established meaning. By analogy, we can speak of economic participation understood as the total sum of forms of social participation in economic life, including both those within and those outside the market,[2] as well as formal and informal participation. This broad perspective allows a certain hypothetical comparison of the two forms of participation: political and economic. I leave my theses on this subject to a later part of the chapter.

The weakness of Polish political participation can be investigated on two levels: first, the engagement of society in politics and, second, the ways in which the political actors themselves, such as leaders or parties, take part in politics. I believe that the weakness of Polish politics results from the weakness of both these elements, which are mutually interconnected.

As regards its weak level of social participation in politics, Poland is no exception among the post-communist countries. Participation in general elections is on the order of 40–50 percent; it is lower in referendums and somewhat higher in the case of direct presidential elections. In addition, interest in politics is not at a very high level, and engagement in party-political activity is weak.

Is this climate of aversion to politics and of political non-participation a typically Polish phenomenon? In order not to go along with the common tendency to explain everything as a so-called Polish peculiarity, it is good to make comparisons. Let us assume that one of the elements that creates a climate of social acceptance of populist politics is a lack of interest in politics. A second element could be the conviction that politicians are concerned with what ordinary people think only to a very small degree or not at all. Furthermore, let us assume that those who are not interested in politics and those who believe that politicians are not interested in them constitute a group within society susceptible to populist slogans. Simultaneous acceptance of both views indicates a double lack of interest and can be defined as an expression of 'symmetrical alienation': people from politics and politics from people. Table 8.1 shows the percentages of people from nineteen different countries who could be considered to suffer from symmetrical alienation.[3]

Without wishing to exaggerate the significance of the multiple factors decisive for the position of any given country in the hierarchy according to these indices, if we examine the responses, we shall see that they reveal an interesting structure. Countries where the feeling of symmetrical alienation is relatively strong (i.e. over the threshold of more than half of the population) are principally those of southern Europe, coming from the Catholic tradition, together with two of the post-communist countries included in the survey. Countries with a relatively low feeling of alienation (below 50 percent) are the group of mainly Protestant, Scandinavian countries representing the northwestern Anglo-Saxon part of Europe together with one of the post-communist countries and Israel. It is hard to talk of a very unambiguous pattern, although certain elements of regularity are visible.

For this analysis, it is significant that Poland has a high level of alienation, although it is far from being the highest. We should add that practically all countries from the group feeling the highest degrees of double alienation

Table 8.1 'Symmetrical Alienation' in Politics in the View of Respondents from Nineteen Countries

Country	Percentage
Spain	72.5
Czech Republic	67.4
Greece	66.3
Italy	62.7
Portugal	60.7
Poland	56.2
Slovenia	55.2
Luxembourg	50.6
Ireland	49.5
Hungary	49.0
Finland	47.1
Britain	44.0
Norway	40.8
Germany	35.3
Israel	34.5
Sweden	34.0
Switzerland	33.8
The Netherlands	30.4
Denmark	29.4

N=1182–2899
Source: Rychard (2004: 177).

have a recent history of autocratic, anti- democratic governments that mobilized populist feeling. There are distinctly fewer countries with this experience in the second group (only Germany and Hungary should be included in that category). It is also interesting to note that three post-communist countries, namely, Poland, the Czech Republic and Hungary, which are normally mentioned in the same breath when analyzing the so-called advanced countries of transformation, are placed at various levels here. Generally, however, the table is perhaps a convincing illustration of the notion that previous institutions and the cultural past weigh heavily on the present.

As regards Poland, some researchers (Ekiert and Kubik 1999) believe that the distinctiveness of Polish political participation is due to a weakness of the conventional forms, such as electoral participation and party membership, combined with the relative strength of engagement in unconventional activity, such as various kinds of protest movement. To a certain degree this is true, but we should remember that, in politics, the conventional and the unconventional are dynamic and variable. Some actions of an initially unconventional nature become conventional in the sense that they become an institutionalized element of political ritual.

It sometimes appears that those taking part in the various types of protest and conflict in Poland are playing long-familiar roles. This weakness in political participation is what leads Pełczyńską-Nałęcz (1998) to assert the empirically supported thesis that both conventional and unconventional participation are more characteristic of groups located high in the social structure. Her research also shows that the present boundary between positive participants and protesters is being eroded, and that both these groups are becoming separated by an increasingly visible boundary from those who do not participate in politics at all. As this is currently one of the most significant divisions in Poland, the problem of non-participation becomes more and more important.

The distinctiveness and weakness of Polish politics are increased by the processes taking place in the political arena. Above all, we should note the paradoxical fact that some politicians would like to present themselves as being above politics. They know that the Polish people are largely averse to politics, and they play on of this aversion. They prefer to appear in the guise of experts, superior to the political quarrelling (a strategy frequently employed by the former president of Poland). When the success of the referendum on Polish accession to the EU was important to the authorities, they did all they could to present the vote as non-political and, on this basis, encourage people to vote. The ploy was successful. At least in the beginning, newly formed political groups will avoid calling themselves 'a political party', knowing that it will prompt bad associations. Playing on anti-party and anti-political feeling results in the further weakening of politics (Rychard 2002, 2003).

Nevertheless, politics is an essential activity that has to take place. It functions mainly through various kinds of informal procedures whereby the demands of different social groups are brought to representatives of the administration. These demands have already acquired a systemic character that has led to the creation of the mechanism of 'negotiation democracy' (Mokrzycki 2002: 140ff.). The author understands this as a system in which, through constant negotiation of their demands with the authorities by powerful social groups, a 'second political system' is introduced that bypasses normal institutions and democratic procedures. Moreover, sociologists (Mokrzycki 2001, 2002; Staniszkis 1999; Zybertowicz 2002) have drawn attention to the fact that alongside the visible, official political arena there is a second, less visible ring in Poland, where informal processes dominate. This is another of the factors contributing to the distinctiveness of Polish politics.

Together, the above-mentioned factors of weak political participation and the psychological climate of 'symmetrical alienation' could create fertile ground for closely linked populist politics. Nevertheless, this is still not the main outcome. Above all, Poland is still a poor country, and the structure of its economic interests is, to a large degree, a structure reflecting the demands of individual groups rather than the interests of 'pro-modernization' groups. What is more, a prominent position in Polish politics can be achieved much more efficiently by championing the interests of groups of losers [from the transformation] – or at least groups claiming to have lost – than those of the groups of winners who are timidly emerging within the structure (Rychard 2003).

However, none of this constitutes a sufficient condition for the emergence of a strong populist offer in politics. One possible reason why these factors are insufficient may be the fact that the Poles who do not participate in political life do not usually have extreme political views but tend to be middle-of-the-road (Markowski 2001). I regard this as very important. Firstly, it shows that the common conviction that non-participants in political life do not usually have political views to be untrue, when clearly this is not the case. Secondly, because their views are moderate, their possible participation in the political process would stabilize the main political currents rather than swing them to the extremes, perhaps of a populist nature.

This empirical result ties in with current observations that some Polish 'non-participants' have abandoned politics not because of a lack of political consciousness but just the opposite: as the result of a conscious – essentially political – decision. Therefore, it is necessary to be very careful when interpreting the above data concerning 'symmetrical alienation' as an inseparable element leading to populism or the acceptance of populist solutions. In fact, it is the contrary phenomenon that awaits explanation: why is it that, in spite of the minimal participation and feelings of alienation from politics that could lead to populism, this is not happening? This indicates that there is some other mechanism of significance for maintaining the stability of the democratic order, which also limits the dangers of populism. In accordance with the thesis of this chapter, this role can be fulfilled by various forms of participation in the market, or, more broadly speaking, in the economy.

Economic Participation: The Chance to Create a 'Citizens' Market'?

The boundary between the market and civil society is not always clearly and sharply defined. There are conceptions that link market activity with the civil sphere, but this relationship is not the main theme of this chapter, which is more concerned with the possible 'civil' consequences of participation in the market. In one analysis of the problem, Kaja Gadowska (2002: 136) deals with the participation of Polish entrepreneurs in civic activity. This is one of the possible approaches. However, I am interested less in the additional civic activities that entrepreneurs undertake, and more in the consequences for civil society of the market activities in themselves.

One should remember that, in Poland, the decision to start up one's own business, especially at the beginning of the transformation, not only had an economic impact but a psychological and cultural one as well (Rychard 1995: 319). Sociologists have concerned themselves with the role of the private sector in generating civil society links (Morawski 1998: 262), and research by Grażyna Skąpska's group repeatedly mentions the search for independence as a motive for undertaking business activity (Sobczak 2002: 53).

Let us now return to a comparison of Polish political and economic participation on a broad scale by considering not only participation but the general relationship of the market to democracy. Here an interesting division is visible, already indicated elsewhere (Domański et al. 2000; Rychard 2002), but which I would like to present more systematically. Poles questioned about their assessment of the economic situation on the one hand and the political situation on the other are very critical of both, but their criticism is differentiated. This is shown in table 8.2.

Table 8.2 Political and Economic Situation: Average Net Assessment from Thirteen Samples between October 2002 and October 2003

Political Situation	–46.7
Economic Situation	–65.2

Source: *Nastroje społeczne w październiku* (2003).

The negative value of both indices shows the strong prevalence of negative assessments, although in the case of politics these are relatively fewer as respondents are less critical. It should be added that calculation of the average index of samples taken over the space of a year do give an approximation to some general pattern, but they obscure the trends concealed within the overall index. To the extent that economic assessments were stable in this period, assessments of the political situation evolved clearly in one direction: they deteriorated. It is true, as the CBOS data show, that over a long period of time (from 1997 to 2003) a clear trend in the growth of negative assessments of the economy is visible, a trend that is less clear in political assessments (*Nastroje* 2003: 2, 5).

In short, in the social *consciousness*, the assessment of the economy is even worse than the assessment of politics. However, if we look at social *behavior* we see that the reverse is true: Poles participate relatively weakly in democracy and decidedly more strongly in the economy. This is equally the case whether they are participating as consumers or producers. Of course, it is possible to argue that participation in the market is largely unavoidable, whereas participation in democracy is a matter of choice. It is true that people's choice of whether or not to be a consumer is limited because they are simply enveloped by the market; and, even as producers, they are sometimes forced by circumstance to engage in private business (Sobczak 2002). Nevertheless, the consequences of the linkage between the market and enforced activity probably do not have strong significance for social assessments. What is fundamental is real involvement in market relationships.

It would seem that this is stronger in Poland than involvement in 'democratic relations'. Could it be that Poles are consumers (and producers) to a greater degree than they are citizens? We shall look at this in more detail but first we would point out that stronger involvement in the market than in democracy is certainly not a typically Polish phenomenon: it results largely from the specificities of political and economic participation. They are not completely balanced forms of civic participation within the institutional order. As I mentioned before, we should remember that market participation is, by its very nature, 'commonplace' whereas political participation has a certain 'celebratory' character.

We shall begin our analysis of market participation by examining how Poles function in the role of producers. It is generally recognized that Polish capitalism is based largely on the small and medium-size business sector. At the end of the year 2000, it employed 65.5 percent of all employees and created 69.4 percent of the gross added value outside agriculture, forestry and fishing (Marody and Wilkin 2003: 151). At the same time, however, this sector is dominated by very small firms (of up to five people). In the view of the above authors, this shows the preservation of the existing set-up in that firms which do not have sufficient potential for innovation are geared mainly toward survival. The upside of this phenomenon is that it does mean a large portion of society is linked to the market.

As many authors have noted, it is an imperfect market with dominant elements of 'pirate capitalism' (Skąpska 2002: 29), where there are clear insufficiencies of social capital (including trust capital) and where individual resourcefulness, sometimes of a parasitic nature, has to prevail because the necessary institutional infrastructures are not developed (Marody and Wilkin 2003: 174–175). This is all true, but we should remember that, in the long term, inclusion of a large section of society at the beginning of market regulation must bring far-reaching changes. That will obviously only happen on condition that this distinctive market does not falter at the current stage and so does not undergo the process that I once defined as 'premature consolidation'. I will return to this problem in a later section.

The extent to which Polish capitalism has become widespread need not be measured only by the scale of entrepreneurship at the small and medium level and its economic role. For the purpose of this chapter, it is perhaps more important to consider the social composition of the Polish entrepreneurial class. This question is vital insofar as a fairly general stereotype existed at the start of the transformation according to which the basis of Polish capitalism was formed by the 'enfranchised nomenclature'. Without denying this phenomenon, it is necessary to put it into perspective. As the results of comparative research show, the process of changing political capital into economic capital certainly happened in Poland, but on a considerably smaller scale than is generally believed (Eyal and Wasilewski 1995: 126–131).

Even if the scale of that capital conversion had been greater, the former party 'nomenclature' comprised a relatively small group which could not have constituted the majority of the large stratum of entrepreneurs. Consequently, the results of another investigation by Henryk Domański (1997: 56) are surprising only at first glance. They show that, in 1994, in the group of males in the employment category 'private entrepreneur', 41 percent were formerly (i.e. in 1988) private entrepreneurs and 38 percent were formerly workers. This means that, apart from self-recruitment, which was the strongest mechanism, the working class constituted a significant recruitment base for Polish business. We should remember this result because it is proof of the 'grass roots' nature of Polish capitalism.

To some extent, both of the above conclusions, one showing the dominance of small-scale entrepreneurship and the other, the blue-collar origins of a large section of Polish business, favor the thesis that Polish capitalism is popular in character ('folk capitalism'). Indeed it is – with all the advantages and disadvantages inherent in such a state of affairs. The advantages include the social rootedness of business, and the bringing together of a large part of society at the beginning of market rule. The disadvantages include the aforementioned deformation of capitalism conducted in the face of a deficit of various forms of capital, among which the biggest seems to be the lack of social capital. Nonetheless, the peculiarity of the Polish market – well-illustrated by the title of a recent book about Polish entrepreneurial activity edited by Skąpska (2002), *The Buddenbrooks or the Pirates* – is an empirical fact.

We cannot exclude that the relative success of market transformation in Poland is not so much the success of changes led from the top, but rather the result of processes of adaptation from the grassroots, during which not only society adapted but also the market. It is often said in Poland that populism is a significant threat to our public life. In fact, however, populism did not lead to the destruction of either politics or the economy. It may be that populism did not destroy the market because it controlled it from within. Precisely in this sense, Polish business, at least at the outset, had a strongly 'popular' character. As a result we are dealing more with market populism than anti-market populism.

We move on now to analysis of the role of the consumer. If we are to seek the main protagonist behind the changes in Poland, having noted the clear role played by workers and the intelligentsia that led to the downfall of the old system, we should turn our attention to consumers. They are particularly important in explaining the relative success of the initial construction of the new system.

Consumers – or, more strictly speaking, consumers' aspirations – also played their role in leading to the change of system because they created the tensions which could not be resolved within a command economy (Sikorska 1998). After the collapse of the system, their role increased due to the fact that the hitherto principal actors such as the Solidarność social movement and the working class, which constituted its main backing, began to suffer internal divisions, and in some cases, disintegration, on account of ever more clearly defined differences of interest. Against the background of these processes, the anonymous mass of consumers trying to adapt to the new market reality became the heroes of transformation.

We noted the significance of the role of consumption in researches carried out by IFiS when, on two occasions (in 1995 and in 1999), we asked respondents in which spheres of daily life they felt they had the greatest possibility of choice. We were anxious to learn about the anthropological climate of 'everyday freedom' experienced by Poles. The results proved interesting from the point of view of their fundamental stability. Poles saw a greater possibility of free choice as consumers rather than as workers or citizens (Rychard 2000). The fact that the consumer market offered a wider possibility of choice than the 'civil society market' is open to many interpretations. We see a fundamental difference in the situation today with respect to the previous period: under the communist system in the economy of 'the producer', the role of the worker provided much greater possibilities for influence.

Today, its significance seems to be diminishing in favor of the role of consumer. This raises interesting questions about the future institutional order if the people building it feel themselves to be consumers rather than citizens. As yet there are no answers, but it is worth noting the changing meaning of the role of the consumer in today's economy. In the view of Jonathan Frenzen, Paul M. Hirsch and Philip C. Zerillo (1994: 405), the sociology of consumer behavior clearly considers that the consumer is now ceasing to be a passive customer and buyer. The consumer is becoming more active and may even be seen as a participant in the production process, which is influenced by the consumer's decisions. The active element of the consumer role is therefore an increasingly important one.

Usually labelled material consumption, the phenomenon of the evolution of the consumer role can also be seen in a far broader aspect, a fact that seems to be particularly apparent in Poland. Having overcome the economic crisis, the Polish people are discovering needs of other kinds, apart from strictly material ones. Something else is becoming a source of dissatisfaction: not the frustration resulting from unequal access to goods of an exclusively material kind, but the frustration connected with inequalities of access to goods such as education, health or a feeling of security. This evolution is perhaps illustrated by the recently published research by OBOP, which compared feelings about what troubled Poles in 2003 with analogous feelings in 1992. Table 8.3 contains examples of the most symptomatic changes of feelings.

We can see distinct changes. Poles are already less concerned about lack of money and high prices. Other fears too are clearer, and some that are less concerned with strictly material matters. The results of research mentioned earlier concerning perceptions of 'everyday freedom' show that, apart from the market for consumer goods where many choices are available, Poles consider there is less possibility for choice with respect to access to the

Table 8.3 Selected 'Difficulties and Fears' Experienced by Poles in 1992 and 2003

	1992	2003
Cost of living, high prices	66	50
Lack of money	50	40
Unemployment	32	43
Bureaucracy/incompetence of officials	23	32
Poor functioning of heath service	14	22
Threat of crime	10	16

Source: 'Co nas męczy, co nas dręczy' (2003).

health service, education, entertainment or influence on local government. This can be an area of new frustration resulting from the non-fulfillment of needs which are becoming increasingly important (Rychard 2000: 190; 2002: 153). These findings may lead to the conclusion that Poland is following the path defined by R. Inglehart (1997) as a shift from materialist to post-materialist values.[4]

We would point out that the Polish system of institutions for conflict resolution is consistently geared towards the institutionalization of industrial conflict. Political authority is also traditionally sensitized to the dissatisfaction manifested by the most vociferous groups of workers. Perhaps it is because we deal with this type of conflict relatively well; in any case, they have not held up the transformation. However, this might indicate unpreparedness for the new frustrations and conflicts arising in their wake. We cannot resist the impression that the institutions of authority and the strong claimant groups of workers are locked in a ritual of dispute negotiation, but that, to a certain extent, such disputes now represent the departing order (though not without drama and noise). Against this background, frustrations of another kind become ever more clearly visible, although the system has not succeeded in channelling them. What is more, even the groups experiencing these frustrations have perhaps not yet learned how to articulate their dissatisfaction and mobilize for protest. Acquisition of the know-how for collective activity is a long-term process of social learning.

These changes in the nature of the role of the consumer in Poland today may lead to the conclusion that we are dealing with a specific process of making consumption 'civil'. The citizen becomes an increasingly active participant in the market, whilst the market expands to include not only material goods, while the non-material goods gain in relative significance. Nevertheless, we should also note that significant changes are taking place in the sphere of civil society as well. Political marketing, and its role in promoting figures who may have little content to contribute beyond the form of their message, indicates a process of the 'marketization' of citizenship.

These two processes run in parallel: perhaps to a certain extent the consumer becomes more of a citizen, and the citizen more of a consumer. That would lead to the erosion of a clear differentiation between the two roles. If it were possible to document this hypothesis, it could provide additional arguments about the significance of economic participation for building links in civil society. Once again, it is necessary to underline that acceptance of a broad definition of consumption seems to be an obvious position since in the modern world this phenomenon goes far beyond the consumption of material goods.

Summing up, it is worth noting that the study of economic behavior may give us important knowledge about society in general. Polish sociology has a tendency to look at society through an excessively political prism. At the same time, as is generally accepted, this is only one fragment of reality engaging in only one fragment of social activity. Economic behavior remains primarily the domain of market research, without leading to the satisfaction of intellectual curiosity. It is sometimes worthwhile to view Poles as consumers, or more broadly as participants in economic life. Then perhaps we have a chance to learn something about ourselves and, indirectly, about something that has an influence on political participation and, more broadly, on participation in public life.

What Prevents a Consumer from Becoming a Citizen?

Without a doubt, it is not only consumers but also producers who are hobbled by the deformities of Polish economic participation mentioned above. These create a series of barriers which are difficult to overcome.

Researchers have noted that, after the first decade of transformation, considerable frustration unexpectedly appeared among the group forming the nascent middle class in Poland (Kolarska-Bobińska 2001). It also turned out that some of its members voted for the populist, Samoobrona (Ziemkiewicz 2001), and, at all events, that many of its frustrated representatives find themselves among his close followers.

We have to agree with the authors of 'EU monitoring' who put forward the thesis that Polish entrepreneurs, after giving impetus to the first stage of the transformation, were not able, in view of the barrier of cultural competence, to 'pass the threshold dividing straightforward management of a small enterprise from the new, more complicated phase of management, based on communication in the process of management and of undertaking organized activity, at best making efforts to improve competitiveness in the market by offering bribes or entering into the local "arrangement" between politics and business' (Marody and Wilkin 2003: 173).

Perhaps this judgement is over-generalized, but it certainly applies to some Polish entrepreneurs and perhaps even to the majority. After all, it depicts a very general phenomenon. In the beginning, social actors are the main dynamic force, but after a certain length of time with their participation, a system is created which begins to outgrow the possibilities of those actors and, instead of being a factor for change, they become a conservative force. To some degree, this is the road travelled by Polish workers: overcoming communism and opening up the way towards a market economy which threatened their interests. Their role then began to be taken over by representatives of the nascent middle class (to a large extent of blue-collar origin) which to some extent met the same fate. The system 'tames' changes and can congeal in the state of premature consolidation I mentioned above. Nevertheless, that stagnation is probably only a stage in a long evolutionary process, because in accordance with its logic, either another group or a new factor will appear after a while, making the situation dynamic again. Who or what will fulfill this role in Poland? Will it be the new frustrations and needs mentioned above? Or perhaps a new institutional situation after accession to the EU? We do not know yet.

In order for economic participation to lead to some form of catalyst for public participation it must become a means for overcoming social disintegration. The social vacuum, cogently identified by Stefan Nowak, still exists in Poland. Given the shortfall of civic engagement, could the impetus from the market help, even partially, to make up for it and to fulfill the role of a factor for social integration?

I do not believe that we can seriously question the existence in Poland of a society, a whole constituted by various social groups and classes: strata that are internally integrated or linked by a variety of relationships between themselves. The alternatives are to accept either the extreme individualist position, claiming – as Margaret Thatcher once did – that there are only free individuals; or else the entirely opposite model of complete totalitarianism where only masses of atomized individuals exist. In neither of those two cases can we say that society does not exist, but for fundamentally different reasons: with full individualism it is 'unnecessary', and under full collectivism it is a threat.

In Poland, as we know, neither the collectivizing plans of totalitarianism were realized in full, nor has nascent capitalism inculcated individualistic habits. The combination of totalitarianism (and so, of the essence of the pathology) with capitalism should not suggest that I am comparing two equally valid systems: obviously this is not the case. Nonetheless, from a historical viewpoint, this is what happened to us and to a large part of Europe: after a long-term experiment with incomplete totalitarianism, capitalism is being created. And as indicated by many authors, and above all by our own experiences of the previous system and of almost fifteen years of building a new system, we find elements of both old and new in social life just as in institutional activity.

In Polish sociology there is no agreement about the basic nature of Polish society. Although there is no dispute (more's the pity), it is possible to find opposing judgements formulated by sociologists – such as Pawel Śpiewak's (2003) opinion (referred to above) that there are two Polands, and also Marody's (2002) concept that there are three. There is also the empirically well-documented opinion of Domański (1995) that the Polish social structure is clearly crystallizing and recomposing after a period of decomposition.

From one point of view, these two sample judgements can be taken as contradictory. The implication of the thesis about two (or more) Polands is an assumption that something like insular development is occurring, where it is difficult to talk about a whole; while the thesis about recomposition implies the opposite: that not only does the whole exist, but that its internal structure is becoming increasingly distinct. But are these two positions necessarily contradictory? Is the implication of judgements of the first kind that there is in fact no society, and does it only exist if we hold the second view?

We can reconcile the two views by demonstrating that there are mechanisms linking these two Polands into one. However, these mechanisms have two particular characteristics: firstly, frequently (although not always), they have a pathological character, or at least hinder the development of society. Secondly, in order to find them, or in other words, to find out what makes a society, you have to go beyond the dominant perspectives. Frequently, society is not where we look for it and sometimes it is where we don't want to see it. The first feature of these mechanisms, which is their informal nature, need not always give rise to the pathological. Unfortunately, it very often does. Researchers draw attention to the usefulness of Adam Podgórecki's category of 'dirty community' for describing the ties in Polish social life, especially when referring to economic life (Skąpska 2002: 29).

This would indicate that we still cannot cross the threshold into market society, in Polanyi's sense, as Mokrzycki noted (see above). Is this an insuperable boundary? The second feature of these intriguing mechanisms is that they often occur in unexpected places. Maria Wieruszewska's group researches show that the beginnings of civic ties may paradoxically be observed to a larger extent in a more traditional Podlaska village rather than in a modernized one in Wielkopolska, which has survived transformation in a worse condition (Wieruszewska 2002: 28). On informal territory, civic ties can also grow from traditional ties. So can these, with all the baggage of distinctiveness and pathology of Polish participation in the market, still constitute an opportunity for future civic ties?

We do not yet know the answer to the question posed in this way. It is known, however, that to understand the specificity of Polish civic ties we should accept a broader definition of civil society. As I indicated earlier, Polish participation in public life is unconventional in character; its informal manifestations are stronger than its formal ones. Consequently, we cannot limit ourselves merely to the study of NGOs, for example, as the basic way in which civil society manifests itself. We should take into account civic ties and initiatives of a much less formal nature. We will then be able to see more easily that market participation has civic meaning. After all, many elements of Polish market participation, bearing in mind its aforementioned 'popular/folk' character, are not completely formal.

Still, taking this in the broad sense of civic consequences gives rise to at least two problems. Firstly, how do we differentiate engagement resulting from ordinary human ability to cope and motivated by economic interest, from engagement of a civic character. Secondly, how do we distinguish 'good' informal ties from bad, pathological ones of a clientelistic or mafioso kind? The first question may be solved by concentrating not so much on the motives for action but on their objective outcome. It may turn out that even actions motivated by economic interest may have civic consequences. The second problem is probably more complicated. As I indicated earlier, in Poland many individual and group actions are integrated into a larger whole with the help of pathological mechanisms. These are the mechanisms of the 'dirty community' described by Podgórecki. They are indeed sometimes the only means for ensuring a particular social unity. We then arrive at the phenomenon of the 'functionalization of pathology' described by Jadwiga Staniszkis (2001: 105–106), where the pathological solution perpetuates itself because it has become vital to the functioning of the system. Certain mechanisms of integration or informal action may have just this kind of character. Let us recall that in the view of Robert Putnam (1995), the means for distinguishing civic from clientelistic ties is their form: civic ties are usually horizontal while clientelistic ones are vertical, linking persons in various positions in a hierarchy.

The issue of the type of tie is important because it leads to the question of what kind of social cohesion is ensured dependent on the different ways of participating in the market. It need not always be cohesion that is based on civic ties, and this is worth remembering.

Concluding Remarks

Finally, let me reflect on the general features of the approach presented here. As I have already mentioned, the dominant perspective in studies of post-communist transition focuses on macro-systemic analyses of the institutional changes, predominantly political and economic ones. As various researchers have already noted, this perspective is usually based on the teleological assumption that it is an ideological goal of a transition (building the market and democracy) which determines and explains its course. One consequence of this assumption is an overestimation of the political and institutional changes as seen 'from above'. The other consequence is that within the limits of this perspective we are not able to explain the spontaneous political and economic processes, which lead to unexpected results (e.g. the low level of socio-economic conflicts or the successful political comeback of post-communist politicians).

As I have written before, it is mainly due to these adaptive strategies and not to successful implementation of designed changes 'from above', that the

market change in post-communist Europe has not been rejected by populations and that there were no serious social conflicts resulting from market
transition. On the contrary, it is owing to the dynamics and creative adaptive
processes of individuals and small groups that economic crises have been
overcome. However, in the course of these processes, market arrangements
have been modified resulting in various deviations, including pathological
ones. One of the goals of future research could be to identify to what extent
these adaptive processes helped to transform the system and to what extent
they have 'frozen' the necessary changes and changed their initial direction. My preliminary hypothesis is that in the first stage of transition (let
us say, from 1990 to 1995) they served as the main agent of the dynamics.
However, after the successful completion of this stage, they slowed down
further changes, contributing to what I call the 'premature consolidation'
of a system. To sum up, according to my approach, what we are witnessing
in Central and Eastern Europe is not the success of the transition itself, but
rather the way the transition has been 'transformed' by societies.

The perspective adopted has involved analysis of various manifestations
of 'everyday transitions', including changes in organizational culture, coping
strategies, and the ways social groups are using (and abusing) the market
and democracy. My initial claim is that post-communist societies seem more
adapted to markets than to democracies, which results in peculiar forms of
social participation that is more consumer-oriented than citizen-oriented.
However, even this consumer-oriented participation has some important
potential civic consequences. The aim of the chapter was to present some
preliminary hypotheses on these consequences.

Notes

1. An earlier version of this text was prepared at the Institute of Philosophy and Sociology
   PAN for the volume Niepokoje polskie ('Polish Anxieties') (Domański, Ostrowska and
   Rychard, eds., 2004). The present text is a modified version and was prepared for the
   CiSoNet conference, Madrid, September 2004.
2. I base my remarks here on the well-known distinction by Polanyi and his collaborators
   (Smelser and Swedberg 1994: 15), according to which there are three mechanisms of
   integration of the workings of economic systems: reciprocity, redistribution and exchange.
   Only the third kind assumes market relationships. This means that market systems constitute only a sub-class of economic systems, and that in fact the three ideal types of
   mechanism may co-exist. In connection with this, economic participation may also, by
   analogy, equally mean market and non-market forms of participation. With reference to
   the situation in Poland, we can note here, for example, Miroslawa Marody's (2002) conception of public and private institutions in Poland and of institutions of social protection
   as a means of multiple participation. Although it seems that Marody assumes rather too

strong a relationship between types of occupation and forms of ownership (e.g. the market with the private sector, and full time employment with the public sector) we cannot, after all, exclude subjection of full-time employment to market regulation, regardless of the sector of ownership.

3. Data from the European Social Survey conducted by IFiS PAN in 2003. The indices shown are the percentages of those who responded negatively to the question 'How would you describe your interest in politics. Are you … ?' by choosing 'not very interested' or 'not interested at all' and also to the question 'Do you think that in general politicians attach any weight to what people like you think' by choosing the responses 'practically no politician' or 'very few' or 'some' attach any weight to what people 'like me' think.

4. However, for Inglehart (1997: 109–119) the values related to fighting crime and maintaining order belong to the sphere of materialist values, the importance of which is rising in Poland. Maybe it is more a shift from narrowly defined materialist values to values of this type understood in the broader sense.

References

'Co nas męczy, co nas dręczy' (What Troubles, What Torments Us). 2003. *Gazeta Wyborcza.* Warsaw.

Domański, Henryk. 1995. 'Rekompozycja stratyfikacji społecznej i reorientacja wartości', in *Ludzie I instytucje: Stawanie się ładu społecznego. Pamiętnik IX Ogólnopolskiego Zjazdu Socjologicznego.* Lublin: Uniwersytetu Marii Curie-Skłodowskiej, pp. 369–397.

_____. 1997. 'Mobilność I hierarchie stratyfikacyjne', in *Elementy nowego ładu*, ed. H. Domański and A. Rychard. Warsaw: IFiS PAN, pp. 47–79.

Domański, Henryk, Antonina Ostrowska and Andrzej Rychard. 2000. 'Wstęp, czyli o życiu w Polsce I życiu Polski', in *Jak żyją Polacy*, ed. H. Domański, A. Ostrowska and A. Rychard. Warsaw: IFiS PAN, pp. 7–16.

Eyal, G., and J. Wasilewski. 1995. 'Pochodzenie społeczne I postkomunistyczne losy nomenklatury', in *Elity w Polsce, Rosji I na Węgrzech: Wymiana czy reprodukcja*, ed. I. Szelenyi, D. Treiman and E. Wnuk-Lipiński. Warsaw: ISP PAN, pp. 105–132.

Ekiert, Grzegorz, and Jan Kubik. 1999. *Rebellious Civil Society: Popular Protest and Democratic Consolidation in Poland, 1989–1993.* Ann Arbor: University of Michigan Press.

Frenzen, Jonathan, Paul M. Hirsch and Philip C. Zerillo. 1994. 'Consumption, Preferences, and Changing Lifestyles', in *The Handbook of Economic Sociology*, ed. Neil J. Smelser and Richard Swedberg. Princeton, NJ: Princeton University Press, pp. 403–426.

Gadowska, Kaja. 2002. 'Społeczne zasoby: Obywatelskie zaangażowanie polskich przedsiębiorców', in *Buddenbrookowie czy piraci: Polscy przedsiebiorcy okresu głębokich przemian*, ed. G. Skąpska. Krakow: Universitas, pp. 129–179.

Inglehart, Ronald. 1997. *Modernization and Postmodernization: Cultural, Economic, and Political Change in 43 Societies.* Princeton, NJ: Princeton University Press.

Kolarska-Bobińska, Lena. 2001. 'Wątpliwości klasy średniej', *Rzeczpospolita*, 12 November.

Markowski, Radoslaw. 2001. 'Dynamika współzawodnictwa w polskim systemie partyjnym 1997–2001', in *System partyjny I zachowania wyborcze: Dekada polskich doświadczeń*, ed. Radoslaw Markowski. Warsaw: Friedrich Ebert Stiftung, ISP PAN, pp. 147–175.

Marody, Miroslawa. 2002. 'Trzy Polski – instytucjonalny kontekst strategii dostosowawczych', in *Wymiary życia społecznego: Polska na przełomie XX I XXI wieku*, ed. Miroslawa Marody. Warsaw: Naukowe Scholar, pp. 252–271.

Marody, Miroslawa, and Jerzy Wilkin, eds. 2003. *Na prostej? Polska w przededniu członkostwa w UE. EU-monitoring VII.* Krakow: Friedrich Ebert Stiftung.

Mokrzycki, Edmund. 2001. *Bilans niesentymentalny*. Warsaw: IFiS PAN.

_____. 2002. 'Demokracja "negocjacyjna"', in *Utracona dynamika? O niedojrzałości polskiej demokracji*, ed. Edmund Mokrzycki, Andrzej Rychard and Andrzej Zybertowicz. Warsaw: IFiS PAN, pp. 129–146.

Morawski, Witold. 1998. *Zmiana instytucjonalna*. Warsaw: Naukowe PWN.

Nastroje społeczne w październiku (Social Moods in October). 2003. Centrum Badania Opinii Społecznej. Warsaw.

Pełczyńską-Nałęcz. 1998. 'Postawy i zachowania polityczne – tendencje zmian w latach 1988–1995', in *Polacy 95. Aktorzy i klienci transformacji*, ed. W. Adamski. Warsaw: IFiS PAN, pp. 219–275.

Putnam, Robert. 1995. *Demokracja w działaniu*. Krakow: Społeczny Instytut Wydawniczy Znak.

Rychard, Andrzej. 1995. 'Posłowie', in *Demokracja w działaniu*, ed. Robert Putnam. Krakow: Społeczny Instytut Wydawniczy Znak, pp. 310–321.

_____. 2000. 'Codzienność świata instytucji', in *Jak żyją Polacy*, ed. Henryk Domański, Antonina Ostrowska and Andrzej Rychard. Warsaw: IFiS PAN, pp. 183–192.

_____. 2002. 'Polityka I społeczeństwo w Polsce: Ewolucja porządku instytucjonalnego', in *Utracona dynamika? O niedojrzałości polskiej demokracji*, ed. Edmund Mokrzycki, Andrzej Rychard and Andrzej Zybertowicz. Warsaw: IFiS PAN, pp. 147–171.

_____. 2003. 'Polska polityka w dobie integracji europejskiej: Analiza instytucjonalna'. Manuscript for the EU-monitoring Project VII, Friedrich Ebert Stiftung.

_____. 2004. 'Konsumenci, obywatele, populiści: czy rynek może pomóc demokracji?', in *Niepokoje polskie*, ed. H. Domański, A. Ostrowska and A. Rychard. Warsaw: IFiS PAN, pp. 171–189.

Sikorska, J. 1998. *Konsumpcja: Warunki, zróżnicowania, strategie*. Warsaw: IFiS PAN.

Skąpska, Grażyna, ed. 2002. *Buddenbrookowie czy piraci: Polscy przedsiębiorcy okresu głębokich przemian*. Krakow: Universitas.

Smelser, Neil J., and Richard Swedberg. 1994. 'The Sociological Perspective on the Economy', in *The Handbook of Economic Sociology*, ed. Neil J. Smelser and Richard Swedberg. Princeton, NJ: Princeton University Press, pp. 3–26.

Sobczak, Jerzy B. 2002. 'Polski small business – proba rekonstrukcji jego kulturowych wzorów', in *Buddenbrookowie czy piraci: Polscy przedsiębiorcy okresu głębokich przemian*, ed. G. Skąpska. Krakow: Universitas, pp. 35–65.

Śpiewak, Pawel. 2003. 'Dwie Polski', *Wprost*, 35.

Staniszkis, Jadwiga. 1999. 'Polityka przyszłości – władza bez polityki', in *Przyszłość polskiej sceny politycznej*. Warsaw: Instytut Spraw Publicznych, pp. 66–71.

_____. 2001. 'Postkomunizm. Próba opisu', Słowo/Obraz, Terytoria, Gdańsk.

Wieruszewska, Maria. 2002. 'Społeczność wiejska – podstawy samoorganizacji', in *Samoorganizacja w społecznościach wiejskich: Przejawy – struktura – zróżnicowania*, Warsaw: IRWiR PAN, pp. 12–90.

Ziemkiewicz, Rafal. 2001. 'Kapitalizm bez kapitalizmu', *Wprost*, 28 October.

Zybertowicz, Andrzej. 2002. 'Demokracja jako fasada: Przypadek IIIRP', in *Utracona dynamika? O niedojrzałości polskiej demokracji*, ed. Edmund Mokrzycki, Andrzej Rychard and Andrzej Zybertowicz. Warsaw: IFiS PAN, pp. 173–214.

Chapter 9

CONCLUSIONS AND SUGGESTIONS FOR FURTHER RESEARCH

Víctor Pérez-Díaz

Although markets, civil societies and liberal democratic polities are part of a unified system of action and meaning, the variety of angles and topics dealt with in the chapters of this book bears witness to a wide range of variations regarding each of these components of the system and the relations among them. Civil societies come in many different ways both historically and geographically, and the same applies to markets (Swedberg 1994, 2005; Uzzi 1997) and to liberal democratic polities (and to their combination); indeed, the very logic of a decentralized system of decisions and experimentations suggests endless variations.

Anchoring the Search in a Conceptual Schema

A Historical, Social Scientific Approach

For a better understanding of these variations, the search should be anchored in a conceptual schema. Even though we must be sensitive to the different ways that a unified system has been articulated throughout the course of history, and to the nuances of meaning linked to specific historical configurations, a social science approach needs a more fixed, relatively context-free definition (Gellner 1985: 101ff.). We should be careful in drawing up an analytical model and, then, applying it to different historical configurations, in order to build an explanatory theory for the purpose of giving a particular account of the matter under consideration; and such a theory would

---

Notes for this chapter are located on page 252.

be either substantiated, or invalidated, by appropriate factual evidence,[1] which would provide a 'reality check' to the theory in question if anything approaching social science is ever to be carried out (ibid.: 21, 63, 76). This is the reason why it has been suggested in this book that a return to the broad composite concept of civil society, with its emphasis on the unity of markets, civil societies qua associations, and liberal democratic polities, as interconnected parts of a whole, may be useful for explaining a variety of historical processes, both past and present, and presumably in the future as our contemporary societies gradually move away from a state-centered world towards more complex forms of social coordination; the point being not so much to take on the old label of 'civil society' to denote the whole, as to take on that whole (the 'thing itself') with one label or another.

We can then explore the character, scope and limits of the relations and correspondences between these institutions, in order to build a set of theories to explain a variety of phenomena, and advance practical recommendations. For instance, we may conjecture that within this broad institutional framework there is more likelihood that violence and fraud will be absent the more government, social and cultural elites are kept at a safe distance from markets, given the tendency of such elites to collude with economic entrepreneurs, who, in turn, may be tempted to control and distort the market so as to avoid competition. Policy-oriented recommendations might follow that could be tested – for instance, those concerned with various forms of market regulations. This kind of theory-building and systematic testing of both hypotheses and institutional arrangements implies the consideration of social, economic, and political relations as parts of an integrated field.

A Note on the Post-Hegelian Tradition and the Limits of Public Deliberation

Tensions between coherence and diversity in the conceptual schema of civil society were already apparent at the time the influence of the Scottish tradition was (partially) replaced in some parts of the European continent by that of Hegel and his followers, right and left. Hegel suggested a sequence of forms of ethical communities in modern times. The broad concept of civil society he inherited from the Scottish philosophers included markets (a system of needs), corporations and a limited state (reduced to the administration of justice and a modicum of public policy); for him, this corresponded, *grosso modo*, to the British experience at the time. Then, he went on to envision an ethical community of a more advanced sort, which, he suggested, pointed to the Prussian state as it was presumably evolving under his very eyes. In it, the state has developed into a complex institutional machine in which the bureaucracy plays a crucial role, particularly that of monitoring the markets and educating the corporations into adopting a view of the whole beyond their particular interests. Hegel ultimately argues in favor of unifying the entire socio-political and socio-economic field by placing that (political) state at the center of the historical process.

The question is, whether modern society is understood better in the light of an idea of society which is made out either of parts that fit to each other or of disjointed parts. The ensuing debate is largely the story of answers to this question, which have oscillated between the view of a radically conflicting society and that of an ordered society; in the last case, there is still an oscillation between those who see the state (or the state cum social and political partners) at the center of the ordering process, and those who don't see the state playing such a central role. In a sense, we may take many contemporary thinkers to be Hegel's descendants (either self-consciously or inadvertently), as if they had received Hegel's legacy *cum beneficio inventarii* and selected different portions of it. They have oscillated between several positions, from 'right' to 'left'.

Thus, the 'Hegelian right' (at first, in the guise of civil servants working from within bureaucratic authoritarian regimes, then, in the guise of social democrats) stuck to Hegel's unifying view and took seriously the steering role of the state for the entire social system under modern conditions, to educate society and instill it with a view of the whole. The state was supposed to be the bearer of a moral project. Civil servants and great statesmen would educate parties to control their own partisan impulses, and make the best of society's diversified energies not to be wasted in merely private pursuits; then, social-democratic leaders and parties could work out a compromise between economic efficiency and social justice of a similar character. Corporatist arrangements and welfare policies suited them all. They could adjust easily to the ways of the time and to the drift of the contemporary world towards increasing state intervention, at least until the partial questioning of the trend took place in the 1970s and 1980s, and since.

The 'Hegelian left' started by questioning Hegel's unifying view of the whole. Initially, they settled for a disjointed view of society, in which its components tended to follow opposite logics and eventually clashed with each other, as they might insist on a fundamental conflict between the logic of a capitalist economy, that of the modern state, and that of the social manifestations of a life-world. But time showed several modalities of a left Hegelian tradition were possible, as we may distinguish a (at first euphoric, now rather extinct) old left, a variety of (melancholy) middle left, and a (more optimistic) new left.

The 'old left' dreamt of a revolution, the abolition of the market economy, the withering away of the state, and the cornucopia of communism, with the results which are well known. For the 'middle left', as the logics of the markets and of the state conflate there is hardly anything that can be done to counter it, except to defend and protect a limited space for the development of the life-world. The contrast should be maintained between, on the one hand, the hard world of naked economic and political interests, and, on the other, a soft social space which could be home to a process of social and cultural deliberation, expressions of personal and group identity, and alternative life-styles. For the adherents to the 'new left' things look different. They see an opening in the possibility of a rapprochement between the social sphere and the state. The state as the bearer of a moral project is replaced, now, by a process of social and political deliberation, in which state and civil society institutions and agents play a role of co-protagonists. The process points to society's ever-greater awareness and self-reflexivity, leading to consensus, which in turn would culminate in public policy (and, eventually, the establishment of ever-better liberal democratic political institutions). By doing so they abandon the disjunctive view of society of the old left and the middle left; in the end, there is indeed a new, unifying picture in which a democratic state and a plural, public-spirited civil society tame the markets.

The new left's final position meets that of the traditional Hegelian right. In the end, a consensus seems to emerge, so that left and right meet in a 'middle way', or a 'third way'. Instead of the intimidating father figure of a powerful state bureaucracy dealing with party oligarchies and big business and big unions, and engaging in a grandiose game of world-politics (à la Alexander Kojève, a rather eccentric but influential Hegelian of our times: Auffret 1990), we get a more gentle relative of the family, with a populist touch and a gregarious communicative attitude: a new mix in which civil servants meet party activists, participants in social movements, public intellectuals, the media and the low clergy, all engaged in an open-ended process of collective deliberation possibly ending in some binding decision, to keep the world in running order, and in peace. The process suggests a deliberative, collective, unitary actor pointing to some form of harmonious, collective self-institutionalization (Terrier and Wagner 2006).

Critics, however, can point to the fact that self-institutionalization may prove to be an elusive goal since neither individuals nor societies, properly speaking, institutionalize themselves, in the same way as they do not give birth to themselves. Rather, they are born of their parents. As every generation is born out of a previous one, it inherits its material basis, its institutions and its culture; and crucial cognitive and moral limitations are part of its legacy. On top of that, no generation is ever able to know what the full consequences are of what it does, nor what are the full implications of what it says, and, therefore, it is unable to know exactly what it does accomplish in its short passage on earth. There are limits, then, to what the most lively and knowledgeable public sphere can deliver. In other words, people come into being in institutional settings that are already established and to which they accommodate themselves, proceed to learn some, if lucky, and then to change some of what they have inherited but, more often, to endure most of it, as best, and as long, as they can.

Those who think in these critical, cautious (and largely pre-Hegelian) terms are keen to point out the limits of human knowledge, good will and deliberation in shaping the long-term prospects of any society. They are prone to be at the same time hopeful and skeptical about the potential of any well-ordered society to stay on course for a long period of time. Hopeful, because they see a real possibility of a more sensible, reasonable society to come through, not as a result of human design but as mostly unintended (and partly intended) consequences of intricate combinations of human actions.

Indeed, the sequence of theorists in the traditions of natural jurisprudence and *societas civilis* from the sixteenth through the late eighteenth centuries suggests the feasibility of a historical path of living with, and gradually reforming, a set of institutions of a particular kind over long periods of time which ends up in what is called an order of freedom, or a natural system of liberty, in which the different spheres of a market economy and liberal polity would fit the public sphere and a world of voluntary associations, and social networks. But this was taken to be no more than a model, a regulatory idea of the actual sequence of world-historical events with no more than a fifty-fifty chance of realization; and this is why, for instance, David Hume's arguments were conditional, and he stated his conditions (with more than a grain of salt of skepticism) in terms of tendencies (Robertson 1983: 155).

Similar expectations could apply to those who engage, today, in a discourse on civil society, and who are sensitive to the dangers of 'unbridled capitalism', alert to the excesses of no less 'unbridled' sectarian social movements (and a 'noisy and deceptive' public sphere), and attentive to the dangers of 'unlimited' democracy, and may even point towards a 'utopia of civil society' (to use the words of Dieter Gosewinkel and Jürgen Kocka).[2] They may get to see the utopia being realized only insofar as all those excesses are continuously watched over, monitored and checked; the chances being, of course, rather limited.

Suggestions for Further Research

Research might, then, proceed in many directions; and at this point I should like to add just a brief comment on the mixed character and language of associations (civil society in the narrow sense), and its relations with politics, as well as the role played by the professions in shaping that language and those relations, and the way associations may learn the language of markets and politics; and on the role of civil virtues.

The Voices and Character of Associations
and the Role of Professions

In the entire social-political-economic configuration of a civil society broadly understood, networks of voluntary associations (the third sector, or civil society in a narrow sense) find their place alongside parties and citizens of liberal democratic polities, and all kinds of economic agents in free markets. They all share some crucial characteristics. All of them engage in strategic as well as communicative activities, and all are subjected to rules requiring them to refrain from using violence and fraud against each other. They also share the complexities of having particular agendas and dimensions that are public as well as private.

In this regard, it may be useful to build bridges between two different ways of understanding voluntary associations, one of which focuses on the public dimension of their activities and the other on the private one. This may prove crucial for dealing with a growing world of voluntary associations that see themselves as belonging to a third sector lying somewhere between markets and state institutions, but refuse to confine their *raison d'être* to activities that take place uniquely or mainly in the public domain. In fact, they are anchored in both public and private domains, as is the case of non-governmental, non-profit organizations, such as churches, ethnic communities, unions, cultural associations, associations defined by gender or age groups *e tutti quanti*; these all express specific identities and defend special interests, at the same time as they articulate their demands both in terms of self-assertion and in the name of some form of common good. Throughout this process, they engage in an inextricable mix of strategic and communicative activities by becoming involved in a conversation that to a certain extent requires them to adopt a public language.

Yet they cannot be faithful to their own roots without nurturing their own particular private languages too. These private languages are, of course, a mark of identity, and therefore of difference. Thus, for instance, in James Ault's (2005) sensitive rendering of life in religious fundamentalist communities in the United States, one of the most thriving kinds of voluntary association on the American scene, and very much a part of American civil society (Ladd 1999: 43ff., 66ff.; Putnam 2000: 65ff.), the point is to recognize the particular voice of those communities and make sense of the way (words, emotional sounds, etc.) in which they try to articulate their thirst for an orderly family life, a moral community and deep religious experience in an uncertain, disconcerting milieu. In the end, what is needed is to follow the transitions between the two languages.

A large network of voluntary associations involves an intricate game of both public and private languages in which many voices are engaged in open-ended, inconclusive conversations. We might believe, as Gellner (1985: 111ff.) does, that we have entered a new historical era in which society is science-based, and that abstract, context-free knowledge rules an ever-larger segment of human experience; but, were this the case (and my guess is that it is not), there would still be enough uncertainty surrounding us to keep the primacy of practical reason, or prudential wisdom, intact. However, in a complex, plural society there is a need for the kind of transversal communication that expertise and professional knowledge can provide us with. This is of some help to us and should be most welcome, even though it is limited, if only because it helps us deal with 'extended orders' as well as with 'small groups' (Hayek 1988: 18).

As associations are intent on expressing the identity, defending the interests and articulating the grievances of particular sets of people, they are out to set a measure of self-governance for their small worlds. But these small worlds are located in the larger landscape of extended orders. The world of associations may be compared to 'a field of mushrooms' (Pérez-Díaz and López Novo 2003: 69ff.), in which a multitude of specimens spring up more or less spontaneously under the right conditions of light and humidity, each one standing on its own. But the scope of this image is limited because associations are engaged with each other as well as with the wider landscape to which they belong. In order to survive and prosper they not only have to manage themselves but need to understand the extended orders. For them, a *modus vivendi* between the discourses (and, eventually the moralities) of their small worlds and that of the extended order is an obvious, albeit difficult, goal to attain. Tensions arise; solving and accommodating such tensions is a matter of practical judgement and prudence. A process of discovery, or of trial and error, may favor the development of this virtue of prudence.

But accommodation and transition between the two worlds can be favored by a number of link mechanisms. Here experts, *amici curiae* and professionals can play a role in reinforcing this mechanism. These professionals should be (or are expected to be) trained in the practice of exercising technical and impartial judgment, but the cultivation of a *techné* is not merely an exercise in instrumental reasoning and applied science; it also involves moral virtues and professional morality. Thus, they should be (or are expected to be) somehow detached from the cult of wealth, power and status at the same time as they are committed to an ideal of social service (to paraphrase the early Parsons' scriptures: Brick 1996: 384ff.). Such experts are expected to help people understand some of the intricate problems of modern life, and, in particular, help associations make the transition from the language of their small worlds to that of the extended orders, and *vice versa*. This is the case, of course, with 'civil' professionals, since the alternative is that of 'uncivil' professionals who become self-interested, predatory animals eager to increase their own power, wealth and status, and willing to use the associations they lead or advise with those ends in mind. The extent to which the spread of a professional culture of service (with or without religious foundations) may be helpful in producing professionals of the right kind, and turning uncivil professionals into civil ones needs to be explored.

On the other hand, expertise, technical and professional knowledge may also go hand in hand with the development of oligarchical tendencies within any kind of organization, including voluntary associations. That much has been known for a long time. More recently, Theda Skocpol (2003: 175ff.) has pointed out the replacement in the United States of representative associations, which put a premium on member participation, by associations managed from the top down. This has been mainly brought about by a convergence of opportunities following changes in the way the political system (Congress, in this case) works, and new technologies favoring a concentration of money management and technical expertise in the higher echelons of organizations.

Finally, a counter-tendency to these oligarchical trends may also be grounded in the professional experience. Again in the United States, Michael Schudson has drawn attention to the vibrancy of grassroots engagement in civic concerns due to the rise of what he calls 'monitorial citizens' (Schudson 1999). This points, in fact, to a way of transferring professional skills from the private arena to the collective arena by concerned citizens and social and political entrepreneurs temporarily attracted to specific issues and opportunities. What is initially seen as an opportunity may become a calling, an obligation or an institutionalized practice (or not, as the development of the blogosphere suggests). Juries and arbitrators may be understood as specifically institutionalized forms of drawing the civic potential of concerned, monitoring citizens into the system of governance. In turn, these, or similar experiences, may be made possible by the law and institutional arrangements within the political system, or hybrids between politics and society that allow for communities of debate on public policy composed of experts, associations, civil servants and politicians, as in the case of the governmental commissions that pervade Swedish political life as a matter of routine (Trägårdh 2007).

Associations' Learning the Language of Markets and Politics: The Case of Solidarność

There is a need to anchor our debate on civil society in time, extending our time frame both towards the past and the future. In order to do this, we may go back to the sources of civil society and explore its history, not only in the natural jurisprudence and civic traditions, but also in those of city guilds and peasant communities, in other words, the medieval and classical past. At the same time, we may project ourselves into the future, and be attentive to the increasing interdependence of different kinds of third-sector organizations, the family, economic firms and various forms of governance particularly at local level, looking for connections, hybrids and correspondences. Looking back and forwards, the point is that discussion on civil society should not be confined to the rather short, largely erratic historical cycle that goes from Hegel to the social movements of the last third of the twentieth century and their legacy in the years immediately following.[3]

Even with regard to the recent past, there is room for further debate to explore new developments that have played a crucial role in the revival of the idea of civil society. To a great extent, these debates have exaggerated the relevance of the languages used by the most articulate participants in associations and social movements involved in these processes, and this may have negatively affected a correct understanding of the situation. This is the case with events in Central and Eastern Europe, which have given apparent plausibility to a discourse on civil society in which too much is attributed to a particular Hegelian and post-Hegelian tradition, at the expense of others. It may also have clouded views concerned with other developments, for instance, in Southern Europe, Latin America and Asia (Pérez-Díaz 1978, 1993).

Let us consider the case of the Polish trade union Solidarność as an example. From the viewpoint of those who see civil society as a locus for public deliberation resulting in consensus that leads to policy, Solidarność may seem like a projection of their dreams of collective self-institutionalization and fate control (even allowing for the prudent, self-limiting character of its first moves). It is supposed to express the voice of a society, eager to define, decide on and implement its true goals, true values, true identity and true interests. However, seen from the viewpoint of those who equate civil society with an order of freedom, a decentralized system of talking and taking action, Solidarność stands out as a process better understood as a gradual unfolding of an exercise involving multiple voices.

The Polish Catholic tradition gave voice to the theory of subsidiarity of the state in a plural, organic society. Here, the state is not the main agent, and fate control is simply not on the cards (let us say, it is more a matter of divine providence). This theory was attuned to a Polish peasant mentality possibly permeated by Catholic ways of thinking and feeling, and was in all likelihood reinforced by the somewhat bitter experience the Polish working and mingling classes had with state socialism, which, in the long run, after many ups and downs, left them with a legacy of disappointed expectations and a readiness to try out exactly the opposite (Barlinska 2006).

In these circumstances, intellectual talk about worker control (with implicit reference to the rather frail Yugoslavian experience), suggesting a refurbishment of the system to provide it with a human face, sounded somewhat empty. However, such talk was not entirely useless. Rhetorical exercises like these, with the vocabulary at hand (a light version of a long-standing Proudhonian tradition, with some Marxist overtones), were useful for people who saw themselves as potential leaders of a new Poland but not responsible as yet for the consequences of any specific public policy. Such rhetoric allowed a new generation of dissidents to gain time while they learned about the basic facts of economic life in the real world, something they expected to do during the transition process.

The fact is, these dissidents, who were a crucial sector of the leaders of Solidarność, could draw little inspiration from their *own* past experience, which was limited to living in an administered economy, earning their living from state wages and subsidies, and spending their spare time talking about transforming the world. They really had no alternative but to use the only language at their disposal, albeit with increasing ambiguity and looseness. They started playing with new words ('inflation', 'prices', 'productivity', etc.) in anticipation of learning the new language of a market economy (syntax and semantics included), and prepared themselves eventually to learn on the job, by doing. In time, for both society and the elite, 'liberation from the communist yoke' gradually acquired the ordinary common-sense meaning of liberation from a planned, administered economy. Thus, the idea of a deliberative democracy leading to a consensus resulting in policy decisions in the crucial arena of economic policy became a non-starter; at the moment of truth, *grosso modo*, liberal ideas (Leszek Balcerowicz's ideas, for instance) soon became the *topoi* of the place, Solidarność included.

On Civil Virtues

Civil society, broadly understood, denotes a coherent set of different institutional arrangements, and civil virtues are moral dispositions that fit in the various domains of that institutional framework. They come in different and complex modalities; for instance, in the political domain, they include both civic virtue, which implies a commitment to a *civitas*, and to its common good, but to a kind of *civitas* which allows for, and rests on, diversity and individual freedom.

We should expect that civil virtues practiced in one domain would prepare the way for the development of other civil virtues in other domains – for instance, that civil habits and dispositions acquired through the economic experience would be put to work in political life, and that properly functioning markets should provide the basis for political education of a liberal polity (and *vice versa*). Thus, the market practice of accountability for freely made decisions, while taking into account the risks and rewards concomitant to these, would prepare the way for political practice that demands responsibility from political leaders, and, at the same time, rejects casting citizens in the role of victims of their freely chosen leaders, if and when these happen to be indecisive, irresponsible, corrupt or worse. The practice of risky decisions may also make for wise decisions in the long run, if the system allows enough room for learning; otherwise, correctives may arise more or less spontaneously, provided *iustitia* is tempered by *liberalitas*, *hospitalitas*, and other complementary social virtues. Market practices are usually embedded in such social virtues, as are other practices, such as trusting or helping people in need or in situations of dependence; in fact, without these virtues, these practices cannot be sustained over the long term.

The practice of civility – meaning the virtue of being able to engage in loyal cooperation and competition with strangers, without fraud and violence – which may be practiced in a market economy, can spill over to politics. In fact, the contrast between *le doux commerce* and the violent, war-like passions of emerging nation-states has been common in academic debates since Montesquieu. Trade was supposed to tame the political passions, although, in fact, it could also be subject to the logic of political interest in the form of 'jealousy of trade' (Hont 2005). The contrast was originally applied to the unstable situation of the post-Westphalia and post-Utrecht intra-European wars, but a case can be made for its application to civil war situations in local European, and non-European, societies at very different times. An argument has been made to the effect that the example of the Spanish situation in the 1930s and the aftermath that led to the transition to democracy in the 1970s suggests a protracted yet virtuous path in which, *inter alia*, prosperity associated with the growth of a market economy, both in Spain and Western Europe (to which the Spanish economy was linked) ensured a taming of the fratricidal dispositions that erupted in the war. Whatever the merits of this argument, it seems to be corroborated by the fact that today many Europeans envision a way to pacify the Balkans, based to a significant extent (although not exclusively) on linking their economies to the European common market and the world economy beyond, in the hope that they will all find a place there. On the other hand, the contrast between the internal (and external) violence of a totalitarian system and the (relative) pacification of social life that comes with the spread of a normal market experience seems corroborated (so far) by the Chinese example, despite ongoing problems; it may even apply, to a point, in the case of today's Russia, at least when it is compared to the previous socialist experiment of an administered economy in which the role played by the gulag was crucial, rather than marginal.

In turn, the different practice of civil virtues makes a difference in the way the institutional framework really functions. Thus, on paper, various forms of statist-corporatist coordination of the economy may look alike, while in fact they cover quite different historical experiences, as suggested by a cursory comparison of social-democratic governance in, say, Nordic countries and European Mediterranean countries. For instance, submission of markets to the state and corporatist arrangements may translate on everyday market practices on the ground that foster political deference of the economic entrepreneurs vis-à-vis the political class and may even go as far as to provide for a pattern of collusion between economic and political entrepreneurs. The practice of business linked to dwelling in the corridors of local, regional and national governments pushes businessmen towards becoming courtiers who look for friends in government in order to make a profit with the smallest possible risk. In such a court society, professionals, teachers, academics, and public intellectuals can gravitate towards the state and educate themselves in the practice of being careful when expressing their political ideas; otherwise their careers could be in jeopardy. They may be inclined to support the official line of the right, the left, or whoever happens to be the relevant aggregate actor or political family they feel closer to.

Loss of civil virtues in various domains may, in a relatively short period of time, spell ruin for a liberal democratic polity, as illustrated by the numerous cases in both Europe and Latin America where democratic regimes have broken down during the last century. In turn, the way to a liberal democracy may be preceded by a diffusion of (civil) cultural themes with frail institutional foundations. As these cultural changes incorporate existential decisions (in which the experience of 'truth' is required to stand against that of 'customs', as in any process of moral conversion), they cannot be deduced from institutional premises. There is therefore a substantial degree of surprise and unpredictability in the cycles of civil progress and uncivil regression, as shown by the rise (often sudden and unexpected) of totalitarian regimes, both right and left, in modern, contemporary twentieth-century Western societies. In fact, one of the most enduring lessons from these experiences is that similar totalitarian experiments could be played out (possibly under different guises) at any time in the future.

Notes

1. The familiar counter-arguments are, of course, well known: evidence may be partially influenced by a prior theory and it should include interpretations made by the participants; and a never-ending round of criticism may follow the examination of evidence and attention to meaning.
2. See the editors' preface to this series of books (pages xi–xiii, this volume) and Kocka (2004, 2005).
3. Nor should it be confined to the Western tradition either (Bruhns and Gosewinkel 2005; Randeria 2006).

References

Auffret, Dominique. 1990. *Alexandre Kojève*. Paris: Grasset.

Ault, James. 2005. *Spirit and Flesh: Life in a Fundamentalist Baptist Church*. New York: Vintage.

Barlinska, Izabela. 2006. *La sociedad civil en Polonia y* Solidaridad. Madrid: Centro de Investigaciones Sociológicas.

Brick, Howard. 1996. 'The Reformist Dimension of Talcott Parsons's Early Social Theory', in *The Culture of the Market: Historical Essays*, ed. Thomas Haskell and Richard Teichgraeber III. Cambridge: Cambridge University Press, pp. 357–396.

Bruhns, Hinnerk, and Dieter Gosewinkel. 2005. 'Europe and the Other: Non-European Concepts of Civil Society', *WZB Discussion Paper*, Nr. SP IV 2005–406.

Gellner, Ernst. 1985. *Relativism and the Social Sciences*. Cambridge: Cambridge University Press.

Hayek, Friedrich. 1988. *The Fatal Conceit*. Chicago, IL: University of Chicago Press.

Hont, Istvan. 2005. *Jealousy of Trade: International Competition and the Nation-State in Historical Perspective*. Cambridge, MA: Harvard University Press.

Kocka, Jürgen. 2004. 'Civil Society from a Historical Perspective', *European Review* 12, no. 1: 65–79.

_____. 2005. 'Commentary on Keane', *Journal of Civil Society* 1, no. 1: 35–37.

Ladd, Everett. 1999. *The Ladd Report*. New York: Free Press.

Pérez-Díaz, Víctor. 1978. *State, Bureaucracy and Civil Society*. London: McMillan.

_____. 1993. *The Return to Civil Society: The Emergence of Democratic Spain*. Cambridge, MA: Harvard University Press. First Spanish edition 1987.

Pérez-Díaz, Víctor, and Joaquín Pedro López Novo. 2003. *El Tercer Sector Social en España*. Madrid: Ministerio de Trabajo y Asuntos Sociales.

Putnam, Robert. 2000. *Bowling Alone: The Collapse and Revival of American Community*. New York: Touchstone.

Randeria, Shalini. 2006. 'Entangled Histories: Civil Society, Caste Solidarities and Legal Pluralism in Post-colonial India', in *Civil Society: Berlin Perspectives*, ed. John Keane. New York: Berghahn Books, pp. 213–241.

Robertson, John. 1983. 'The Scottish Enlightenment at the Limits of the Civic Tradition', in *Wealth and Virtue: The Shaping of Political Economy in the Scottish Enlightenment*, ed. Istvan Hont and Michael Ignatieff. Cambridge: Cambridge University Press, pp. 137–178.

Schudson, Michael. 1999. *The Good Citizen: A History of American Civic Life*. Cambridge, MA: Harvard University Press.

Skocpol, Theda. 2003. *Diminished Democracy: From Membership to Management in American Civic Life*. Norman: University of Oklahoma Press.

Swedberg, Richard. 1994. 'Markets as Social Structures', in *The Handbook of Economic Sociology*, ed. Neil J. Smelser and Richard Swedberg. Princeton, NJ: Princeton University Press, pp. 255–282.

_____. 2005. 'Markets in Society', in *The Handbook of Economic Sociology*, 2nd ed., ed. Neil Smelser and Richard Swedberg. Princeton, NJ: Princeton University Press, pp. 233–253.

Terrier, Jean, and Peter Wagner. 2006. 'The Return of Civil Society and the Reopening of the Political Problematique', in *The Languages of Civil Society*, ed. Peter Wagner. New York: Berghahn Books, pp. 223–234.

Trägårdh, Lars. 2007. 'Democratic Governance and the Creation of Social Capital in Sweden: The Discreet Charm of Governmental Commissions', in *State and Civil Society in Northern Europe*, ed. Lars Trägårdh. New York: Berghahn Books, pp. 254–270.

Uzzi, Brian. 1997. 'Social Structure and Competition in Interfirm Networks: The Paradox of Embeddedness', *Administrative Science Quarterly* 42: 35–67.

INDEX